A
FINGERTIP GUIDE
TO
CRIMINAL LAW

A
FINGERTIP GUIDE
TO
CRIMINAL LAW

J Ross Harper
Peter Hamilton
with
Michael Allen

Third edition

Butterworths
Law Society of Scotland

Edinburgh   1994

Butterworths

United Kingdom	Butterworth & Co (Publishers) Ltd, 4 Hill Street, EDINBURGH EH2 3JZ and Halsbury House, 35 Chancery Lane, LONDON WC2A 1EL
Australia	Butterworths, SYDNEY, MELBOURNE, BRISBANE, ADELAIDE, PERTH, CANBERRA AND HOBART
Canada	Butterworth Canada Ltd, TORONTO and VANCOUVER
Ireland	Butterworth (Ireland) Ltd, DUBLIN
Malaysia	Malayan Law Journal Sdn Bhd, KUALA LUMPUR
New Zealand	Butterworths of New Zealand Ltd, WELLINGTON and AUCKLAND
Puerto Rico	Butterworth of Puerto Rico, Inc, SAN JUAN
Singapore	Butterworths Asia, SINGAPORE
South Africa	Butterworths Publishers (Pty) Ltd, DURBAN
USA	Butterworth Legal Publishers, CARLSBAD, California, and SALEM, New Hampshire

Law Society of Scotland
26 Drumsheugh Gardens, EDINBURGH EH3 7YR

First published 1986

A CIP Catalogue record for this book is available from the British Library.

ISBN 0 406 04496 1

Typeset by Phoenix Photosetting, Chatham, Kent
Printed and bound in Great Britain by Mackays of Chatham PLC, Chatham, Kent

PREFACE

'What's that case? It's almost at my fingertips.' How often have we asked that question as we appear in court?

Many lawyers keep notes of their favourite cases but their summaries are rarely comprehensive or well organised, nor is it always easy in a busy practice to keep them up to date. The first edition of this book started life as an extension of the authors' private notebooks and was an attempt to provide a considerable body of criminal law at one's fingertips.

We repeat our original warning that this case book is by no means a complete statement of the law. In the first place the choice of the areas of substantive law covered was, and is, dictated by the frequency of their encounter in today's legal practice. In the second place, extract from cases have had to be kept brief. While attempting to highlight the salient point at issue there is not room to list the qualifications and provisos with which the case may be surrounded. Our extracts provide a point of reference and a starting point for the detailed research which the solicitor must then pursue in the preparation of his case.

This third edition is justified primarily by the need for any such guide to be kept up to date. A considerable body of cases has come before the courts since our second edition. The sections on evidence, sentencing and road traffic have been extensively revised and this edition includes new sections on homicide and on sexual offences.

We were deeply indebted to many people for their assistance in the preparation of the first edition. For this edition we are indebted to Michael Allen who has looked at every reported case since May 1990 and adjusted the text accordingly. We also thank our publishers Butterworths.

The law is stated as at 30 September.

J Ross Harper
Peter Hamilton
November 1994

CONTENTS

TABLE OF STATUTES

LIST OF CASES

List of Cases

M

List of Cases

SUBSTANTIVE LAW

ASSAULT

A **deliberate attack** on the person of another which may be **aggravated.** There may be **defences.**

COMMENTARY	CASE LAW	STATUTE LAW
Deliberate The mens rea of assault is the intention to injure. It is not a crime which can be committed through recklessness.	*David Keay* (1837) 1 Swin 543 K whipped and alarmed a pony which bolted and threw its rider. Per Lord Moncreiff: 'I cannot see what purpose the panel could have except to do him a direct injury or to put him in alarm . . . if a person throws a stone out of a window into the street [causing injury] done without intention to hurt anybody he could not be charged with assault.' *John Roy* (1839) Bell's Notes 88 R maliciously broke glass which hit the eye of a girl whom he did not know to be in the vicinity. Acquitted of assault. *HMA v Phipps* (1905) 4 Adam 616 P, to frighten off salmon poachers, fired a sporting gun in their direction. Some of the shot lodged in the eye of one of them. Accused maintained this was accidental. Per Lord Ardwall: 'Evil intent is the essence of the charge.' Acquitted. *Note:* But could be convicted of reckless conduct. But see: *Connor v Jessop* 1988 SCCR 624 C charged with assaulting S by throwing tumbler at her. Tumbler thrown at someone with whom C fighting earlier, but had missed and hit S. C convicted. *Held* on appeal that circumstances were such that what happened was likely to occur as result of what appellant did and appeal refused. *Roberts v Hamilton* 1989 SCCR 240 R charged with assaulting C by striking him with a stick. C was attempting to separate two other men who were fighting, one of whom R had intended to strike. R convicted of assault and appealed on ground that she lacked the necessary mens rea to assault C. *Held* that where A intends to assault B and strikes C instead he is guilty of assaulting C; and appeal refused. *Lord Advocate's Reference (No 2 of 1992)* 1992 SCCR 960 Accused entering shop with imitation gun, telling shopkeeper to empty the till, then saying 'I'm only kidding'. Acquitted. *Held* that evil intention is the essence of assault which cannot be committed recklessly. Accused was acting deliberately with necessary intent, motive irrelevant. See also: *Quinn v Lees* 1993 SCCR 159 *Gilmour v McGlennan* 1993 SCCR 837	

Attack

Attack must be physical in character but need not have a physical result.

Stewart v PF Forfarshire (1829) 2 SJ 32
S aimed a blow at someone but missed. Convicted.

Ewing v Earl of Mar (1851) 14 D 314
Accused rode horse at victim to alarm him. Convicted.

Kay v Allan (1978) SCCR Supp 188
K set dog on two young boys in garden. Assault constituted by establishing intention to use dog to frighten person. Fact that dog caused injury is aggravation of that assault.

Uttering threats is a separate crime.

James Miller (1862) 4 Irv 238
Per LJ-C Inglis: 'The use of threats is in certain well-known cases a crime in the eye of the law of Scotland.'

The attack need not be direct *qui facit per alium facit per se.*

David Keay, supra

Injury to the victim is unnecessary (Gordon, p 815).

HMA v Jane Smith or Thom (1876) 3 Couper 332 (see infra)

Aggravated

An assault may be aggravated by various factors, eg, by the nature of the injury caused.

Kay v Allan (1978) SCCR Supp 188, supra

or by the identity of the person assaulted, eg officers of the law in the execution of their duty,

Monk v Strathern 1921 JC 4
M seriously injured a police constable returning home who prompted M and others to go home at a late hour of the night. The constable was in uniform. Conviction quashed on appeal on grounds that constable had left beat and was no longer on duty, although still in uniform. Accordingly, he was not assaulted in the execution of his duty.

Police (Scotland) Act 1967, s 41

Criminal Procedure (Scotland) Act 1975, s 312(*t*). If the evidence demonstrates that the police officer was not in the execution of his duty there can be a conviction for assault at common law.

Smith v Hawkes (1980) SCCR Supp 261
A police officer who has reasonable grounds for making proper inquiries is acting in the execution of his duty.

Annan v Tait 1981 SCCR 326
Knowledge of fact that victim is a police officer is essential to the statutory charge.

Stocks v Hamilton 1990 SCCR 190
Assault on constable when accused attempting to leave a room in police station.
Held on appeal that accused unlawfully detained, constable not in the exercise of his lawful duty so statutory charge not available.

and by use of weapons,

HMA v Fitchie (1856) 2 Irv 485
By throwing acid on victim.

HMA v Morison (1842) 1 Broun 394
Assault, especially when committed by presenting a loaded firearm.

although merely presenting a weapon at someone may or may not be an assault,	*Mackenzie v HMA* 1982 SCCR 499 Accused presented a knife onto which victim impaled himself in course of a scuffle. *Held* that the trial judge had misdirected the jury in withdrawing the defence of accident and verdict set aside but Crown given leave to raise fresh indictment. Per LJ-C Wheatley: 'I am not prepared to say that in every situation, irrespective of the facts, where a person presents a weapon at another with the intention of frightening him off from further violence, an assault is committed.'	
by circumstances of indecency,	*Sweeney and Another v X* 1982 SCCR 509 Intercourse with drunken woman incapable of consent held to be an indecent assault.	Sexual Offences (Scotland) Act 1976, s 15
by intention, eg, assault with intent to ravish,	*John Hosie* 1826 Alison I 186 Pursued woman into a pond where she had run to avoid his advances: assault with intent to ravish.	
or by the nature of the injury caused.	*Jane Smith or Thom*, supra Assault to the danger of life. Charged with throwing a child out of a railway train. Although child uninjured, held relevant to libel that the assault had been to danger of life.	
	Kerr v HMA 1986 SCCR 91 K convicted of assault by stabbing to severe injury and the danger of life. Medical evidence that complainer's life had not in fact been endangered. K appealed on that ground against the retention of the aggravation of danger to life in the verdict. *Held*, following *Thom* supra, that jury entitled to convict where the inference of danger to life had been drawn, even if the complainer's life was not in fact at risk.	
Defences Generally where there is evil intent to injure, consent is not a defence to assault.	*Smart v HMA* 1975 SLT 65 Victim accepted challenge to a 'square go'. *Held* that state of mind of victim irrelevant and that consent was not a defence where there was an evil intent to inflict injury. Opinion of the court: 'It is in the public interest that it should be decided and made known that consent to a "square go" is *not* a defence to a charge of assault based on that agreed combat.'	
	C v HMA 1987 SCCR 104 C aged 14 charged with indecently assaulting girl aged 11. His defence was that she had consented, or at least that he believed she had so consented. *Held* that as an eleven-year-old girl incapable in law of giving consent, C's state of mind as to conduct irrelevant.	
A physical attack may not be assault where it is so justified as to be protected by statute,	*Skinner v Robertson* 1980 SLT (Sh Ct) 43 Nurse in mental hospital charged with assaulting certain mentally handicapped children by throwing water over them, striking them on the face and head with his knuckles. *Held* that use of force reasonably required to control the children and in circumstances protected by s 107(1) of Mental Health (Scotland) Act 1960. Compare: *Norman v Smith* 1983 SCCR 100 Nurse at a mental hospital held to have exceeded the limits of reasonable restraint in relation to a patient.	Mental Health (Scotland) Act 1960, s 107(1), now Mental Health (Scotland) Act 1984, s 122(1)

or where it constitutes reasonable chastisement,	*Stewart v Thain* 1981 SLT (Notes) 2 Headmaster held *not* to have exceeded the limits of proper chastisement of a 'difficult and fractious' pupil. *Peebles v McPhail* 1989 SCCR 410 P charged with assaulting her two-year-old son by slapping him on the face. Child having a temper tantrum and P became angry. The force of the slap knocked him off balance and left red mark on face. *Held* that to slap child aged two on face, knocking him over, is an act as remote from reasonable chastisement as one could imagine and conviction upheld.
or carried out in *self-defence*,	See Special Defences, p 119.
or in exercise of citizen's right of arrest.	*Codona v Cardle* 1989 SCCR 287 Force used must not be excessive, and arrest by a private citizen only justifiable where the citizen has witnessed the crime or has 'information equivalent to personal observation'. *Bryans v Guild* 1989 SCCR 569 B chased group of youths who had been throwing things at his house. B mistakenly took hold of a youth who had not been part of the group and twisted his arm up his back, bruising his arm. B convicted of assault and admonished. On appeal *held* (1) B had not witnessed offence committed by complainer and had no right of citizen's arrest but (2) sentence quashed and absolute discharge substituted.
Note: Recklessness. Culpable, reckless acts which may or do cause injury to others may incur criminal liability.	*RHW v HMA* 1982 SCCR 152 W charged with causing culpable and reckless injury by dropping a bottle from a fifteenth-floor flat. *Held* (1) mens rea required was total indifference to and disregard for public safety, and (2) appellant had shown recklessness so depraved as to be regardless of consequences. *MacPhail v Clark* 1982 SCCR 395 (Sh Ct) Culpably and recklessly endangering lieges. Farmer set fire to straw in field. Fire spread to verge of road. Smoke obscured visibility on road and collision resulted. *Held* that to allow the fire to spread demonstrated reckless indifference to the consequences for the public and road users. Convicted. *Khaliq v HMA* 1983 SCCR 483 Shopkeepers charged that they did culpably, recklessly and wilfully supply children with solvents in the knowledge of the intended use, that use being injurious to health and dangerous to lives. Convicted. On appeal, sentence reduced (see *Khaliq v HMA* 1984 SCCR 212, infra). See also: *Ulhaq v HMA* 1990 SCCR 593. *Normand v Morrison* 1993 SCCR 207 (Sh Ct) Accused charged with culpably and recklessly denying there was an unprotected needle in her handbag, permitting police officer to place his hand in the bag, exposing him to risk of infection. Plea to relevancy repelled. Accused has total disregard for health and safety of the officer.

Assault

See also:

Kimmins v Normand 1993 SCCR 476
—relevancy of similar charge upheld on appeal.

HMA v Harris 1993 SCCR 559
Doorman pushing girl down stairs onto a road where she was struck by a car. Charged with assault or alternatively with culpably and recklessly causing injury. Plea to relevancy.
Held on appeal (five judge bench) that conduct can be criminally reckless either where there is danger to the lieges or reckless conduct causing actual injury. To be distinguished from assault which must be deliberate and cannot be committed recklessly.

See also:

Normand v Robinson 1993 SCCR 1119.

References: Macdonald, 115; Alison I, 175; Gordon, 815; Gane and Stoddart, 383.

SENTENCING POLICY

Brown v Normand 1988 SCCR 229—Assault resulting in permanent disfigurement. B sentenced to 240 hours of community service and ordered to pay £650 compensation. Appealed, submitting sentence excessive in light of fact that he was first offender and conduct of complainer. Appeal allowed: community service reduced to 100 hours, and as complainer's conduct would have prevented him from recovering compensation from CICB, compensation order quashed.

Stirling v Stewart 1988 SCCR 619—Appellants (aged sixteen) pleaded guilty to assaulting lone US serviceman at Dunoon pier. Sheriff imposed sentence of thirty days' detention as short, sharp shock and as deterrent to the frequency of such attacks. *Held* that appeal court could not interfere with sheriff's sentence.

Mays v Brown 1988 SCCR 549—M convicted of assaulting water bailiff in course of his duty by throwing lamp at him. Fined £250. On appeal against sentence fine increased to £500.

Dick v Jessop 1989 SCCR 258—D convicted of assault by kicking A on head. D, aged twenty-five, in good employment, had no previous custodial sentences and no previous convictions for crimes of violence. Sheriff imposed a two months' custodial sentence. On appeal *held* that although the assault was serious, careful weight should be given to the fact that D would lose job if imprisoned; and appeal allowed with hesitation and fine of £500 substituted.

McCardle v Douglas 1989 SCCR 262—Similar facts to *Dick v Jessop* supra. McC seventeen years old. Sentence of thirty days' detention quashed, compensation order of £200 substituted.

Ferguson v Lowe 1989 SCCR 281—F (aged seventeen, in employment, no previous convictions, but convicted of minor assault and two breaches of peace after offence in question) convicted of assaulting bus driver by knocking him down and repeatedly punching and kicking him. Sheriff sentenced to sixty days' detention. On appeal *held* that sheriff had exercised discretion properly. Appeal refused.

Pearson v HMA 1990 SCCR 125—P, a first offender, pleaded guilty to three assaults on his wife, the first two involving only punching and kicking. The third was an assault with knife to injury and permanent disfigurement. Fined on first two charges and sentenced to 15 months' imprisonment on third charge.
Held that as it was a domestic issue, parties were now divorced, assault out of character and P a first offender, appropriate disposal was probation for 18 months in place of imprisonment.

Murchie v McGlennan 1990 SCCR 533—Assault with cricket bat and meat tenderiser. Victim alleged to have used lewd practices toward's appellant's children. Three years' imprisonment on the basis that court could not tolerate people taking law into their own hands.

Galloway v Mackenzie 1991 SCCR 548—Careers officer admonished on minor assault on youth scaring his children. Job exempt from Rehabilitation of Offenders Act 1974, admonition a conviction. On appeal *held* that an absolute discharge would be more appropriate.

Leslie v HMA 1992 SCCR 880—punching glass into the face of victim to his severe injury. Eighteen months' imprisonment appeal.
Held that custody appropriate but given accused's good background, no material previous convictions and six months served prior to appeal that sentence quashed. 240 hours community service and £1,500 compensation order.

McKay v HMA 1992 SCCR 584—striking victim with glass to severe injury. Fifteen months' imprisonment *held* on appeal to be severe but not excessive. Alternatives looked to but not appropriate.

Modiak v HMA 1992 SCCR 572—acid attack on wife to her permanent severe injury and loss of sight. Trial judge said it was hard to think of a more cowardly, wicked and premeditated crime. On appeal, no difficulty in upholding twenty years' imprisonment, devastating injuries.

Garrett v HMA 1993 SCCR 1044—G striking solicitor on face in the cells. Twelve months' detention upheld on appeal. Officers of court must be able to carry out their duties free from violence at hands of clients.

Andrews v HMA 1994 SCCR 191—indecent assault on thirteen-year-old boy by twenty-seven-year-old intellectually impaired stepbrother. On appeal *held*, custodial sentence inevitable, serious assault by person in position of trust but sentence too long. Two years' imprisonment reduced to nine months.

McGowan v HMA 1994 SCCR 217—M assaulting sixty-three-year-old shopkeeper, threatening her with a needle and AIDS, pushing her to ground breaking her hip. Seven years' imprisonment upheld on appeal. Serious injury and public anxiety about such matters.

BREACH OF THE PEACE

Disorderly conduct causing or likely to cause public disturbance.

COMMENTARY	CASE LAW	STATUTE LAW
Disorderly conduct Conduct is disorderly when it is in breach of public order,	*Mackie v MacLeod* 1961, High Court, unreported, Gordon, 988 M, infatuated with a young woman, habitually waited for her outside her workplace and followed her and her fiancé about. Convicted.	
or public decorum.	*Docherty v Thaw* 1962, High Court, Gordon, 985 D, a participant in a sit-down demonstration, obstructing street traffic. Convicted.	
	Palazzo v Copeland 1976 JC 52 P, a shopkeeper, discharging shotgun into the air to scare off 'a number of unsavoury and drunken youths' engaged in a fracas outside his premises. Argued that that which was calculated to stop a breach of the peace was not itself a breach. 'A man may not take the law into his own hands . . . a man may not commit an offence to stop another.' Convicted.	
	Jas Ainslie (1842) 1 Broun 25 A took off his clothes in public and uttered threats. Convicted.	
	Raffaelli v Heatly 1949 JC 101 R, a 'peeping tom', staring at women through chink of curtains at lighted window of dwellinghouse late at night. Convicted.	
	MacDougall v Dochtree 1992 SCCR 531 'Peeping tom', accused looking into solarium from locked toilet cubicle, discovered when suspicious attendant looked under door. On appeal *held* that a member of the public could have discovered conduct and become alarmed. Observed: okay to look into cubicle when suspicious. If no-one could see into the cubicle, might not be a breach of the peace. (Per Lord McCluskey) Even if unlikely to be discovered might be shamelessly indecent conduct.	
	Young v Heatly 1959 JC 66 Y, a depute headmaster of technical school, at four separate interviews with adolescent pupils made 'grossly improper remarks and suggestions' to them. Convicted.	
	Lauder v Heatly 1962, unreported L, a 'kerb-crawling' motorist, stopped his car opposite two women, opening nearside door; no evidence that he spoke to them. Convicted.	
	McAvoy v Jessop 1989 SCCR 301 M in charge of orange procession accompanied by band. Police officer asked band to stop playing as procession neared Catholic church outside which worshippers were being greeted by the priest. M ordered band to resume playing and convicted of breach of the peace.	
	Fisher v Keane 1981 SLT (Notes) 28 Glue sniffing in absence of evidence of alarm or annoyance. *Held* not to be a breach of the peace.	

Substantive Law

Hughes v Crowe 1993 SCCR 320
Playing music and making banging sounds in flat between 7.15–8.15 am 'all exceedingly loudly'. Convicted. Upheld on appeal, facts show a gross lack of consideration for others present.

Taylor v Hamilton 1984 SCCR 393
Breach of the peace. T and another seen sniffing glue from plastic bags in public; woman saw them swaying, staggering and walking round in circles; she phoned police. T convicted.
Per Sheriff Forbes (quoting LJ-G in *Montgomery v McLeod* 1977 SLT (Notes) 77; (1977) SCCR Supp 164): 'There is no limit to the kind of conduct which may give rise to a charge of breach of the peace. All that is required is . . . some conduct such as to excite the reasonable apprehension . . . or . . . create disturbance and alarm to the lieges. . . .'
On appeal, the sheriff's verdict upheld: there was sufficient evidence that a breach of the peace had taken place.
Fisher v Keane supra, distinguished.

Thompson v MacPhail 1989 SCCR 266
T charged with breach of the peace in that he injected himself with an unknown substance in the locked toilet cubicle of a restaurant. When manager became suspicious he alerted police who unlocked door and found T removing syringe from arm. There was blood on the walls and floor. Convicted. On appeal *held* that while there might be circumstances where similar conduct would constitute breach of the peace, in the present case there was insufficient evidence: no evidence of what was in syringe; activities had taken place behind locked door; no evidence as to length of time T was in cubicle or what the demand for cubicles was.

Causing or likely to cause
Where actual disturbance does not occur disorderly conduct constitutes breach of the peace if, viewed objectively, it is likely to provoke such disturbance or cause alarm or annoyance to others.

Turner v Kennedy (1972) SCCR Supp 30
T distributed to schoolgirls aged twelve–fourteen pamphlets referring inter alia to adolescent sex. Convicted.

Sinclair v Annan 1980 SLT (Notes) 55
S made indecent remarks to a woman in the hearing of a girl of 18 who was embarrassed. Convicted.

Wilson v Brown 1982 SCCR 49
Gesturing and swearing at opposing team supporters at football match. Acquitted by sheriff, but convicted on appeal by Crown.
Per Lord Dunpark 'test . . . is whether the proved conduct may reasonably be expected to cause any person to be alarmed, upset or annoyed.'

See also:

Raffaelli, supra
Evidence that one of the women stared at was afraid to inform her husband in case he was tempted into a breach of the peace.
Per LJ-C Thomson: 'Where something is done in breach of public order or decorum which might reasonably be expected to lead to the lieges being alarmed or upset or tempted to make reprisals at their own hand the circumstances are such as to amount to breach of the peace.'

See also Civic Government (Scotland) Act 1982, s 54

8

Butcher v Jessop 1989 SCCR 119
B and W, both professional footballers, convicted of breach of peace in the course of a football match between Rangers and Celtic. As result of incident on pitch, there was a disturbance among spectators, which led police to fear invasion of pitch.
Held (diss Lord Murray) that sheriff had taken proper account of context of 'physical contact' sport, that test of breach of peace was objective, that actions of appellants were deliberate and likely to cause alarm. Appeals refused.

Young, supra
No finding of alarm being created to spectators or the public, none of whom either saw or heard what took place, nor was there any finding of alarm to the boys themselves.
Per LJ-C Clyde: '. . . it is not essential . . . that witnesses should be produced who speak of being alarmed or annoyed . . . if the nature of the conduct giving rise to the offence [is] so flagrant as to entitle the court to draw the necessary inference from the conduct itself.'

Stewart v Lockhart 1990 SCCR 390
Man dressed as a woman in an area frequented by female prostitutes. Conviction upheld on appeal. Red light area, real possibility of public disturbance.

HMA v Forbes 1994 SCCR 163
Housebreaking with intent to rape. F entering house, removing clothes, prowling around and making a hood.
Held on appeal, could be a breach of the peace but motive irrelevant.

See also:

McKenzie v HMA 1992 SCCR 14
Wyness v Lockhart 1992 SCCR 808
Cameron v Lockhart 1992 SCCR 866.

Swearing at the police.

Logan v Jessop 1987 SCCR 604
Appellants convicted of causing breach of the peace by shouting and swearing at two police officers and then running off.
Held that in the absence of any finding that the words complained of were uttered in the presence of others who might have been expected to react to them, there was insufficient evidence to justify conviction.
Logan v Jessop has not been followed in subsequent cases, and appears to be a special case.

Compare:
Norris v McLeod 1988 SCCR 572
Accused verbally abused police officers who were themselves annoyed and upset, although no members of the public present.
Held to amount to breach of peace.

Cardle v Murray 1993 SCCR 170
M 'breakdancing' in street. Police officer holding his arm attempting to warn him after he bumped into shopper. M resisted, shouted and swore. Acquitted.
Held that as the original breakdancing could not be regarded as a breach of the peace, the officer's action was unjustified. M entitled to refuse to accept detention as the officer was not acting under a warrant or exercising a statutory right on suspicion of M having committed some offence.

But see:

Woods v Normand 1992 SCCR 805.

Saltman v Allan 1988 SCCR 640
Held that it was not the law that if the only persons present at the scene were police officers there can be no breach of the peace nor that a police officer is not to be regarded as liable to be affected by disorderly conduct.

Mens rea or motive is irrelevant.

Ralston v HMA 1988 SCCR 590
R charged with breach of the peace by mounting protest on prison roof. R stated that his actions were a peaceful protest against prison conditions. Sheriff directed jury that they were entitled to convict even if R's motives were blameless.
Held on appeal that R's behaviour deliberate and sheriff's direction adequate. Appeal refused.

Public disturbance
Can result from disorderly conduct taking place in private.

Ferguson v Carnochan (1889) 2 White 278
The holding of a noisy party in a private dwellinghouse caused disturbance of the peace to those in neighbouring dwellinghouses, and in the street outside, and conviction followed.

Can result if the disorderly conduct taking place in private is likely, viewed objectively, to provoke public alarm and annoyance and thereby public disturbance.

Young, supra
Per LJ-G Clyde: 'It is well settled that [breach of the peace] can take place in a private house.'

Part of a disorderly crowd.

MacNeill v Robertson & Others 1982 SCCR 468
Charge libelling that accused did form part of a disorderly crowd, members of which did shout, swear and commit a breach of the peace.
Held on appeal by Crown, charge irrelevant.

Tudhope v Morrison 1983 SCCR 262 (Sh Ct)
Disorderly crowd.

Montgomery v Herron (1976) SCCR Supp 131
M was member of crowd preventing access to public meeting.
Held that findings showed that appellant formed part of crowd and in absence of any explanation by him the only reasonable inference was that he participated in breach of the peace.

Tudhope v O'Neill 1983 SCCR 443
A breach of the peace can be constituted by forming part of an 'amorphous group' of people; even where there is no evidence as to how each accused behaved.

Threats of violence by police officer; whether breach of the peace.

Carey v Tudhope 1984 SCCR 157
Police officer convicted of breach of the peace committed in course of his duty. Appeal against conviction dismissed.
Per LJ-C Wheatley: 'In many cases it becomes a matter of judgment for the judge to decide whether in the context and atmosphere of what occurred the facts did constitute the offence of breach of the peace in the law of Scotland.'

Provocation cannot operate in exculpation.

MacNeill v McTaggart (1976) SCCR Supp 150
McT charged with breach of peace by fighting with R in public place. McT argued he was responding to R's provocation.
Held that provocation cannot be pled in charge of breach of the peace.

References: Hume I, 439; Macdonald, 137-138; Gordon, 985; Gane and Stoddart, 693.

SENTENCING POLICY

Tait v Allan 1984 SCCR 385—Sheriff accepted that allowances should be made in sentencing otherwise respectable citizens for offences committed in the course of an industrial dispute. However, different considerations applied in this case and sixty days' imprisonment imposed.
Per LJ-G Emslie, upholding sentence. '. . . he was not in any sense an official picket engaged on what could fairly be regarded as a picketing activity. . . .'

Donaghy v Tudhope 1985 SCCR 118—D convicted of breach of the peace in that in pursuit of CND objectives he climbed up onto and remained on crane at Ministry of Defence premises. Sentence of sixty days' imprisonment upheld on appeal.
Per LJ-G Emslie: '. . . this was a very bad example of the offence of breach of the peace. . . . We are not concerned with the motive which led to the commission of this offence.'

McGivern v Jessop 1988 SCCR 511—M convicted of breach of peace by taunting rival football supporters and shouting and swearing.
Held that three months' detention not excessive as conduct could lead to serious consequences and must be severely discouraged.

Worsfold v Walkingshaw 1987 SCCR 17—Appellant pleaded guilty to swearing at police officer and police cadet who had warned him that he was parking illegally. Sheriff fined him £100.
Held that £100 excessive, fine reduced to £25.

Linton v Ingram 1989 SCCR 487—L pleaded guilty and admitted three analogous previous convictions. Sentence deferred for one year for him to attend alcohol education course. He did so and was of good behaviour. When he reappeared for sentence he was fined and appealed against sentence on ground that having complied with conditions of deferment he should only have been admonished.
Held court still has discretion as to appropriate sentence, and justice entitled to impose fine.

Smillie v Wilson 1990 SCCR 133—S pleaded guilty to breach of the peace by driving car in a way which placed occupants of another car in state of fear and alarm. Sheriff made compensation orders of £100 in favour of each of four occupants of other car.
Held that as no personal injury, loss, or damage, there was no justification for compensation order. Fine of £200 substituted.

Cameron v Lockhart 1992 SCCR 866—Kicking ball in street causing hindrance to vehicles and pedestrians. On appeal £60 fine reduced to £25.

Public Disorders

Meetings, street processions and **offences occasioned by procession or assembly** are covered in various statutes.

COMMENTARY	CASE LAW	STATUTE LAW
Meetings Permission must be sought to hold a meeting. Holding a meeting on or in private premises without consent of owner or occupier is an offence.		Public Order Act 1936 Civic Government (Scotland) Act 1982 *Note:* Provisions of Civic Government (Scotland) Act 1982 are intended to be complementary to Public Order Act.
Public parks, open spaces, etc, are invariably governed by local bye-laws or local legislation.	*Aldred v Miller* 1925 JC 21 Accused challenged bye-law requiring that permission be sought from local authority before holding meeting. Conviction upheld.	
Streets and roads, too, are subject to local regulations.	*Aldred v Miller* 1924 JC 117 A began lecturing in a street, causing a large number of people to assemble, and thereby occasioning obstruction. A convicted under Glasgow Police Act 1866. Per LJ-G Clyde: 'If anybody causes an obstruction in a public street or hinders other members of the public in exercising the public right of free passage upon it—he selfishly engrosses the public right to himself, and his action is justly condemned.'	
Street processions No such prior sanction is required for a procession although powers exist to prohibit or regulate proposed march or to prevent march actually taking place. Notice of intention to hold a procession is required.	*Loyal Orange Lodge v Roxburgh District Council* 1981 SLT 33 Power of district council to issue orders prohibiting or regulating processions is a wide one.	Public Order Act 1936, s 3 Civic Government (Scotland) Act 1982: s 62, requirement to give notice to regional council of a public procession; s 63, power of chief constable to prohibit and impose conditions; s 64, appeals against power granted by s 63.
Offences occasioned by procession or assembly		Public Order Act 1936, s 6 Civic Government (Scotland) Act 1982, s 25 sets out penalties relating to offences committed by disregard of conditions laid down in ss 62 and 63 of the same Act.
	Deakin & Others v Milne (1882) 10 R (J) 22 Salvation Army parade. Officers convicted of commiting a breach of the peace. *Marr v McArthur* (1878) 5 R (J) 38 M and another convicted of statutory breach of the peace in that they played flutes in a public place. Tune played was of political nature. *Held,* on appeal, that the mere playing of such a tune, without further proven detail of actual breach of the peace, was insufficient and conviction quashed.	

References: Gordon, 971; J.L. Murdoch, 144.

The **wearing of certain forms of uniform, provoking a breach of the peace, stirring up racial hatred** or **disrupting a lawful public meeting** may each in themselves be statutory offences.

COMMENTARY	CASE LAW	STATUTE LAW
Wearing of certain forms of uniform	*O'Moran v DPP; Whelan v DPP* [1975] 1 All ER 473 O'M and others arrested at funeral of Irish Republican hunger-striker, wearing dark berets, dark glasses and black pullovers. Similar items worn on separate occasion during Sinn Fein rally by W and others. Conviction upheld, per Widgery CJ.	Public Order Act 1936. Section 1 prohibits wearing of uniforms which signify association with a political organisation or object, in a public place or at any public meeting.
Provoking a breach of the peace	*Jordan v Burgoyne* [1963] 2 QB 744 A speaker must take his audience as he finds them; test *not* of a hypothetical audience of reasonable citizens. Section has also been used against disorderly football fans, 'streakers' and persons disrupting an Armistice Day silence.	Section 5, as substituted by Race Relations Act 1965, s 7 prohibits in any public place or at a public meeting use of threatening, abusive or insulting words or behaviour or distributing or displaying any such form of writing or sign with intent to provoke a breach of the peace or whereby a breach of the peace is likely to be occasioned.
Stirring up racial hatred	*R v Britton* [1967] 1 All ER 486 B smashed windows of M.P.'s flat and left racialist poster on door. *Held* no distribution to public; conviction fell. *R v Malik* [1968] 1 WLR 353 Black Power leader jailed for using words at a public meeting of a threatening, abusive and insulting nature. Both cases prosecuted under Race Relations Act 1965, s 6(1).	Section 5A, as inserted by Race Relations Act 1976, s 70, makes it an offence to publish or distribute written matter which is threatening, abusive or insulting, or to use in a public place or at a public meeting words of like character, where hatred is likely to be stirred up against any racial group.
Meaning of 'public place'.	*Cawley v Frost* [1976] 3 All ER 743 Track between spectators' area and football pitch at stadium held 'public place' even though public not ordinarily permitted access thereto.	Section 9: includes any highway or any other premises or place to which at the material time the public have or are permitted to have access whether on payment or otherwise.
Disrupting a lawful public meeting	*Burden v Rigler and Another* [1911] 1 KB 337 Meaning of 'lawful public meeting' considered. *Held*, on appeal, that the fact that a public meeting is held on a highway does not necessarily make it unlawful; whether or not an obstruction is caused will depend on the circumstances in which it is held.	Public Meeting Act 1908, Representation of the People Act 1983, s 97. Any person at a lawful meeting acting in a disorderly manner to prevent transaction of business commits an offence and any person who incites others to commit such offence.

Reference: Gordon, 971.

BROTHEL KEEPING

Sexual Offences (Scotland) Act 1976, s 13(1)
(a) The **keeping or management** or acting or assisting in the management of a **brothel.**
(b) A tenant, lessee, occupier or person in charge of any premises, **knowingly permitting** premises or part thereof to be used as a brothel or for the purposes of **habitual prostitution,** *or*
(c) The letting of premises or part of premises with the knowledge that such premises are to be used as a brothel *or* wilfully being a party to the continuing use of such premises as a brothel, by a lessor or landlord or the agent of a lessor or landlord of premises.

COMMENTARY	CASE LAW	STATUTE LAW
Keeping or management		
	Vaughan v Smith 1919 JC 9 Per LJ-G Strathclyde: 'One who assists in the management of a brothel manages a brothel only with aid, but he is none the less managing a brothel.'	Section 13(1)(*a*)
Brothel Definition: 'Open and notorious house of lewdness, for the reception of loose and dissolute visitors' (Hume I 468).	*Winter v Woolfe* [1931] 1 KB 549 Place where persons of opposite sexes are permitted to resort for illicit intercourse, whether or not the women are common prostitutes.	
	Milne v McNicol (1965) SCCR Supp 8 M convicted of managing boarding house as a brothel, after typhoid outbreak in Aberdeen caused scarcity of tourist business. No evidence that M had sought business from prostitutes but ample evidence that boarding house acquired notoriety as place where prostitutes could obtain room.	
More than one woman using premises.	*Singleton v Ellison* [1895] 1 QB 607 House occupied by one woman only for purpose of prostitution (with no other women being allowed to use the premises for a similar purpose). *Held* not a brothel.	
Individual rooms in a house let out to individual prostitutes may constitute a brothel.	*Donovan v Gavin* [1965] 2 QB 648 Landlord let out separate rooms to separate tenants. Three rooms on ground floor let to prostitutes, who used them to ply their trade. Lord Parker CJ: 'It seems to me that . . . whether they were independent and separate lettings is an immaterial matter.'	
	R v Tan [1983] 3 WLR 361 (and Lord Parker CJ in *Donovan,* supra, at p 661).	
Knowingly permitting	*Mattison v Johnson* (1916) 26 Cox CC 373	
Habitual prostitution Includes habitual prostitution in premises by an *individual* prostitute.	*Girgawy v Strathern* 1925 JC 31 Over a period of time, a large number of prostitutes resorted to a furnished flat of which two men were the tenants and occupiers. Several of the prostitutes went repeatedly. Occupiers were convicted of knowingly permitting premises to be used for habitual prostitution. Case observes that (1) if prostitution had been with the occupiers of the flat only, no offence would have been committed, in respect that the occupiers could not 'permit' their own acts; (2) immaterial that accused made no profit.	Section 13(1)(*b*)

'Keeping open and notorious house of lewdness.'	*Herron v Macdonald* 1973, unreported Occupier of house in which pornographic films shown, and live sexual display performed, prosecuted in sheriff court for 'keeping an open and notorious house of lewdness for the reception of loose and dissolute visitors' (Hume I, 468). But quaere: now would he be prosecuted under 'shameless indecency'?	
Other statutory offences.		Theatres Act 1968
		Indecent Displays (Control) Act 1981
		Post Office Act 1953 Indecent matters not to be sent by post.
		Unsolicited Goods and Services Act 1971, s 4(1), prohibits sending of unsolicited sex manuals.
Living on immoral earnings.	*Soni v HMA* 1970 SLT 275 Landlord convicted of living on immoral earnings. *Held*, on appeal, that it did not have to be proved that rents charged were exorbitant, if it could be proved otherwise that the accused was participating or assisting in activities of the prostitute.	Sexual Offences (Scotland) Act 1976, s 12(1)
Homosexual brothels.		Criminal Justice (Scotland) Act 1980, s 80(13)

References: Hume I, 468-469; Gordon, 909.

CONTEMPT OF COURT

Contempt of court is conduct offending against the **dignity** or **authority** of a court, **within or outwith its precincts.**

COMMENTARY	CASE LAW	STATUTE LAW
The **dignity** of a court is offended by disorderly conduct.	*John Allan* 1826 Shaw 172 A, a witness, attended court so drunk as to be unable to give evidence. *Robert Clark or Williamson* 1829 Shaw 215 'Rudely, indecently and contemptuously addressed the court . . . to be a gross contempt.'	Criminal Procedure (Scotland) Act 1975. Section 145(4): 'Any person who interrupts or disturbs the court shall be liable to imprisonment or a fine or both as the judge thinks fit' (solemn procedure).
	McKinnon v Douglas 1982 SCCR 80 Solicitor, due to misunderstanding, arrived late at district court. Opinion of the court: '. . . to arrive late in the circumstances . . . was not contempt . . . no neglect of the obligation to support the dignity of the court. There was no wilful or reckless interference with the administration of justice. All there was, was a late arrival [which was] wholly excusable.'	Section 145 of the 1975 Act, as amended by Criminal Justice (Scotland) Act 1980, s 21, now also makes provisions for an accused to be removed and for trial to proceed in his absence, where he misconducts himself to the extent of making a proper trial impossible. Legal representation is essential during such absence.
The **authority** of the court is challenged, when a witness prevaricates, refuses to answer questions or to take an oath or affirmation when required to do so,	*Caldwell v Normand* 1993 SCCR 624 Accused half an hour late, slept in. *Held* on appeal that mere lateness not contempt unless wilful defiance of the order of the court. *Aitken v Carmichael* 1993 SCCR 889 Spectator found in contempt for putting on headphones when leaving court at an adjournment. *Held* on appeal that sheriff had grossly overreacted.	Section 344. (Summary procedure.) A witness who fails to attend after due citation, refuses to be sworn or to answer proper questions or prevaricates, or refuses to produce documents when required by court may be punished forthwith for contempt, or prosecuted by way of formal complaint.
	McMillan v Carmichael 1993 SCCR 943 Accused awaiting trial, yawned 'openly and unrestrainedly', found in contempt. *Held* on appeal that there was no intention to affront the authority of the court. A warning would have been enough.	
	Mowbray v Valentine 1991 SCCR 494 Party defender found in contempt for time wasting, asking obscure, rambling questions and ignoring directions. *Held* on appeal that some latitude is required with party litigants. Behaviour not designed to insult the court.	
	Bacon, Petitioner 1986 SCCR 265 B, a defence witness, prevaricated in answer to question which he believed would incriminate him. Judge held him to be in contempt of court. On petition, held that in these circumstances it could not be affirmed that his conduct amounted to contempt.	
	Dawes v Cardle 1987 SCCR 135 Complainer refused to leave cell to appear before sheriff. Sheriff and other court officials visited cells to warn that she might be in contempt if she failed to appear. She then appeared in court but refused to tender a plea. *Held* that sheriff was entitled to find complainer in contempt.	

or where an order of the court is not implemented.

HMA v Airs 1975 SLT 177
A, a journalist, a prosecution witness at a trial, refused to say whether he had met one of the accused.
Opinion of the court: 'Subject only to the single qualification [ie, s 344 Criminal Procedure (Scotland) Act 1975] contempt of court is not a crime within the meaning of our criminal law. It is the name given to conduct which challenges or affronts the authority of the court or the supremacy of the law itself whether it takes place in or in connection with civil or criminal proceedings. The offence of contempt of court is an offence sui generis . . . any witness . . . who declines to answer a competent and relevant question in court must realise that he will be in contempt.'

Contrast:
Macara v MacFarlane 1980 SLT (Notes) 26
M, a solicitor at one court unable to get to another court on time, had anticipated this and arranged for a replacement solicitor to take his place if necessary. When case called M did not appear and replacement took the case. Sheriff convicted M of contempt.
Conviction quashed on appeal on basis that M having taken the proper steps to ensure that the business of the court would be able to proceed, the sheriff had no material before him at all which justified a finding of contempt of court.

or where, for example, a witness ignores citation to appear.

HMA v Bell 1936 JC 89
Witness failed to attend. Guilty of contempt and sentenced to one month's imprisonment.

McGlinchy or Petrie v Angus (1889) 2 White 358
P cited to appear as witness in trial of her brother for assault. She failed to heed adequate citation and did not turn up at court. Convicted of contempt and conviction upheld on appeal.
Per LJ-C Macdonald: 'In all such cases it is in the power, and, indeed, it is the duty of the court, in order to protect the dignity, quietness, and regularity of its proceedings, and to prevent defiance of its orders, to deal with such acts of contempt . . .'

The conduct may be **within the precincts of the court** either wilfully

Pirie v Hawthorn 1962 JC 69; 1962 SLT 291
Accused failed to appear in sheriff court to answer summary complaint, the explanation being that his father omitted to inform him of the date. On appeal his conviction quashed.
Per LJ-G Clyde: 'There was no wilful defiance of the court. The essential element of contempt of court is thus absent.'

Leys v Leys (1886) 13 R 1223
Non-delivery of child to be handed over held to be contemptuous.

See also:

McKinnon v Douglas, supra

See also Contempt of Court Act 1981, s 15, re penalties for contempt in all Scottish courts.
Section 10: No court may require a person to disclose, nor is any person guilty of contempt of court for refusing to disclose, the source of information contained in a publication for which he is responsible, unless it is established to the satisfaction of the court that disclosure is necessary in the interests of justice or national security or for the prevention of disorder or crime.

or carelessly,

Muirhead v Douglas 1979 SLT (Notes) 17
M, a solicitor, due to defend an accused in a trial second on a list of three, absented himself from court after the first trial started anticipating that it would last two hours. Court business was delayed for half an hour when the first trial finished earlier than expected. He appealed unsuccessfully against conviction for contempt of court.
Per Lord Cameron: 'The variety and quality of the acts or omissions which in particular cases may fall within "contempt of court" are not capable of precise delimitation or formulation. On the other hand, it may be said that where there has been a failure to obey or obtemper an order or requirement of a court, such a failure demands satisfactory explanation and excuse, and in the absence of such may be held to constitute a contempt of court of varying degrees of gravity. I can see no reason in principle, and there is certainly none in authority, for an assertion that failure due to carelessness alone may, in no circumstances, constitute contempt of court.'

or the conduct may be **outwith the precincts of the court**, for example, where the administration of justice is prejudiced by publishing material calculated to cause prejudice.

Stirling v Associated Newspapers Ltd 1960 SLT 5
Newspaper printed a photograph of accused a day after his initial detention along with an article about him and the crime.
Held to be contempt. Test was: Is the course adopted by the newspaper such as to prejudice the impartiality of the trial?

Hall v Associated Newspapers Ltd & Others 1978 SLT 241
Accused in police custody in connection with a murder inquiry. While in custody newspaper published extensive reports about the inquiry and the accused.
Held that from the moment of arrest, or the moment the warrant to arrest is granted, the person concerned is under the care and protection of the court. At either of these points relevant proceedings have commenced so as to bring into play the contempt jurisdiction of the court where prejudicial publication is concerned.

In summary matters, jurisdiction starts from the time of arrest or service of the complaint, whichever is the earlier.

See also:

Kemp, Petitioner 1982 SCCR 1
Press reports during a conspiracy trial indicated that witnesses who had given evidence were at a secret address under police custody. Trial judge's finding of contempt quashed by appeal court, as the reports were narratives of fact not likely to prejudice the minds of the jury.

HMA v Stuurman & Others 1980 SLT 182
Prejudicial pre-trial publicity, even if it constitutes contempt, does not necessarily bar the subsequent trial taking place. Plea in bar of trial rejected.

Contempt of Court Act 1981, ss 1 and 2, strict liability provisions in relation to publications which create a substantial risk that course of justice in particular proceedings will be seriously impeded or prejudiced; s 4, postponement of reporting of proceedings.

For discussion of provisions, see *New Law Journal*, 1981, pages 923, 1167 and 1191.

HMA v News Group Newspapers; HMA v Scottish Express Newspapers Ltd 1989 SCCR 156

Man arrested and charged with attempted murder. Article in *Sun* and *Scottish Daily Express* next day reported arrest and described the attempted murder as the attempted political assassination of a Yugoslav political exile. Impression given by article that the arrested person was guilty.

Held that publisher must not only try to avoid committing contempt of court but must succeed in doing so. Having regard to the spectacular nature of the crime and the 110 day rule, time lag between publication and trial not long enough to avoid prejudice. Found guilty.

Moot point whether contempt of court extends to public inquiries, etc, as not strictly courts of law.

But see:

HMA v Airs, supra

Contempt: 'Conduct which challenges or affronts the authority of the court or the supremacy of the law itself whether it takes place in or in connection with civil or criminal proceedings.'

Restriction on press and TV in proceedings involving person under sixteen.

Criminal Procedure (Scotland) Act 1975. Sections 169 (solemn) and 374 (summary), both as substituted by Criminal Justice (Scotland) Act 1980, s 22, make it an offence to publish the identity, or picture of a person under sixteen years in any newspaper where that person is involved in any proceedings in a Scottish court. (This includes radio and television reporting.) The court or the Secretary of State may lift such reporting restrictions.

Note: This protection extends to a witness who is under sixteen years where the accused is also under sixteen. It does not apply where the accused is over sixteen and the witness is under sixteen, unless the court so directs.

Facts which constitute contempt may also constitute crime, eg perjury.

Manson, Petitioner (1977) SCCR Supp 177.

References: Gordon, 1088-1096; Hume I, 405-406; Gane and Stoddart, 718.

SENTENCING POLICY

Ellen Hislop, Petitioner 1986 SCCR 268—H was defence witness in drugs trial. Refused to name those who had supplied her with drugs other than one man whom she did name. Sentenced to nine months' imprisonment for contempt.

Held not to be excessive.

Contempt of Court Act 1981, s 15(2) provides that maximum imprisonment for contempt of court in Scottish proceedings shall be two years.

McInally, Petitioner 1993 SCCR 212, supra—Witness prevarication. Seventeen-year-old, first offender. Eighteen months' detention on appeal reduced to nine months. Contempt as bad as it could be, custody inevitable but some appreciation now of the gravity of her conduct.

Forrest v Wilson 1993 SCCR 631—Witness prevaricating given 42 days' summary imprisonment. On appeal *held* that the restrictions on first imprisonment did not apply as court not sentencing but summarily punishing. Period should have been 21 days under s 334 of the 1975 Act.

FIRE RAISING

Fire raising is the **wilful or reckless setting alight** of the **property of another.**

COMMENTARY	CASE LAW	STATUTE LAW
Wilful or reckless If the fire is not started deliberately the mens rea—that it must be started intentionally—will be found if it is started with a high enough degree of recklessness.	*HMA v Geo MacBean* 1847 Ark 262 MacB set fire to house by setting alight some straw and paper in a garret room with a lighted candle. Fire spread through his and neighbours' houses. *Held* that if fire is raised in such a state of reckless excitement, to show that the person raising it does not know or care what may result, the requisite degree is attained.	Criminal Justice (Scotland) Act 1980. Section 38: wilful fire raising may be prosecuted summarily in the sheriff court. Section 78(2): acts constituting wilful fire raising may not be charged as vandalism.
But carelessness alone will not provide the necessary mens rea.	*Carr v HMA* 1994 SCCR 521 C setting fire to church hall into which he had broken. Sheriff directed the jury that if the fire was caused accidentally then the crime could not be wilful fire raising but could be culpable and reckless fire raising. Direction upheld on appeal in this regard but court said that in considering recklessness it was important to focus on whether C's actions showed complete disregard for any dangers which might result from what he was doing.	
Setting alight The fire must have taken hold, no matter how minimally,	*John Arthur* (1836) 1 Swin 124 Chemist tried to set shop alight by igniting various chemicals. However, fire was discovered when only a part of the door was alight. *Held* to be sufficient to constitute fire raising, if proved.	
	Peter Grieve (1866) 5 Irv 263 Door of the premises found to be charred. Jury question as to whether that implied fire had actually taken hold. Convicted. However, court observed that charring of a door did not necessarily mean that it had been *set* on fire.	
	Alexander Pollock (1869) 1 Couper 257 P set stock and materials alight. However, building itself did not seem to be on fire. Some time after extinction of the fire, smouldering joist discovered. Lord Ardmillan: 'To constitute fire raising, a portion of the fabric must actually have been on fire, through the act of the accused.'	
although it may not have been applied directly or initially to the property alight.	*Margaret Anderson* 1826 Hume I 130 Set fire to furniture in room from which the fire then spread through the house.	
	Janet Hamilton & Another 1806 Hume I 129 H set fire to a cart-house adjoining a dwellinghouse which was subsequently burned down.	

Property

The nature of the property does not now determine whether the fire raising is wilful or reckless, although certain property is protected by statute.

Angus v HMA (1905) 4 Adam 640
Conviction of wilful fire raising of a haystack upheld in the circumstances although haystack is not heritable property.

Blane v HMA 1991 SCCR 576
Hostel going on fire after the accused set fire to his bedding. Sheriff convicted, sufficient if the premises burnt as a result of the bedding being set on fire. Appeal.
Held that there could be no transferred intent. Sheriff should have looked to the likely consequences, reckless indifference. Conviction for setting fire to bedding substituted.

Of another

It is not fire raising to set own property alight but may be the crime of fire raising with the intent to defraud insurers.

HMA v Paterson (1890) 2 White 496

Hannah McAtamney & Others (1867) 5 Irv 363
McA set alight stock in store in her shop, intending to claim insurance.

In both the above cases it was made clear that the crime was fire raising to defraud insurers.

HMA v Bell 1966 SLT (Notes) 61
B charged with setting his hotel alight with the intent to defraud his insurers. Despite Crown's failure to libel alleged intimation by B of claim to insurance company, charge held relevant, but proceedings later withdrawn and B found not guilty.

It is probably also a crime to endanger life or property by setting fire to one's own property.

John Arthur, supra

Setting fire to moorland or land covered with heath except during specified period is an offence. (Specified period usually 16th April–30th September.)

Hill Farming Act 1946, s 25

References: Hume I, 122; Alison I, 429; Gordon, 719.

SENTENCING POLICY

Donaldson v HMA 1983 SCCR 216—D convicted of seven charges of fire raising. Had a bad record. Life sentence in young offenders institution imposed. Appeal refused. Sentence not excessive. Indeterminate life sentence different from determinate sentence of preventive detention.

FRAUD

By **false pretence,** the **achievement** of a **definite practical result.**

COMMENTARY	CASE LAW	STATUTE LAW
False pretence The false pretence must be an essential, not collateral, matter.	*Tapsell v Prentice* (1910) 6 Adam 354 T pretended that she would be buying considerable amounts of provisions from a shopkeeper who bought a rug from her 'in excess of its value'. Per Lord Ardwall: 'There can be no crime in such a sale unless the fraudulent misrepresentations relate directly to the articles to be sold.' Conviction quashed.	
	Strathern v Fogal 1922 JC 73 Misrepresentation made in relation to leasing of a shop. Charge irrelevant. Per Lord Hunter: 'The misrepresentation if made did not in any real sense affect the subject of the bargain but was essentially collateral.'	
	Hood v Young (1853) 1 Irv 236 Misrepresentation was that two horses being sold for a 'knocked down' price were only parted with because the owner was about to emigrate. Convicted.	
It may be explicit,	*Turnbull v Stuart* (1898) 25 R (J) 78 Misrepresentation was that a horse being sold had been owned by people well known for their expertise in matters relating to horses. Convicted.	
or by implication,	*Alex Bannatyne* 1847 Ark 361 Misrepresentation that a mixture of grains in chiding oats was pure oats. Nothing actually said but way mixture 'got up' implied it. Convicted.	
	Jas Paton (1858) 3 Irv 208 Prizes won by cattle at a show by inflating their skins and putting false horns on them. Charge relevant—not proven.	
	Steuart v Macpherson 1918 JC 96 Misrepresentation by two men intent on cheating a third at cards by acting as if they were strangers to each other. Convicted.	
or result from silence when there is a duty to furnish information.	*Strathern v Fogal*, supra Non-disclosure of grassum exacted from tenants for renewal of lease. Charge relevant.	
	HMA v Pattisons (1901) 3 Adam 420 Non-disclosure of liabilities in balance sheets.	
The misrepresentation may be as to future conduct.	*Richards v HMA* 1971 JC 29	
Achievement Unless it is as an outcome of the false pretence that the result is achieved, there is no fraud as there must be a causal connection between the two.	*Mather v HMA* (1914) 7 Adam 525; 1914 SC(J) 184 Cheque tendered *after* delivery of goods and subsequently dishonoured. *Held* that the indictment did not contain a relevant charge of fraud. It did not set forth that the accused had obtained delivery of goods by reasons of worthless cheque. Per LJ-G Strathclyde: 'Telling a falsehood simpliciter is not a crime by the law of Scotland', although observed 'if a person obtain goods or money by issuing a cheque, he having no funds in bank and knowing the cheque will not be honoured, he commits a fraud'.	

Definite practical result
If the false pretence achieves something which would not otherwise have been achieved, that is fraud.

Adcock v Archibald 1925 JC 58
A misrepresented amount of coal which he had produced by substituting his own marker on fellow miner's batch of coal. A convicted of fraud even though he made no financial gain, because the company had to pay statutory minimum wage which was in excess of sum due even on misrepresented amount. Conviction upheld on appeal.
Per LJ-G Clyde: 'It is, however, a mistake to suppose that for the commission of a fraud it is necessary to prove an actual gain by the accused or an actual loss on the part of the person alleged to be defrauded. Any definite practical result achieved by the fraud is enough.'

McKenzie v HMA 1988 SCCR 153
Appellants charged with attempting to defraud a company in that they instructed solicitors to raise civil actions against the company based on false averments.
Held that dishonest representations had been made to solicitors which had a practical effect, ie the raising of an action, and that was sufficient to make relevant case of attempted fraud.

A person charged with fraud may be convicted of a different charge.

Criminal Procedure (Scotland) Act 1975, ss 60 (solemn) and 312(*m*) (summary). Where an accused is indicted for fraud he can be convicted of theft or reset.

Certain frauds are covered by statutory provisions and most frauds in connection with the sale and purchase of motor vehicles are prosecuted under statute.

Tarleton Engineering Co Ltd v Nattrass [1973] 3 All ER 699
Mileage shown on milometer amounts to a trade description.

Norman v Bennett [1974] 3 All ER 351
Unsuccessful attempt to use disclaimer to defeat protective provisions of the 1968 Act.
Held that to be effective such a disclaimer had to be made before goods supplied: to be as bold and compelling as the description of the goods itself and to be effectively brought to the buyer's attention.

Trade Descriptions Act 1968. Section 11 deals with false and misleading representations as to price. Section 13 deals with false representations concerning the supply of goods or services. Section 14 deals with false and misleading statements as to services.

Limited company can be charged with fraud

Purcell Meats (Scotland) Ltd v McLeod 1986 SCCR 672
Attempted fraud. Central issue is whether the facts show that the persons by whose hands the acts were performed were of such a status that the acts fell to be regarded as the acts of the company.
Tesco Supermarkets Ltd v Nattrass [1972] AC 153; [1971] 2 WLR 1166; [1971] 2 All ER 127 applied.

References: Hume I, 172; Alison I, 362; Macdonald, 52; Gordon, 588; Gane and Stoddart, 401.

SENTENCING POLICY

Scott v Lowe 1990 SCCR 15—S and three others pleaded guilty to fraud. S earned £120 per week and was fined £600. Co-accused were fined varying sums amounting in each case to five weeks' income.
Held that sheriff had assessed fines in correct manner; and appeal refused.

Caldwell v Jessop 1991 SCCR 323—Community national, sixteen charges of obtaining money by false hard luck stories. Three previous convictions for dishonesty. Sentenced to 60 days' imprisonment and deportation recommended. Upheld on appeal.

McLean v HMA 1991 SCCR 972—Seven charges of 'clocking cars', nine months' imprisonment. Upheld on appeal, public interest required effective deterrence against such offences and restitution would not meet that need.

HOMICIDE

Homicide, the killing of another, is murder when the perpetrator **intends to take life** or is **wickedly reckless** as to the consequence of those actions which result in death. Homicide is culpable homicide where either the perpetrator intends to kill but there are **mitigating factors** relating to the act or where the perpetrator did not intend to kill but has been **criminally negligent** as to his actions.
Homicide will not be criminal when **casual** or **justifiable.**

COMMENTARY	CASE LAW	STATUTE LAW
Homicide The destruction of a human life other than one's own.	*HMA v Scott* (1892) 3 White 240 Accused strangled child immediately on birth. Evidence that the child breathed. *Held*, could be culpable homicide. Did not matter that child not fully born at the time. *Jean McCallum* (1858) 3 Irv 187 LJ-C Inglis stating that child must have separate existence from its mother.	
Destruction of foetus not homicide.		Abortion Act 1961 Concealment of Birth (Scotland) Act 1809.
Injuries sustained in utero.	*McCluskey v HMA* 1989 SLT 175 Charge of causing death by reckless driving. Child in utero born but dying of injuries sustained in utero. *Held* on appeal, charge competent. Following Hume (I, 189) culpable homicide charge might be relevant in such circumstances.	
Wickedly reckless Involuntary murder.	*Cawthorne v HMA* 1968 JC 32 Attempted murder charge, C firing shots into a room containing four people. Per LJ-G Clyde: 'The mens rea which is essential to the establishment of such a common law crime may be established by satisfactory evidence of a deliberate intention to kill or by satisfactory evidence of such wicked recklessness as to imply a disposition depraved enough to be regardless of the consequences.'	
Shown by intention to do serious bodily harm (sometimes seen as a separate aspect of mens rea).	*Brennan v HMA* 1977 JC 37 Full bench. B killing father while in a state of self-induced intoxication. Murder conviction upheld. Intention to do serious injury sufficient for mens rea. See also: *Broadley v HMA* 1991 SCCR 416	
Shown by the use of weapons.	*HMA v McGuinness* 1937 JC 37 Victim killed by knife. *Held* that people using deadly weapons guilty of murder.	
Homicide during the course of robbery.	*Miller and Denovan v HMA* 7 December 1960, unreported, C of CA Blow to the head of victim with block of wood during robbery causing death. *Held*, no room for culpable homicide. Homicide in course of robbery due to serious and reckless violence is murder.	

Mitigating factors
Pleas of diminished responsibility and provocation may reduce a charge of murder to one of culpable homicide.

HMA v Blake 1986 SLT 661
Attempted murder, attack with an axe.
Held that diminished responsibility requires some sort of mental illness, that is '. . . unsoundness of the mind bordering on but not amounting to insanity.'

See also:

Connelly v HMA 1990 SCCR 358
LT v HMA 1990 SCCR 540
Martindale v HMA 1992 SCCR 700

Provocation: See Special Defences (Self-Defence) pp 120–121

Criminally negligent
Involuntary homicide may be culpable where the person is deemed criminally negligent.

Homicide in the course of a lawful act.

Paton v HMA 1936 JC 19
Charge of culpable homicide by reckless driving.
Held that criminal negligence amounting to criminal indifference must be shown.

Homicide in the course of an unlawful act.

Mathieson v HMA 1981 SCCR 196
Culpable homicide by culpable and reckless fire raising.
Held that if the act causing death was unlawful, crime would be culpable homicide.

Bird v HMA 1952 JC 23
Accused assaulting a woman who collapsed and died. Judge in charge including directions that death resulting from any assault would be culpable homicide. Attacker must take the victim as he finds him or her.

Casual

HMA v Rutherford 1947 JC 1
Per LJ-C Cooper quoting with approval from Alison I, 139: 'It is casual homicide where a person kills unintentionally, when lawfully employed and neither meaning harm to any one nor having failed in the due degree of care and circumspection for preventing mischief to his neighbour.'

Justifiable
'. . . committed in the necessary prosecution of that which the killer is bound or hath a right to do.' Hume I, 195.

Armed forces.

HMA v Sheppard 1941 JC 67
Soldier shooting a prisoner he was escorting who tried to escape.
Held that if soldier acting in line of duty jury should acquit.

References: Hume I, 179; Alison I, 1; Macdonald, 87; Gordon, 727; Gane, 479; McCall Smith and Sheldon, 151.

SENTENCING POLICY

LT v HMA 1990 SCCR 540—Mother setting fire to home killing two children. Mentally disturbed but no diminished responsibility. Ten years' imprisonment upheld on appeal. No need for life sentence, sentence reflecting public outrage and the need for treatment of the accused.

RJK v HMA 1991 SCCR 703—Twelve-year-old convicted of culpable homicide of three-year-old. Sentence to be detained 'without limit of time'.
Held on appeal that it was competent under s 206 of the Criminal Procedure (Scotland) Act 1975 and appropriate here where the child needed psychiatric assessment over several years.

Substantive Law

Casey v HMA 1993 SCCR 453—Murder in the course of a violent robbery. Trial judge under s 205A of the 1975 Act ordering minimum recommended sentence of twenty years. Appeal.
Held that recommendations may be made where crime particularly brutal or where accused a danger to the public. No recommendations of less than twelve years and normally will be fifteen to thirty years. Fifteen years appropriate here.

Beddie v HMA 1993 SCCR 970—Culpable homicide. B killing victim by driving his car at him causing him to fall on the bonnet then braking so he fell on the road and fractured his skull. Four years' imprisonment. Appeal.
Held that the culpability was slight, six months substituted.

Baillie v HMA 1993 SCCR 1084—Culpable homicide. Twenty-two-year-old assaulting and killing twenty-month-old child of cohabitee. Sentenced to life imprisonment to protect the public. Appeal.
Held that there was no evidence that public needed such protection, fifteen years substituted.

INDECENT OR OBSCENE PUBLICATIONS

Indecent or obscene publications are those which have a **tendency to deprave and corrupt** the minds of those into whose hands the publication may fall and the **sale, publication or display** of which may be held to be **shamelessly indecent conduct.**

COMMENTARY	CASE LAW	STATUTE LAW
		Provisions of Burgh Police (Scotland) Act 1892 and local statutory provisions repealed by s 137 of Civic Government (Scotland) Act 1982 subject to provisions for postponement of repeal contained in s 134 of same Act.
Indecent or obscene Terms once generally held to be synonymous must now be viewed independently subject to distinctions implied by separate provisions of Indecent Displays (Control) Act 1981, s 1(1), and Civic Government (Scotland) Act 1982, s 51, although see:	*Watt v Annan* 1978 JC 84 Complaint of shameless indecency alleged that the accused had exhibited 'a film of an obscene or indecent nature'.	
	Ingram v Macari 1981 SCCR 184; 1982 SCCR 372 Words 'indecent or obscene convey a single idea'. 1981 report relates to relevancy; 1982 report relates to final disposal.	
Indecent What constitutes indecency remains a question of fact.	*Galletly v Laird* 1953 JC 16 G convicted of exhibiting for sale 'indecent or obscene books'. Per LJ-G Cooper: 'Inevitable that the character of the offending books or pictures should be ascertained . . . by reading the books or looking at the pictures. The book or picture itself provides the best evidence of its own indecency or obscenity or the absence of such qualities.'	Indecent Displays (Control) Act 1981. Offence of making, causing or permitting the display of indecent matter in, or so as to be visible from, any public place. Section 1(3) makes provisions for the exclusion in certain limited circumstances from the provisions of s 1, where specific requirements as to warning notices, etc, are complied with, although such a warning may be viewed as incriminating evidence in a charge of shameless indecency.
Exposing for sale.	*Robertson v Smith* 1979 SLT (Notes) 51 *McGowan v Langmuir* 1931 JC 10 Per LJ-G Clyde: 'Everything depends on the mode and circumstances of each act of sale, loan or exhibition and on the character and circumstances of the persons who are parties to these acts.'	
Obscene Again, question of obscenity remains one of fact to be considered in all the circumstances.	*Galletly v Laird*, supra *McGowan v Langmuir*, supra	Civic Government (Scotland) Act 1982. Section 51 creates offences relating to publication, sale, distribution or display of obscene material. Section 51(5) allows court to convict a person found not guilty under s 51(1) on the basis that the material was indecent and not obscene, of the offence under s 1(1) of the Indecent Displays (Control) Act 1981 of displaying indecent material. (Provisions of this section indicate, therefore, that the terms 'indecent' and 'obscene' can no longer be treated as synonymous.)

Obscenity may be of a non-sexual nature.	*John Calder (Publications) Ltd v Powell* [1965] 1 All ER 159 Book dealing with drug-taking and addiction. *Held* obscene. *DPP v A & BC Chewing Gum Ltd* [1968] 1 QB 159 Bubble gum cards depicting battles. *Held* that magistrates were wrong in excluding evidence of child psychiatrists.	
Publications Applies particularly to books, pictures, drawings, films and articles of such nature which are capable of exhibition, display or sale.		Section 51 of Civic Government (Scotland) Act 1982 and s 1(1) of Indecent Displays (Control) Act 1981 do not apply to broadcasts by the BBC or IBA, nor do they apply to performances of a play which are regulated under s 2(2) of Theatres Act 1968.
May take form of electronic pulses or similar.	*Smith v Downie* 1982 SLT (Sh Ct) 23 Video-cassette.	Civic Government (Scotland) Act 1982, s 51(8), gives definition of 'material'.
Essence is 'publication' to general public or part thereof by exhibition or sale.	*Annan v Nolan* 1980 Crown Office Circular Record by the Sex Pistols. *Galletly v Laird*, supra Per LJ-G Cooper, two elements in offence: (1) 'book or picture is of such a nature as to be calculated to produce a pernicious effect in depraving and corrupting those who are open to such influences; and (2) such book or picture is being indiscriminately exhibited or circulated or offered for sale in such circumstances as to justify the inference that it is likely to fall (and perhaps intended to fall) into the hands of persons liable to be so corrupted'.	
Publication to private groups or individuals also criminal.	*Watt v Annan*, supra Indecent films shown behind locked doors of public house. *Held* to constitute shamelessly indecent conduct at common law. Per Lord Cameron: 'Neither publicity nor privacy of locus of conduct necessarily affects . . . criminal quality of conduct.'	
Generally the circumstances of the publication must be taken into account.	*McGowan v Langmuir*, supra Per Lord Sands: 'There is always an element of relativity. Charts and realistic coloured illustrations which might be exhibited in a medical classroom, might be grossly indecent as adornments of a place of public worship or even of a private sitting-room.'	
Tendency to deprave and corrupt Criteria satisfying this qualification follow those necessary for indecent or obscene.	*Ingram v Macari*, supra Attempted to introduce expert evidence on question of whether or not magazines were liable to deprave and corrupt the morals of the lieges. *Held*, on appeal, that such evidence could not be admitted. 'It was the duty of the sheriff to make up his own mind from examination of the magazines whether they were indecent or obscene in the sense of being likely to deprave and corrupt the morals of their readers.'	

Sale, publication or display

Provisions of Civic Government (Scotland) Act 1982 supplement those of the common law and extend liability to situations not previously covered.

Tudhope v Barlow 1981 SLT (Sh Ct) 94
Held, inter alia, that shameless indecent conduct was a crime of intent and could not be committed recklessly or negligently and accordingly in view of the accused's ignorance of the contents of the magazines in question the necessary criminal intent had not been established and accused found not guilty. This was a common law charge.

Indecent Displays (Control) Act 1981, s 1
Civic Government (Scotland) Act 1982
Section 51(2): publishes, sells, distributes, or with a view to eventual sale or distribution, makes, prints, has or keeps obscene material.
Section 51(4): due diligence to avoid committing the offence is a defence to the charge.

Shamelessly indecent conduct

This common law offence has now been applied to indecent or obscene publications.

Robertson v Smith 1979 SLT (Notes) 51
Shopkeeper charged with shamelessly indecent conduct by selling, exposing for sale and having for sale indecent and obscene magazines. Conviction by sheriff confirmed on appeal.

Ingram v Macari, supra

'All shamelessly indecent conduct is criminal' (Macdonald, 150).

McLaughlan v Boyd 1934 JC 19
Publican convicted of lewd and libidinous practices towards a number of persons. Lord Clyde approving statement by Macdonald to cover such conduct.

Intention or knowledge for this common law crime must be proved.

Watt v Annan, supra
W showed an obscene film to a number of persons in a hotel. Convicted of shameless indecency.
Lord Cameron: 'Conduct to be criminal must be directed to some person or persons with an intention or knowledge that it should corrupt or deprave those towards whom the indecent or obscene conduct was directed.'

Dean v Menzies 1981 JC 23
Held a company could not be deemed to possess the necessary mens rea for the offence at common law.

Civic Government (Scotland) Act 1982, s 51, and Indecent Displays (Control) Act 1981, s 1, now obviate this gap in the common law since the statutory offence does not require mens rea.

Exposing for sale.

Scott v Smith 1981 SLT (Notes) 22
Police constable purchased obscene magazine produced from a drawer.
Held that stock held in readiness for sale was being 'exposed for sale'.

Tudhope v Sommerville 1981 SLT 117
Obscene publications—possession for circulation and distribution to retailers.
Held that mere possession without any exposure to the public does not constitute a crime at common law.

References: Gordon, 991; Gane and Stoddart, 680; Macdonald, 152-153.

MALICIOUS MISCHIEF

Malicious mischief is the **damaging** in part or in whole of **another's property.**

COMMENTARY	CASE LAW	STATUTE LAW
Damaging May be achieved intentionally,	*Forbes v Ross* (1898) 2 Adam 513 An appeal against conviction of having wilfully, maliciously and mischievously broken down a wall. *Held*, that since appellant caused the wall to be destroyed in the knowledge that it was not his property, conviction should be upheld, although it was not clear to whom the wall belonged, the wall was of little value and the appellant claimed the destruction was to vindicate a right of way.	
	But contrast: *Black v Laing* (1879) 4 Couper 276 Conviction quashed where removal of a fence which formed an obstruction to one of the entrances to the accused's property was not considered to warrant crime of malicious mischief, since in the circumstances the removal was justified as the gap was the only access to the garden and that question of rights was one to be determined by a civil court.	
	Clark v Syme 1957 JC 1 Farmer shot and killed sheep which strayed from adjoining land under mistaken belief that he was legally entitled to do so. *Held*, on appeal by Crown, that wilful disregard of the property rights of another was sufficient to make the destruction of that property an act of malicious mischief.	
or result from deliberate disregard of another's property rights and therefore cannot be caused accidentally or unwillingly.	*Ward v Robertson* 1938 JC 32 Trespassers crossed an unfenced field of growing grass, on foot. Conviction of causing malicious mischief to the crop of grass quashed on appeal. It is essential that the accused had or should have had knowledge that he was likely to cause damage.	
Damage need not be physical.	*HMA v Wilson* 1983 SCCR 420 W activated emergency stop button of power station generator, causing loss of electricity costing £147,000 to replace. Sheriff held that the indictment of malicious mischief was irrelevant in the absence of an averment of physical damage. Overturned on appeal. *Held* that an element of physical injury is not necessary. Malicious mischief may be constituted by any patrimonial injury. Indictment held relevant.	
Another's property A belief that the goods are one's own is also a good defence provided it is not held recklessly.		
Malicious mischief different from vandalism.	*Black v Allan* 1985 SCCR 11 Accused charged with vandalism contrary to s 78(1) of Criminal Justice (Scotland) Act 1980: breaking window as result of horseplay. Court of appeal made it plain that this statutory offence different from common-law crime of malicious mischief. Opinion of the court: 'The statutory offence is an offence standing in its own language and is committed if the conduct in question resulting in damage to property is wilful or . . . reckless.'	Criminal Justice (Scotland) Act 1980, s 78(1). Any person who without reasonable excuse wilfully or recklessly destroys or damages any property belonging to another shall be guilty of the offence of vandalism, but fire raising is excluded (s 78(2)).

References: Hume I, 122; Alison I, 448; Gordon, 711.

MISUSE OF DRUGS

Production, supply and possession of controlled drugs

(1) It is an offence for a person **to produce** a **controlled drug** unlawfully or to be so concerned.
(2) It is an offence to **supply** or offer to supply a controlled drug to another unlawfully or to be so concerned, or to be concerned in the making unlawfully of an offer to supply such a drug.
(3) It is an offence for a person to have a controlled drug in his **possession**.
(4) It is an offence for a person to have a controlled drug in his **possession**, whether lawfully or not, **with intent to supply** it to another unlawfully.

COMMENTARY	CASE LAW	STATUTE LAW
Produce (or be so concerned)	*R v Farr* [1982] Crim LR 745 CA F allowed C and A to use F's kitchen knowing that C and A were producing pink heroin there. *Held*, allowing F's appeal against conviction of producing a controlled drug contrary to s 4(2) of the 1971 Act, that there had to be some identifiable participation in the process of producing a controlled drug before a conviction under s 4(2) could be sustained. Appropriate charge should have been under s 8, allowing premises to be used for production of the drug. F had made no prior arrangements with C and A, and the evidence showed only passive presence.	Misuse of Drugs Act 1971 Sections 4(2) and 37(1): produce 'by manufacture, cultivation or any other method'.
Controlled drug	*Mieras v Rees* [1975] Crim LR 224 DC Defendant supplied a drug to X believing it to be a controlled drug, but said he later discovered that it was not. *Held*, allowing defendant's appeal against conviction, that as the prosecutor could not prove the drug to have been in fact a controlled drug no actus reus could be proved and accordingly no offence or attempted offence could be proved.	Section 2(1): Any controlled drug, ie, substance or product specified in Sched 2 to 1971 Act.
Supply	*R v Mills* [1963] 1 QB 522 Lord Parker CJ at 572: '. . . "supply" must denote the parting of possession from one person to another . . .'. *R v Harris (Janet)* [1968] 1 WLR 769 *Held* that the administration of a controlled drug to another who is already in possession of it does not constitute supplying of the drug by the person administering it. *Kerr (DA) v HMA* 1986 SCCR 81 The offence of being concerned in the supplying of a controlled drug to another, contrary to s 4(3)(*b*), may be established even though there has been no actual supply to another person. Per Lord Hunter 'I consider that section 4(3)(*b*) was purposely enacted in the widest terms . . . to cover a great variety of activities both at the centre and on the fringes of dealing in controlled drugs. It would include . . . the activities of financiers, couriers and other go-betweens, lookouts, advertisers, agents and many links in the chain of distribution.	Section 4(3): '. . . it is an offence for a person—(*a*) supply . . . a controlled drug to another. . . .'

Possession

Possession requires more than mere control, ie, knowledge.

Lockyer v Gibb [1966] 2 All ER 653; [1967] 2 QB 243
Per Lord Parker CJ: 'It is quite clear that a person cannot be said to be in possession of some article which he or she does not realise is, or may be, in her handbag, or in her room, or in some other place over which she has control. It is necessary to show that the appellant knew that she had the article which turned out to be a drug.'

Warner v Metropolitan Police Commissioner [1969] 2 AC 256
Defendant found with a parcel containing a controlled drug and convicted.
Held, on appeal to the House of Lords, that though there was a very strong inference of fact that a man who possesses a package also possesses its contents, he is entitled to be acquitted if he can show that he genuinely believed the parcel to contain an innocent substance and that he had no reasonable opportunity of examining its contents.

Gill v Lockhart 1987 SCCR 599
Cannabis resin found in accused's golf bag. Accused claimed he had placed it there two years ago and forgotten it. Convicted.
Held on appeal that once a person knowingly has possession of a drug, his possession persists even if he forgets its presence. Appeal refused.

Hughes v Guild 1990 SCCR 527
Possession, drugs found in the living room of flat occupied by two persons.
Held on appeal that drugs lying in the open in room enough for inference of knowledge and control.

Feeney v Jessop 1990 SCCR 565
Possession. Drugs found in F's towel in cell.
Held on appeal that F must have known of them and had control over them.

Davidson v HMA 1990 SCCR 699
Possession. Drugs found in co-accused's room next to scales bought by D.
Held on appeal that given D tried to escape when police raided house there was just sufficient evidence for knowledge and control.

Murray v MacPhail 1991 SCCR 245
Possession. Accused allowing a friend to hide drugs in his room. Convicted.
Upheld on appeal, sufficient knowledge and control.

White v HMA 1991 SCCR 555
Possession. Drugs found in W's flat to which others had access, made statement 'I'm saying nothing about it.' Conviction quashed on appeal, statement not special knowledge.

See also:

Martin v HMA 1992 SCCR 356
Bain v HMA 1992 SCCR 705

Possession while in the custody of another.

Amato v Walkingshaw 1989 SCCR 564
A a seaman employed on ship plying between Larne and Cairnryan. Posted envelope containing drugs to himself at Larne. Purser kept it for him but became suspicious and handed it to authorities in Cairnryan. Convicted.
Held that A must have known that purser would hold envelope on his behalf, element of knowledge and control present and appeal refused.

See also:

R v Marriott [1971] 1 All ER 595
McKenzie v Skeen 1983 SLT 121

Misuse of Drugs Act 1971, s 37(3): 'For the purpose of this Act the things which a person has in his possession shall be taken to include any thing subject to his control which is in the custody of another.'

Onus.

R v Cugullere [1961] 1 WLR 258; [1961] 2 All ER 343
The onus remains throughout on the Crown to prove knowledge.

See also:

Inferences.

Warner, supra
DPP v Brooks [1974] 2 All ER 840
Held, that running away may justify the inference.

Although no provisions as to quantity, important in cases re minute quantities of drugs.

R v Worsell [1970] 1 WLR 111; [1969] 2 All ER 1183
W charged with unlawful possession of a tube containing droplets of heroin.
Held that as the tube was in reality empty (ie, the droplets were invisible to the human eye and could only be discerned under a microscope and could not be measured or poured out), it was impossible to hold that there was any evidence that the tube contained a drug.

However:
Bocking v Roberts [1973] 3 All ER 962
Per Lord Widgery CJ: 'When dealing with a charge of possessing a dangerous drug without authority the ordinary maximum of de minimis is not to be applied.'

The quantities of drug found may be small but must be capable of being weighed, measured and identified to sustain prosecution.

R v Frederick 53 Cr App R 455 CA; [1970] 1 WLR 107; [1969] 3 All ER 804
Direction that if the jury thought the defendant was in possession of traces they should find him guilty because one must not have any dangerous drug in one's possession, no matter how small the quantity. Upheld.

See also:

R v Graham [1969] 2 All ER 1181 CA; [1970] 1 WLR 113
Scrapings in defendants' pockets sufficient to be measured.

R v Colyer [1974] Crim LR 243
Traces measurable in the sense that they represented the minimum weight capable of being detected.

Marriott, supra
Traces of drug found on penknife; although it was also necessary to show that the defendant had reason to know there was foreign matter on the knife.

Hambleton v Callinan [1968] 2 QB 427; [1968] 2 All ER 943
Held that when a drug is consumed, it changes its character and it cannot be said that the drug is then in a person's possession, although traces of it are found in his urine.

Keane v Gallacher 1980 JC 77; 1980 SLT 144
Police discovered on top of sideboard a small quantity of resinous material which was visible and could be measured. Argued by defence that the quantity was not 'useable'. Sheriff acquitted. G convicted on appeal. 'It is possession of the drug which is an offence, not its potential use.'

Murdo McKay v Hogg (1973) SCCR Supp 40; 1973, Crown Office Circular 1224
Appellant asleep naked on couch. Search of his clothes on the chair disclosed nothing. After he had dressed, sixteen tablets of LSD were found on seat cover. No one had anything to do with the chair except the appellant. He must have had the tablets for a second or two.
Held that such fleeting contact was not enough to justify possession in terms of the 1971 Act.

Defence to 'possession' offence

Section 5(4)(*a*): It is a defence to prove that the accused 'took possession [of the drug] for the purpose of preventing another from committing . . . an offence . . . and that as soon as possible . . . he took all such steps as were reasonably open to him to destroy the drug or to deliver it into the custody of a person lawfully entitled to take custody of it; or (*b*) that . . . he took possession of it for the purpose of delivering it into the custody of a person lawfully entitled to take custody of it . . . '

Possession for valid medical reason must be proved by defendant.

Wood v Allan 1988 SCCR 115.

Regulation 10(2) of Misuse of Drugs Regulations 1985, SI 1985/2066.

Possession with intent to supply

Morrison v Smith 1983 SCCR 171
M admitted unlawful possession of a controlled drug, but denied knowledge of a large amount of other drugs found in house. Convicted.
Held, in absence of an explanation for possession, that the sheriff was entitled to infer intention to supply from the value, quantity and diversity of the drugs.

Section 5(3): '. . . it is an offence for a person to have a controlled drug in his possession, whether lawfully or not, with intent to supply it to another in contravention of section 4(1) . . . '

Haq v HMA 1987 SCCR 433
H convicted of possessing cannabis resin with intent to supply. H in possession of large block of the drug weighing 91 g. No evidence of intent to supply other than size of block and evidence from one police officer that block too large for personal use. Appeal against conviction refused.
Held to be sufficient evidence to infer intent.

See also:

Bauros v HMA 1991 SCCR 768

Donnelly (Mary) v HMA 1984 SCCR 419
Heroin. Possession with intent to supply. D occupier of house where 'considerable quantity' of diamorphine found in separate envelopes with street value of £10 or £20 each. Appeal against conviction refused.
Per Lord Dunpark: '. . .where a large quantity of controlled drugs, separately packaged in quantities normally sold in the streets, are found in the possession of a person, it is open to a jury to infer that that person intended to supply them to another. If the appellant . . . did no more than allow [S] to uplift drugs in her physical possession, she was thereby supplying them to another, namely, [S].'

References: Gordon, 1000; Bovey, 6, 7; 20-39; 55-85.

Cultivation of cannabis

Misuse of Drugs Act 1971, s 6. It is an offence to **cultivate** any **plant of the genus** *Cannabis* unlawfully.

COMMENTARY	CASE LAW	STATUTE LAW
Not lawful to **cultivate** any **plant of the genus** *Cannabis*.		
	Tudhope v Robertson 1980 JC 62; 1980 SLT 60 *Held* that the position of plants to secure the light (ie, at a window) necessary to the growth, the condition of the plants, the presence of the seeds and the accused's objective in having the plants in the house, all pointed to the conclusion that the plants were being 'cultivated' and the offence was thus being committed.	Section 6.
Reference: Bovey, 27-29.		

Offences committed by occupiers etc of premises by permitting certain activities to take place there

Misuse of Drugs Act 1971, s 8: A person commits an offence if, being the **occupier** or concerned in the **management of** any **premises**, he **knowingly permits** or **suffers** any of the following activities to take place on those premises, ie,

(*a*) producing or attempting to produce a controlled drug contrary to s 4(1);
(*b*) supplying or attempting to supply a controlled drug to another or offering to supply a controlled drug to another contrary to s 4(1);
(*c*) preparing opium for smoking;
(*d*) smoking cannabis, cannabis resin or prepared opium.

COMMENTARY	CASE LAW	STATUTE LAW
Occupier		
	Christison v Hogg 1974, Crown Office Circular 1281 *Held* that the word occupier must be given its ordinary meaning: 'It is a person who has possession of the premises in question—in possession in a substantial sense involving some degree of permanency and who as a matter of fact exercises control of the premises and dictates their use.' Every case will depend on its own facts.	Misuse of Drugs Act 1971, s 8
	Bruce v McManus [1915] 3 KB 1 Lusk J at p 8: '. . . the person indicated by those words ["occupier of premises"] is the person who is in legal occupation and in control of the premises'.	
	R v Mogford [1970] 1 WLR 988 Two sisters, aged twenty and fifteen, were charged with permitting premises to be used for the purpose of smoking cannabis at their parents' home when they were away on holiday. *Held* that the defendants' control did not amount to the nature and measure of control envisaged by the Act.	
Management of premises		
	Sweet v Parsley [1969] 1 All ER 347; [1970] AC 132 The defendant, the tenant of a farm, sublet rooms there, while living elsewhere. She used her own room occasionally when collecting rent, letters,etc, and rarely stayed overnight. Unknown to her, a sub-tenant used cannabis and the defendant was convicted under the Dangerous Drugs Act 1965, s 5 (equivalent of s 8 of the 1971 Act). *Held* that her appeal be allowed since: (1) the offence was not absolute and (2) she had no mens rea.	
Knowingly permits		
	Sweet v Parsley, supra Per Lord Diplock: '. . . where the prohibited conduct consists in permitting a particular thing to be done, the word "permit" connotes at least knowledge or reasonable grounds for suspicion on the part of the permittor that the thing will be done and an unwillingness to use means available to him to prevent it . . .'.	
Suffers		
	Rochford RDC v Port of London Authority [1914] 83 LJKB 1066; [1914] 2 KB 916 If a person is in a position to prevent a thing without committing a legal wrong and does not do so, then in the common use of language, that person suffers that thing. Of course, one cannot be said to suffer a thing which one cannot prevent, or, which by law one ought not to prevent.	

Yeandel v Fisher [1966] 1 QB 440
Per Lord Parker CJ: 'It seems to me that the legislation had in mind making those . . . who were on the spot and concerned with the management of premises absolutely liable if those premises were used for those purposes, whereas they had in mind that in the case of the occupier who might be an absent occupier . . . he would only be guilty if he wilfully and knowingly permitted.'

Sweet v Parsley, supra
Lord Parker CJ: 'If somebody is a mere occupier he can only be guilty of an offence if it is proved that he permitted, which as we all know involves some knowledge or constructive knowledge.'

Reference: Bovey, 86-92.

Drug enforcement: statutory powers

COMMENTARY	CASE LAW	STATUTE LAW
Corporate liability Drugs offence committed by a body corporate either with the consent or due to the neglect of a director, manager, secretary or similar officer.		Misuse of Drugs Act 1971, s 21 The officer involved, as well as the body corporate, shall be guilty of the offence committed.
Police powers The police have powers to search and arrest those suspected of committing drugs offences.		Section 23(1): gives power to enter the premises of drugs producers to inspect drugs and stock.
Reasonable grounds of suspicion required.	*Weir v Jessop* 1991 SCCR 242 Section 23(2) reasonable grounds for search. Police given anonymous evidence that a person at a certain locus in possession of drugs. W found, admitted being involved with drugs in the past, searched and drugs found. Appeal. *Held* that constable had reasonable grounds. See also: *Campbell v HMA* 1992 SCCR 35 *Wither v Reid* 1980 JC 7 *Held*, clear distinction between power under ss 23(2) and 24(1). A purported arrest under s 23(2)(*a*) was unlawful as the section only contains power to detain.	Section 23(2): 'where a constable has reasonable grounds to suspect a person is in possession of controlled drugs, he may— (*a*) search the person and detain him for that purpose (*b*) search any vehicle or vessel in which he believes drugs may be found (*c*) seize and detain anything which he believes to be evidence.'
	Stuart v Crowe 1992 SCCR 181 Accused coming to house the police were searching, under s 23(3) warrants, for drugs. S searched then separate warrants obtained to search his house and garage where drugs were found. Warrants upheld on appeal. S at house of known drug dealer without valid reason, police entitled to suspect that he was involved with drugs.	Section 23(3). Justice of the Peace may grant warrant for search of premises if he is satisfied by information on oath of reasonableness of grounds.
	Normand v McCutcheon 1993 SCCR 709 Section 23(4) obstructing a search, M swallowing drug when approached by the police. Only one constable gave evidence that M told why he was being detained. Acquitted. *Held* on appeal, accused knew why they were being detained, conviction substituted. See also: *Annan v McIntosh* 1993 SCCR 938	Section 24(1): 'Constable may arrest without warrant a person he reasonably suspects to have committed an offence under the 1971 Act if: (*a*) he believes the person will abscond; or (*b*) name and address of the person are unknown to him and cannot be ascertained; or (*c*) he is not satisfied the name and address given are true.'
Retention of drugs proceeds Assisting another to retain drug trafficking proceeds is an offence.		Criminal Justice (Scotland) Act 1987 Section 42(1): it is an offence to knowingly prejudice an investigation into drug trafficking; (2): it is a defence that the person did not know or have reasonable grounds to suspect he was likely to prejudice the investigation or that he had lawful authority so to do.

Confiscation orders

Prosecution authorities may seek to confiscate the proceeds of drug dealing from an offender.

HMA v McLean 1993 SCCR 917
Supply of drugs valued at £270,000. Confiscation order sought. Deemed proceeds well in advance of the realisable property so order made for the value of the property. No fine imposed.

Sections 1-7: Confiscation orders
Section 1: Person convicted of producing, importing or supplying drugs. Court may on the application of the prosecutor make an order for the offender to pay a sum of money not exceeding either
(*a*) the value of the trafficking or,
(*b*) the value of the offender's realisable property.

(Section 1(2) details offences where confiscation appropriate.)

Sections 2-7 lay out the procedure to be adopted in using these powers.

SENTENCING POLICY

Meighan v Jessop 1989 SCCR 208—M pleaded guilty to possessing heroin and disubstituted barbituric acid contrary to s 5(2) of Misuse of Drugs Act 1971. Placed on deferred sentence to be of good behaviour for a year. By time of deferred diet he had obtained employment as a drugs counsellor. Sheriff imposed fines of £150 and £50, and M appealed against these as excessive. *Held* that had M not been of good behaviour he could have expected custodial sentence. Fines relatively small, and appeal refused.

Bates v HMA 1989 SCCR 338—Possessing heroin with intent to supply. B and C each sentenced to ten years' imprisonment. B appealed on ground that C nine years older than B and had been sentenced to six years' imprisonment for assault and robbery in 1976. B had number of minor convictions, one previous sentence of three months' detention and fined for drugs offences in 1985.
Held that distinction should have been made between B and C, and B's sentence reduced to seven years.

Hemphill v HMA 1989 SCCR 433—H sentenced to three years' imprisonment for possessing canabis resin with intent to supply. No previous convictions.
Held that sentence not excessive.

Hudson v HMA 1990 SCCR 200—H pleaded guilty to possessing cannabis with intent to supply. Non-commercial supply to friends. Sentenced to four years' imprisonment. On appeal *held* sentence not excessive.

Smith v HMA 1990 SCCR 251—Supplying drugs. Whether account has to be taken of the fact that one accused older and had supplied the purchasing funds.
Held on appeal that there was not need to differentiate.

Kennedy v HMA 1990 SCCR 417—Possession of £15 worth of lysergide and cannabis. Sentenced to eighteen months' imprisonment. Appeal.
Held that the sentence was excessive, nine months substituted. Possession of 0.1 grammes of cocaine. First such charge in the area, sheriff imposing six months' imprisonment as a deterrent. Upheld on appeal.

Isdale v Scott 1991 SCCR 491—Possession of cannabis. Sixty days' imprisonment after failing to tell court who was his supplier. Appeal.
Held that providing such information could have mitigating effect but failure didn't provide justification for imprisonment. One year deferred sentence substituted.

Kerr v HMA 1991 SCCR 774—Supplying small amounts of cannabis and buprenorphine to a prisoner. Sentenced to two years' and 18 months' consecutively. Appeal.
Held that this was a serious known evil that required to be dealt with severely. Sentence upheld.

McQueen v Hingston 1992 SCCR 92—Possession of 9.5 grammes of cannabis, previous convictions. Sentenced to sixty days' imprisonment. Appeal.
Held that as M had a family, was unemployed and last offence was three years ago, the sentence was excessive and £1,500 fine substituted.

Howarth v HMA 1992 SCCR 855—Three accused convicted of importing 0.5 million tonnes (£100 million worth) of cocaine. Accused sentenced to twenty-five, fifteen and fifteen years' imprisonment respectively. Upheld on appeal, sentence reflecting the fact that it was Class A drugs, their amount and value.

Gibson v HMA 1992 SCCR 855—First offender supplying cannabis to friends only. £35 worth found. Sentenced to nine months' imprisonment. Appeal.
Held that sentence should be severe but not excessive. 180 hours community service substituted.

Substantive Law

Ravenall v Annan 1993 SCCR 658—First offender, thirty-five-year-old, employed, family. Possession of £20 of Class A Ecstasy. Sentenced to six months' imprisonment. Appeal.
Held that the sheriff had not treated the case on its merits, £250 fine substituted.

Stephen v HMA 1993 SCCR 660—Supplying Class B drug, packaged and ready for sale at folk festival. Valued at £370. Sentenced to twelve months' imprisonment. Increased on appeal to two years.

MOBBING

A mob is a **gathering,** intent on a **common purpose** to be effected illegally and to the alarm of the public, in which **mere presence** may be sufficient for guilt.

COMMENTARY	CASE LAW	STATUTE LAW
Gathering The number needed to constitute a mob is determined by their conduct and is not fixed.	*Sloan v Macmillan* 1922 JC 1 Per LJ-C Scott Dickson: 'The law is that the number of people required to constitute a mob depends on what these people do, the violence they show, the threats they use.'	
There need be no actual violence.	*Sloan v Macmillan*, supra Per LJ-C Scott Dickson: '. . . lied persistently . . . in order to produce terror . . . by saying that there were hundreds of desperate men outside. That seems to me to be enough to make the appellant constitute part of a riotous mob.'	
Common purpose Unless there is a common purpose there is no mob.	*Daniel Blair & Ors* (1868) 1 Couper 168 Crowd assembled to pull down all gates. Per Lord Deas: 'The mere number of people, there may be thousands and thousands, does not constitute a mob. In order to constitute a mob there must be not merely a great number of people but a *common purpose*—and that common purpose must be illegal.'	
	Francis Docherty & Ors (1841) 2 Swin 635 Per Lord Hope: 'Mobbing is not simply a breach of the peace by a number of persons; to constitute that crime it is absolutely necessary that there should be a common object.'	
But the purpose need not be antecedent to the formation of the mob,	*Alex Orr and Ors* (1856) 2 Irv 502 Accused attacked and burned a chapel. Also charged with mobbing and rioting. Per Lord Hope: 'If a mob take up a purpose, although it may not have been concerted beforehand, or may not at first have been known to the individuals at the bar; if the persons at the bar accompany that mob . . . they are guilty of the outrages committed by that mob.'	
and need have no motive other than to engage in disruptive behaviour.	*Michael Hart and Ors* (1854) 1 Irv 574 H was charged with forming part of a mob whose purpose was to attack Orangemen. There was insufficient evidence to support latter part of the libel but the jury were directed that they could nevertheless convict of mobbing and rioting.	
Evidence necessary to prove common purpose,	*Hancock & Ors v HMA* 1981 SCCR 32 Convictions of mobbing quashed on appeal. Crown failed to prove accused intent on a common purpose, but only 'a series of unconnected and fortuitous events . . . without any evidence of preknowledge or support or encouragement or countenance'.	
but when proved, **mere presence** in a mob may be sufficient for guilt,	*HMA v Cairns & Ors* (1837) 1 Swin 597 Person can be guilty of mobbing by mere presence alone. But he may also be the very soul of the mob without doing much—a word, a nod may excite the mob and be the cause of all the mischief that follows.	
and where a mob arises there is a duty to quell or at least withdraw from it (Alison I, p 520).		

Macdonald (5th edn), p 135; also Hume I, 421. It is not necessary to infer guilt that the accused should have been present at the moment when a particular act was committed, or that he should have been personally present at all. The rule that the instigator be as guilty as the perpetrator applies with special force to the case of mobbing.

'It is no defence that the mob's purpose was to prevent something being done by others which the mob thinks to be contrary to what the law allows' (Macdonald, p 132).

References: Hume I, 416; Alison I, 509; Macdonald, 131; Gane and Stoddart, 691.

OFFENSIVE WEAPONS

The **carrying** of an **offensive** weapon, or a weapon **intended for use** as such, in a **public place** without lawful authority or **reasonable excuse.** It is now also an offence to carry a knife in a public place.

COMMENTARY	CASE LAW	STATUTE LAW
Carrying The offence under the Act is the carrying, not the use, of a weapon.	*Bates v Bulman* [1979] 3 All ER 170 Nature of offence under s 1(1) is the carrying and not the use of a weapon. Person who borrowed a clasp knife, not offensive per se, with the immediate intention of using it as an offensive weapon is not guilty of an offence under this Act (in England at least). See also: *R v Jura* [1954] 1 QB 503 Airgun held not be offensive weapon.	Prevention of Crime Act 1953 Section 1(1): 'Any person who without lawful authority or reasonable excuse, the proof whereof shall lie on him, has with him in any public place any offensive weapon shall be guilty of an offence.'
Offensive (1) Offensive per se, eg, swords, daggers, coshes, knuckledusters.	*Tudhope v O'Neill* 1982 SCCR 45 *Held*, a flick knife is an offensive weapon intended for use for causing injury and was therefore an offensive weapon per se. *Woods v Heywood* 1988 SCCR 434 W charged with possessing machete. Sheriff held that machete offensive weapon per se. *Held* on appeal that machete had twofold purpose, ie as a weapon and as a tool, and could not be described as an offensive weapon per se, and conviction quashed. *McGlennan v Clark* 1993 SCCR 334 Shuriken Chinese throwing star is an offensive weapon per se. Only purpose was for causing personal injury.	Section 1(4): ' "offensive weapon" means any article made or adapted for use for causing injury to the person or intended by the person having it with him for such use by him.'
(2) Adapted for use for causing injury, eg, bicycle chain with razor-blade attached, or broken bottle.		
(3) Not offensive per se but intended for use for causing personal injury.	*R v Petrie* [1961] 1 WLR 358 *Held* that an ordinary razor was not an offensive weapon per se but would be offensive under s 1(4) if intention proved. *Glendinning v Guild* 1987 SCCR 304 Flail not per se offensive. Waving it in the air does not render it offensive. *Coull v Guild* 1985 SCCR 421 Sheath knife not per se an offensive weapon. *Houston v Snape* 1993 SCCR 995 Seven-inch dagger did not stop being an offensive weapon per se just because it was in a sheath.	
Intended for use	*R v Petrie*, supra If not per se an offensive weapon the Crown must prove the intent to use to cause injury.	

Statutory question of intention to use is one to be drawn from all the circumstances.

Lopez v MacNab 1978 JC 41
Accused convicted of possession of a kitchen knife in a public place. Argued, Crown failed to prove intention to use it offensively.
Held that intention was to be inferred from the facts and circumstances of the case.

Normand v Matthews 1993 SCCR 856
Accused said he had clasp knife for 'protection'. On appeal *held* that this statement corroborated by two witnesses was sufficient evidence of accused's intention.

Ralson v Lockhart 1986 SCCR 400
R charged with having an offensive weapon, viz a modelling knife, with intention to use it for causing personal injury. R was driving stolen car and when stopped by police, ran off. Sheriff inferred from these facts that he intended to use knife as offensive weapon. *Held* on appeal that it could not be inferred from his flight from the car that he intended to use knife and sheriff had inverted onus of proof which lay on prosecution to prove R had necessary intention. Conviction quashed. *Lopez v McNab* distinguished.

Intention must be to cause injury.

R v Rapier (1979) 70 Cr App R 17 CA
Rapier convicted of possession of carrying knife, having threatened a doorman with it.
Held, on appeal, that intimidation was not enough unless the person intended to cause injury to the person (in England at least).

Farrell v Rennicks 1959 SLT (Sh Ct) 71
Knife found on accused who pleaded guilty to a housebreaking charge. Accused explained in evidence that knife was to be used as a housebreaking tool.
Held that knife not in accused's possession for the purpose of causing personal injury. Acquitted of offensive weapons charge.

Public place

Normand v Donnelly 1993 SCCR 639
Treatment cubicle in a casualty department necessarily private but conviction upheld on the inference that the accused walked through a public place to get there.

Section 1(4): ' "public place" includes any highway and any other premises or place to which, at the material time, the public have or are permitted to have access whether on payment or otherwise.'

R v Theodoulou [1963] Crim LR 573
T convicted of carrying an offensive weapon, namely, an open razor in a public place, namely, a coffee bar. The trial judge assumed this was a public place rather than leaving it to the jury and because of this the conviction reluctantly quashed on appeal.

See also:
R v Mehmed [1963] Crim LR 780; [1963] CLY 791

Reasonable excuse

Grieve v MacLeod 1967 JC 32
Taxi driver carried a piece of rubber hose tipped with metal. Argued that it was for defensive purposes, taxi drivers often being subject to attack.
Held that he had contravened the Act.
Per LJ-C Grant: 'One object of the Act is to ensure that ordinary citizens do not, unless in exceptional and justifiable circumstances, take the law into their own hands.'

See also:

Hemming v Annan 1982 SCCR 432
Nunchaca sticks being carried home very late at night with no reasonable excuse. Convicted.

Concealment. The offence under the Act is obstruction of, or concealment from, a PC who is exercising his powers of search for an offensive weapon under the Act.

Burke v MacKinnon 1983 SCCR 23
The offence of concealment of an offensive weapon under s 4(2)(*b*) can only be established where it is shown that active steps were taken to conceal the weapon; thus failure to reveal possession would not likely lead to a conviction under the section.
Sheriff Gordon in his commentary at p 25 states that whether or not a carrier will be prosecuted under this section, as well as, or instead of, under the Prevention of Crime Act 1953 will depend on the policy of the prosecutor.

Criminal Justice (Scotland) Act 1980, s 4(2)(*a*) and (*b*): it is an offence to obstruct a PC or conceal an offensive weapon from him in the exercise of his powers of search under s 4(1) of the Act.

Knife or other sharply pointed article

Lister v Lees 1994 SCCR 548
L carrying metal spike in railway station, said he had forgotten to throw it away after opening the tin of glue he was sniffing.
Held on appeal that the question was whether at the time of his arrest L had a 'good reason'. Explanation not sufficient here. 'Good reason' different from 'reasonable excuse' under the 1953 Act but will still depend on the facts and circumstances of each case.

Carrying of Knives etc (Scotland) Act 1993, section 1
(1-3) carrying of knife or other sharply pointed article (not a pocket folding knife with a blade of less than three inches) is an offence,
(4) defence that the person had 'good reason' or lawful authority for having the article,
(5) examples of potential 'good reasons', ie religious reasons, part of national costume.

Reference: Gordon, 861-865.

SENTENCING POLICY

Jacobs v Wilson 1989 SCCR 9—J, first offender, pleaded guilty to having butcher's knife with ten-inch blade in street at 4 am. He stated he had been chased by two youths and had entered his house and come out with the knife, by which time the two youths had gone. Sheriff sentenced J to three months' imprisonment following the sentence in *Smith v Wilson* 1987 SCCR 191.
Held on appeal (1) that sheriff must not be seen to be fettering his discretion, and had come close to suggesting that all offensive weapons should be dealt with by a custodial sentence and (2) that *Smith v Wilson* was distinguishable because weapon not per se offensive. Sentence quashed and order for 120 hours' community service substituted.

Mir v Normand 1993 SCCR 654—Second conviction for possessing a knife. Sentenced to six months' imprisonment and deportation order recommended. Upheld on appeal.

Noble v Lees 1993 SCCR 967—Sixteen-year-old convicted of possessing a knife. Had armed himself to 'settle the score' after an earlier assault. Sentenced to three months' detention. Appeal.
Held that not enough account taken of N's good background. 180 hours community service substituted.

Prior v Normand 1993 SCCR 118—Possession of lock knife in centre of Glasgow. P telling police he would use it on them. Three months' imprisonment increased to six months' imprisonment on appeal. Carrying knives '. . . always been a problem in Glasgow'.

Reid v Normand 1994 SCCR 475—Breach of the peace, vandalism and offensive weapon charge regarding a baseball bat. Six months' imprisonment on weapon charge upheld on appeal.

PERJURY

Perjury is the **deliberate falsification** of **material, relevant and competent** evidence given on oath or affirmation in **judicial proceedings.**

COMMENTARY	CASE LAW	STATUTE LAW
Deliberate falsification Express denial of a fact under oath,	*HMA v Cairns* 1967 JC 37 C gave evidence at his own trial under oath that he did not stab the deceased. Found not proven. Later tried for perjury on basis of this denial. *Held* to be nothing contrary to natural justice in prosecuting a false denial of guilt in a trial.	False Oaths (Scotland) Act 1933 Section 1: wilfully making an untrue statement on oath is a crime.
or express assertion of a fact under oath.	*Elizabeth Muir* 1830 Alison I 469–470 M gave false evidence that the police officer arresting the accused in the trial where M was a witness had been drunk. *Held* to be perjury.	
	Simpson v Tudhope 1987 SCCR 348 S, police officer, charged with perjury in that he deponed he was accompanied by a female officer JD, when he knew that he did not know whether he had been accompanied by her. *Held* to be guilty of perjury. Sheriff Gordon comments 'It is perjury to state that one cannot recollect something when one can . . .' conversely it is perjury to claim one does recollect something of which one had no recollection.'	
It is not constituted by omitting to volunteer evidence in one's possession.		
Material, relevant and competent	*Hall v HMA* 1968 SLT 275 H, in evidence, falsely denied making a particular statement to the police, a matter relevant only to credibility. *Held* that this evidence was both material and relevant to the perjury charge.	
	Aitchison v Simon 1976 SLT (Sh Ct) 73 S deponed that he had not made a certain statement to a police constable. The evidence contained in the statement was material evidence in the trial, and the question of whether statement was made was material to S's credibility as a witness. Argued as evidence given by S in the original trial related to a conversation by S outwith the presence of the accused, it therefore could not have been competent evidence against accused and no perjury could attach. *Held* that evidence was relevant for testing S's credibility, therefore competent to support charge of perjury.	
	Lord Advocate's Reference (No 1 of 1985) 1986 SCCR 329 Per LJ-G Emslie 'Whether a false statement is material and relevant to the issue in the proceedings in which it is made is a question of law. . . . It would be well if the word "material" ceased to be employed in describing the crime. All that is required is that it should be clearly understood that a charge of perjury will not lie unless the evidence alleged to be false was both competent and relevant at an earlier trial, either in proof of the libel or in relation to the credibility of the witness.'	

Normally an opinion cannot constitute perjury. However, the corrupt
origin of a pretended opinion may
infer perjury or a professional person may take a bribe to give false
evidence on opinion (Macdonald,
p 164; Alison I, p 468).

Judicial proceedings
Occurs not only in law courts but
before tribunals where an oath can
be administered.

Section 7: (*a*) form of an oath
immaterial if accepted as
binding; (*b*) affirmation
equivalent in effect to oath.

Oaths Act 1978, s 5: witness
may be required to affirm if
impractical to administer oath.

References: Hume I, 366; Alison I, 465; Gordon, 1063; Gane and Stoddart, 701.

SENTENCING POLICY

Hagen v HMA 1983 SCCR 245—Perjury in course of trial. Sentence of four years' detention imposed. Appealed. In view of H's age, and background of threats, sentence was excessive, and one of three years' detention substituted.

Gordon v Hamilton 1987 SCCR 146—G was seventeen years of age and unemployed. At trial refused to inculpate accused in assault case. Sentenced to three months' detention. By time of appeal had obtained employment and sentence of £500 fine substituted.

RESET

Reset is taking **possession** of, or **being privy** to the **retention** of, property **dishonestly appropriated** by another, **knowing** it to have been so appropriated and **intending** that the owner be deprived of its recovery.

COMMENTARY	CASE LAW	STATUTE LAW
Possession is the control of the property and occurs as soon as there is **retention.**	*Robert Finlay and Ors* 1826 Alison I 333 Stolen property was thrown on bed by thieves and covered over by one of the accused who was convicted of reset. 'If he once acquiesce in the placing of the goods there under circumstances inferring his guilty knowledge, and still more if he lend any aid towards their concealment . . . his guilt is incurred.'	Criminal Procedure (Scotland) Act 1975, ss 7 and 292. Any person who, in Scotland, receives property stolen in any other part of the United Kingdom may be dealt with in like manner as if it had been stolen in Scotland.
	HMA v Browne (1903) 6 F(J) 24 B participated in arrangements for banking of stolen money. Per LJ-C Macdonald: 'Not necessary . . . that the property passed into the personal possession of the receiver.' Accused convicted.	Road Traffic Act 1988, s 178(1)(*b*): driving or allowing oneself to be carried in a motor vehicle taken away without lawful authority.
Privity Where the dishonestly acquired property has not been handled, it requires an overt positive act in connection with it to demonstrate privity or connivance,	*McCawley v HMA* (1959) SCCR Supp 3 McC a passenger in stolen car. *Held* thereby privy to its retention and convicted. *McNeil v HMA* 1968 JC 29 McN a passenger in car transporting stolen property and convicted. 'Reset consists of being privy to the retaining of property that has been dishonestly come by.' but compare: *Clark v HMA* 1965 SLT 250 C present at, but not participating in, negotiations for the sale of stolen cigarettes. *Held*, a misdirection that non-reporting of dealings in stolen property could constitute connivance in its retention. Per LJ-C Grant: 'It was a direction that connivance could be inferred from mere inactivity and I do not think it properly can.' *Girdwood v Houston* 1989 SCCR 578 G convicted of reset of number of articles. When police first questioned G, he denied all knowledge of theft. Subsequently made statement that he knew where articles were and knew who had stolen them. Took police to hiding place. *Held* that as reset could be committed by being privy to retention of stolen goods and in light of G's initial denial, sheriff correct in convicting.	
Dishonestly appropriated Reset was at first restricted to reset of theft. Then extended to robbery and now by statute extends also to property appropriated by breach of trust and embezzlement, or by falsehood, fraud and wilful imposition.	*Isabella Cowan and Ors* (1845) 2 Broun 398 *Daniel Clark* (1867) 5 Irv 437	Criminal Procedure (Scotland) Act 1975. Sections 59 and 312(L) provide that there may be a conviction for reset where the property was obtained by robbery, theft, breach of trust and embezzlement, or by falsehood, fraud and wilful imposition.

But the dishonest appropriation must be complete before reset can occur.

Robert and Agnes Black 1841 Bell's Notes 46
RB convicted of theft, not reset, because intention to appropriate pocket-book found by AB not formed until she had taken it home to him. RB could not reset property not yet stolen although physically in possession of AB. AB also convicted of theft.

Reset and theft are mutually exclusive.

Backhurst v MacNaughton 1981 SCCR 6
B charged with reset of a number of articles. Gave evidence admitting theft of some of the articles. Convicted of reset of them all.
Held, on the concession of the Crown, that person admitting to theft of articles cannot be guilty of resetting them. Conviction quashed quoad the articles admittedly stolen.

Knowing

Guilty knowledge is the first of the two constituents of the mens rea of reset. If possession is innocent at first, there is no reset until the property is known to have been dishonestly appropriated.

Latta v Herron (1967) SCCR Supp 18
L, a solicitor, bought two guns at 11 pm at a price about one-third of their true value. The transaction was arranged by a former client of L. In the case stated for appeal, the sheriff, who convicted, found 'although I was inclined to believe that when [he] purchased the firearms he was not conscious of the fact that they had been stolen, after a reasonable time for reflection he must have come to realise that they had been dishonestly obtained'. Conviction upheld.

Friel v Docherty 1990 SCCR 351
F obtaining prima facie valid HGV MOT certificates by means other than standard procedure. Convicted on the grounds that he must have known them to be stolen. Appeal.
Held the sheriff was entitled to find as he did on the facts.

Forbes v HMA 1994 SCCR 471
Guilty knowledge. Lowry painting found in F's car sandwiched between sheets of cardboard, painting partly visible.
Held on appeal that given the possession and the awkward account given for the presence of the painting and the cardboard, sufficient for guilty knowledge.

See also:

Nisbet v HMA 1983 SCCR 13
Awkward explanation of acquisition of goods enough when corroborated by statement of the thief.

Davidson v Brown 1990 SCCR 304
McKellar v Normand 1992 SCCR 393
Murray v O'Brien 1993 SCCR 90

Intending

An intention to prevent the owner recovering his property is the second of the two constituents of the mens rea of reset. Therefore, if it is absent, there is no reset.

If the intention is present there need be no motive of personal profit from the possession of the property dishonestly appropriated.

Cook's Case 1917, unreported; Macdonald, p 67
C, a law agent, negotiated with a thief to buy stolen property from him. However, since he was doing so on behalf of the owner, who was his client, he was acquitted on a charge of reset.

Husband

A wife cannot be charged with reset for receiving or concealing stolen goods brought in by her husband, with the purpose of protecting him from detection or punishment, unless she made a trade of the crime and has taken part in disposing of the stolen goods (Alison I, 338).

Smith v Watson 1982 SCCR 15

Accused was wife of man sentenced and imprisoned for robbery. Received money from the robbery through the letter-box and retained it awaiting husband's release.

Held, sustaining an appeal by the Crown, that accused should be convicted, and that wife's exemption should be restricted to cases where (*a*) the property is brought into the matrimonial home by the husband and (*b*) the wife conceals it to protect her husband from detection.

Decision in *Clark v Mone* 1950 SLT (Sh Ct) 69 doubted.

References: Hume I, 113; Alison I, 328; Macdonald, 67; Gordon, 683; Gane and Stoddart, 612.

SENTENCING POLICY

Bennett v Tudhope 1987 SCCR 203—B, first offender, convicted of resetting shotgun and of possessing it without a firearms certificate. Sheriff took view that danger of shotguns getting into wrong hands was such that offender should be dealt with severely. Sentenced to three months' imprisonment, upheld on appeal.

Rankin v McGlennan 1990 SCCR 607—Convicted of resetting £200, sentenced to 240 hours community service. Order breached and three months' detention substituted. Appeal.
Held that appellant could now pay a fine. £300 substituted.

ROAD TRAFFIC

Definitions

Road Traffic Act 1988, ss 185–192 provides a series of definitions of important terms.

COMMENTARY	CASE LAW	STATUTE LAW
Driver Includes separate person engaged in steering the vehicle as well as another person engaged in controlling the vehicle.		Road Traffic Act 1988 Section 192(1)
More than one person may drive the car at the same time,	*Tyler v Whatmore* [1976] RTR 83 One person controlling the steering of the car from passenger seat, while person in driver's seat controlled propulsion. Both held to be driving. *Langman v Valentine* [1952] 2 All ER 803 Learner driver and instructor in dual-control car. Both held to be drivers.	
but each must be exercising some degree of control,	*Evans v Walkden* [1956] 3 All ER 64 Qualified driver simply sat beside learner driver. Although able to reach brake and steering wheel did not do so. *Held* not to be in control, thus not driving.	
although the degree may be minimal.	*Ames v MacLeod* 1969 JC 1 A car ran out of petrol. Pushed car down straight incline while walking alongside it with one hand on the wheel to steer. *Held* to be driving, because 'in a substantial sense controlling the movement and direction'. But see: *R v MacDonagh* [1974] RTR 372 States differing English approach. In *McArthur v Valentine* 1989 SCCR 704 a five-judge appeal court held that the test applied in *Ames v MacLeod* is to be preferred to the English test in *R v MacDonagh*. M had been drinking and arranged for S to drive him home. In course of helping S to start car by jump starting, M pushed car with one hand on steering wheel. *Held* to be driving.	
Mechanically propelled vehicle Test of mechanical propulsion—will be regarded as mechanically propelled, even if broken down, unless there is no reasonable prospect of the vehicle ever being made mobile again.	*Newberry v Simmonds* [1961] 2 QB 345; [1961] 2 All ER 318 Engine removed from car. Evidence showed that it might be replaced shortly and power restored. *Held* still to be a mechanically propelled vehicle. *Smart v Allan* [1962] 3 All ER 893; [1963] 1 QB 291 Vehicle had no gearbox and engine in such bad repair that future mobility was not possible. *Held* not to be mechanically propelled. *Tudhope v Every* 1977 SLT 2 Car had clutch slipping. Gear box stuck in second gear. *Held* that this car was a motor vehicle and ought only to be released from that classification when it reached such a state of structural or mechanical decrepitude that it would offend common sense to call it a 'mechanically propelled vehicle'. It was also held that the vehicle required to be insured although only parked.	Section 185(1)

Intended or adapted for use on roads

Nichol v Heath [1972] RTR 476
Car rebuilt solely for auto-cross racing.
Held still to be for use on road, although owner did not intend to use it for such.

Section 185(1)

Test is objective.

Woodward v Young 1958 SLT 289
Agricultural tractor may be a vehicle intended or adapted for use on roads.

Childs v Coghlan (1968) 112 SJ 175
Held that a machine whose primary use was not on roads, which regularly went on roads from one site to another, was intended for use on roads.

Holliday v Henry [1974] RTR 101
Roller skates placed under each wheel of a vehicle so that it was not actually 'on' the road.
Held still to be on the road for purposes of s 8, Vehicles (Excise) Act 1971.

Roads
Any highway and any other road to which the public has access.

Roads (Scotland) Act 1984, s 151(1); Road Traffic Act 1988, s 192(2)

Public access may be a matter of fact or circumstance.

Harrison v Hill 1932 JC 13; 1931 SLT 598
Any road may be regarded as a road to which the public have access where members of the public are to be found who have not obtained access either by overcoming a physical obstruction or in defiance of prohibition express or implied.

'Private' notes are not conclusive proof that the road is not public.

Hogg v Nicholson 1968 SLT 265
Road marked 'Private'. However, used by police cars and delivery vans, and also for access to post office.
Held to be a road.

Public access to, eg, car parks and forecourts does not render them roads per se, unless they could be naturally and ordinarily described as such.

See:
Purves v Muir 1948 JC 122; 1948 SLT 529
Henderson v Bernard 1955 SLT (Sh Ct) 27

Griffin v Squires [1958] 3 All ER 468
Car park held not to be a road simply because public had access. 'Nobody . . . would think of a car park as a road.'

But see:

Paterson v Ogilvy 1957 JC 42
Held that a private field being temporarily used as a car park was a 'public place'.

Brown v Braid 1984 SCCR 286
Held that garage forecourt is a public place if there is a high probability of the presence of pedestrians on it.

Beattie v Scott 1992 SCCR 435
Young v Carmichael 1992 SCCR 332

Dangerous and careless driving

Road Traffic Act 1988, as amended by Road Traffic Act 1991:
Section 1: 'A person who **causes** the death of **another** person by driving a mechanically propelled vehicle **dangerously** on a road or other public place is guilty of an offence.'
Section 2: 'A person who drives a mechanically propelled vehicle **dangerously** on a road or other public place is guilty of an offence.'
Section 3: 'If a person drives a mechanically propelled vehicle on a road or other public place **without due care and attention,** or **without reasonable consideration for other persons using the road** or place, he is guilty of an offence.'

COMMENTARY	CASE LAW	STATUTE LAW
Causes Accused's driving need not be a substantial cause of the accident, only a material cause.	*R v Hennigan* [1971] 3 All ER 133 H drove dangerously fast but other motorist he killed was also blameworthy. Per Lord Parker CJ; 'so long as the dangerous driving is a cause and more than de minimis the statute operates.' *Watson v HMA* [1978] SCCR Supp 192 Jury directed by trial judge that W could only be acquitted if other party 'wholly to blame'. *Held* that this was a misdirection and conviction quashed.	
Another Can be a passenger in same car.	*R v Klein* The Times 3 April 1960 K's passenger died as a consequence of K's reckless driving. *McCluskey v HMA* 1989 SLT 175 Driver who caused injuries to unborn child which died as a result, convicted under this section.	
Dangerous	*Abbas v Houston* 1993 SCCR 136 A driving at 108 mph on motorway in good road conditions. Conviction upheld on appeal. Such a conviction possible under s 2A when accused driving at a grossly excessive speed. *Mitchell v Lockhart* 1993 SCCR 1070 Dangerously driving. M driving 61 mph on 15 mph esplanade. Esplanade empty at the time. Convicted. Upheld on appeal. Under s 2A a driver must have regard to potential dangers, in this case of pedestrians walking onto the esplanade. Observed that s 2A based on the language in *Allan v Patterson* 1980 JC 37.	Section 2A(1) of the 1988 Act; Person driving dangerously if (*a*) driving far below that expected of a competent and careful driver and (*b*) it would be obvious to such a driver that such driving would be dangerous.
Note: Alternative verdicts		Road Traffic Act 1991, s 24 Various alternative verdicts open eg conviction for careless driving competent in a charge of dangerous driving.
If accused charged with s 1 and the evidence showed he did not cause the death, he can still be convicted under s 2.		
It can be a defence to a charge of dangerous driving that the driver without fault of his own was deprived of control of the vehicle by a mechanical defect which he did not know about or could not with reasonable diligence have discovered.	*R v Spurge* [1961] 2 All ER 688 Driver convicted—knew of defect but continued to drive.	

It is unclear whether there can be a defence of necessity.	*McNab v Guild* 1989 SCCR 138 *Held* that if defence of necessity is available, it could only be made out if immediate danger to life or of serious injury at the material time, which was not the case here.	
Court cannot assume without evidence that vehicle must have developed defects.	*Rabjohns v Burgar* [1972] Crim LR 46 B's car hit bridge wall on dry road on a clear day. Two skid marks behind car. B gave no explanation for collision. Prosecution did not have to prove that there was no steering defect.	

Without due care and attention

Standard of due care and attention is an objective one, inferred from the circumstances and is therefore a question of fact.	*Jarvis v Williams* [1979] RTR 497 Solitary car damaged in accident. Unexplained accident not attributable to road surface, weather or defect in vehicle. *Held*, on appeal, that the inference was that the defendant was not driving with due care and attention.	Section 3
Careless driving.	*Sigournay v Douglas* 1981 SCCR 302 Careless driving. Driver hit pedestrian who ran in front of her on dual carriageway. Convicted. Appealed. *Held* that the appellant had reasonable grounds for believing that the risk of pedestrian crossing road had passed and had no reason to anticipate pedestrian's actions; there was no evidence to support the suggestion that a swerve could have avoided the accident. Conviction quashed. *MacPhail v Haddow* 1990 SCCR 339 H using a hand-held telephone while driving. No evidence of lack of control or danger to others. Convicted. On appeal *held* that although such driving is contrary to the Highway Code, unless there is actual or potential danger demonstrated it is not an offence in itself. See also: *Rae v Friel* 1992 SCCR 688 *Stock v Carmichael* 1993 SCCR 136	Section 3
Inexperience or error of judgment is not an excuse to this offence.	*McCrone v Riding* [1938] 1 All ER 157 Learner driver found guilty of offence under s 3. *Held* irrelevant that carelessness was due to inexperience. *Simpson v Peat* [1952] 1 All ER 447 If a driver does not exercise that degree of care and attention which a reasonable and prudent man would exercise in the circumstances, he is guilty, whether or not committing an error of judgment.	
Knowledge of the carelessness not an essential element of careless driving.	*Hampson v Powell* [1970] 1 All ER 929 Lorry driver who was not aware he had hit a stationary vehicle was held to be rightly convicted of careless driving. *Farquar v McKinnon* 1986 SCCR 524 Driver of large articulated vehicle reversed slowly along road without assistance, using only mirrors, in area where he was aware children were playing. Ran over child and found guilty of careless driving because he had reversed without clear vision to rear, notwithstanding that lorry showing hazard light. *Brunton v Lees* 1993 SCCR 98 Speeding, 60 mph in 40 mph zone. Speed held to be excessive but not grossly so. Conviction upheld on appeal. Speed in itself sufficient for careless driving.	

No exemption from prosecution exists for emergency services.

Wood v Richards [1977] Crim LR 295
Police officer convicted of careless driving.
Held that there is no special exception or standard to be applied to emergency services.

Without reasonable consideration

Dilks v Bowman-Shaw [1981] RTR 4 DC
Motorway with two-lane carriageway. Accused moved into left-hand lane and overtook. No inconvenience caused to other driver.
Held that although the manœuvre was in contravention of the Highway Code, no one was actually endangered or inconvenienced. No conviction and appeal court upheld decision of lower court and rejected Crown appeal.

but see Wheatley, p 36. This authority might not be followed in Scotland.

Other persons using the road
Includes passengers in the vehicle being driven by the accused.

Pawley v Wharldall [1966] 1 QB 373
Driver of double-decker bus. Five passengers gave evidence that accused's driving caused panic and alarm to them. No evidence that anyone else outside the bus was treated without reasonable consideration. Convicted.

Proof by road marks.

Ryrie v Campbell 1964 JC 33
Tyre impression on wrong side of road and matching paint on lamp-post and at collision were enough to convict despite no eye-witnesses.

No offence of 'causing death by careless driving'.

McCallum v Hamilton 1985 SCCR 368
Careless driving. McC drove car in such manner that it collided with another car causing the latter to mount pavement thereby injuring two pedestrians and killing another. Details of these consequences in complaint objected to as irrelevant. Sheriff repelled objection.
Held, on appeal, that the consequential injuries were relevantly detailed in complaint. However, the word 'fatal' was irrelevant and must be deleted. To do otherwise would effectively create by the back door offence of causing death by careless driving-a crime unknown to statute.
Per LJ-C Ross ('. . . the complaint reads as though it were libelling an offence of causing death by careless driving. There is no such offence under the Road Traffic Acts. . . .'

Sharp v HMA 1987 SCCR 179
Held that it was wrong for sheriff to take into account the fatal consequences of a piece of careless driving in considering sentence.

Drink related offences

Road Traffic Act 1988, s 4.
Section 4(1) **Driving** or **attempting to drive** a motor vehicle while **unfit to drive** through **drink or drugs**.
Section 4(2) **Being in charge of** a motor vehicle while **unfit to drive** through **drink or drugs**.
Section 4(3) It is a defence to a charge under s 5(2) that there is **no likelihood of driving** while unfit through drink or drugs.
Road Traffic Offenders Act 1988.
Section 15(3) provides a defence of **post-incident drinking** if the prosecution relies on analysis of breath, blood or urine specimen.

COMMENTARY	CASE LAW	STATUTE LAW
Driving When motor vehicle moving subject to one's control and direction.	*R v Kitson* (1955) 39 Cr App R 66 K was a passenger in car and awoke to find car moving with no one in driving seat and no key in ignition. K steered car onto grass verge. *Held* that K was driving.	Road Traffic Act 1988 Section 4(1)
	Ames v MacLeod 1969 JC 1 A walking beside car. Car engine not running. Guided car downhill by use of steering wheel. *Held* driving.	
Attempting to drive Intention may be inferred from the circumstances.	*R v Cook* [1964] Crim LR 56 C found in front seat of car fiddling with dashboard which was lit up. Later admitted would have driven away if not caught. *Held* attempting to drive.	
	Guthrie v Friel 1992 SCCR 932 G found in car asleep with engine and lights on. Convicted. *Held* on appeal that the facts showed that G may have been preparing to drive but not actually attempting ie would need handbrake to be off.	
but there must be de facto control.	*Harman v Wardrop* [1971] RTR 127 Motorist effectively prevented from driving at time of breath test as his keys had been taken by another person. *Held* not driving.	
Driving as result of coercion or necessity may prove a valid defence.	*Tudhope v Grubb* 1983 SCCR 350 (Sh Ct) G locked himself in car to avoid violent attack by several persons. Drove off to escape further injury to car and self. *Held* attempted to drive to avoid further injury following unprovoked assault. Acquitted.	
	But see *MacLeod v MacDougall* 1988 SCCR 519 Driving must cease as soon as necessity is over.	
Driving in an emergency.	*Watson v Hamilton* 1988 SCCR 13 Court must be satisfied that no other reasonable alternative has been ignored. Pregnant guest in W's house awoke bleeding heavily and fearing miscarriage. W attempted to find phone and get help but at 2 am set off to hospital. It was *held* that it was not reasonable to have expected W to rouse his neighbours at 2 am.	
Unfit to drive High alcohol content in blood may not indicate unfitness.	*MacNeill v Fletcher* 1966 JC 18 *Held* that although urine sample showed high alcohol content, doctor was entitled not to certify accused as unfit to drive.	Section 4(5)

Normal driving does not raise presumption of fitness.	*Murray v Muir* 1949 JC 127; 1950 SLT 41 *Held* that fact that accused drove 200 yards in proper manner did not create presumption of sobriety which medical evidence could not disprove.	
Drink	*Armstrong v Clark* [1957] 2 QB 391 Diabetic took dose of insulin and became incapable of driving properly. Charged under section similar to present s 4(1). *Observed* that 'drink' probably means alcoholic drink.	
or drugs	*Armstrong v Clark*, supra 'Drug' means any medicine given to cure, alleviate or assist an ailing body, and includes insulin.	
Solvents having drugging effect.	*Duffy v Tudhope* 1983 SCCR 440; 1984 SLT 107 *Held* that driver whose capacity to drive is impaired because he has been inhaling solvents cannot claim that such solvents are not drugs, if they have a drugging effect.	
Being in charge of motor vehicle.	*Macdonald v Crawford* 1952 SLT (Sh Ct) 92 Taxi driver sitting in taxi which had broken down, waiting for tow. *Held* in charge. *Lees v Lowrie* 1993 SCCR 1 Accused supervising 'L' driver, not a lesson. Evidence led that he would not have taken over driving. *Held* that the accused was in charge of the vehicle but no likelihood of driving.	Section 4(2)
Not in charge.	*Adair v McKenna* 1951 SLT (Sh Ct) 40 *Held* that motor mechanic engaged in repairing fault in vehicle by roadside not in charge. *Crichton v Burrell* 1951 JC 107; 1951 SLT 365 Car owner waiting for another person with duplicate keys to drive him home. *Held* not in charge of vehicle, as not in de facto control. *Dean v Wishart* 1952 JC 9; 1952 SLT 86 *Held* that person insensible in back of vehicle which had been immobilised by removal of rotor arm not in charge. *Winter v Morrison* 1954 JC 7 Car owner in front passenger seat. Wife in driving seat with engine running. Wife's provisional licence expired. *Held* that car owner not in charge.	
No likelihood of driving Defence to s 4(2) charge.	*Neish v Stevenson* 1969 SLT 229 *Held* that burden of proof, on a balance of probabilities, is on accused. *Morton v Confer* [1963] 2 All ER 765 *Held* that court must be satisfied that, on balance of probabilities, there was no likelihood that intention not to drive would be departed from. *Northfield v Pinder* [1969] 2 QB 7 Driver found near his car so drunk as to be incapable of driving, finding car, or walking to it. *Held* no defence; no evidence that driver would not have driven when worst effects had worn off.	Section 4(3) *std defence rule* (handwritten)

Post-incident drinking

Defence to section 4(1) and (2) as well as section 5(1)(*a*) and (*b*)

Neish v Stevenson, supra
Standard of proof as in this case.

Hassan v Scott 1989 SCCR 49
Accused may not have to prove exact amount of ale subsequently consumed. If defence evidence demonstrates that there is a reasonable doubt about Crown case, accused entitled to acquittal.

Road Traffic Offenders Act 1988
Section 15(3)

Alcohol concentration above prescribed limit

Road Traffic Act 1988, s 5.
Section 5(1)(*a*) Driving or attempting to drive motor vehicle or
(*b*) in charge of motor vehicle
after consuming so much alcohol that **proportion in breath, blood or urine exceeds prescribed limit**.
Section 5(2) Defence to s 6(1)(*b*)) that **no likelihood of driving** vehicle while proportion of alcohol in breath, blood or urine remained likely to exceed prescribed limit.
Road Traffic Offenders Act 1988.
Section 15(3) Defence of post-incident drinking.

COMMENTARY	CASE LAW	STATUTE LAW
Proportion in breath, blood or urine		
		Road Traffic Act 1988 Section 11(2). Prescribed limits are: (*a*) 35 microgrammes of alcohol in 100 millilitres of breath, or (*b*) 80 milligrammes of alcohol in 100 millilitres of blood, or (*c*) 107 milligrammes of alcohol in 100 millilitres of urine, or such other proportion as may be prescribed by the Secretary of State.
Court may discount evidence if, for example, specimen obtained illegally by deception or under duress.	*R v Fox* [1985] RTR 337 Lord Fraser 'If the appellant had been lured to the police station by some trick or deception, or if the police officers had behaved oppressively towards the appellant, the justice's jurisdiction to exclude otherwise admissible evidence . . . might come into play.'	Road Traffic Offenders Act 1988 Section 15(2). All readings, no matter how they were obtained, must be considered. Section 15(4). Specimen of blood will be disregarded unless taken from accused, with consent, by medical practitioner.
Exceeds prescribed limit	*R v Coomaraswamy* [1976] RTR 21 *Held* that if driver's specimen discloses an excess over prescribed limit, it is not necessary to prove a particular degree of excess. *Lockhart v Deighan* 1985 SCCR 204; 1985 SLT 549 It was made clear in this case that because of a letter from the Crown Agent to the Law Society of Scotland, published in the September issue of JLSS, the Crown has effectively barred itself from prosecuting where the breath alcohol level is less than 40 microgrammes. This delimitation was strictly construed in this case and held not to extend to blood alcohol levels. *McConnachie v Scott* 1988 SCCR 176 Motorist provided two specimens of breath of less than 40 milligrammes. *Held* to be incompetent for police officer to require motorist to provide specimen of blood or urine in these circumstances.	
No likelihood of driving Defence to s 5(1)(*b*) charge.	See: *Neish v Stevenson*, supra, p 57 *Morton v Confer*, supra, p 57 *Northfield v Pinder*, supra, p 57	

Preliminary breath test

Road Traffic Act 1988, s 6.

Section 6(1) Constable may require driver to provide specimen of breath for breath test where he has **reasonable cause to suspect** that:
(*a*) person driving or attempting to drive, on a road or other **public place** or in charge of a motor vehicle, has alcohol in body or has committed traffic offence while vehicle in motion, or
(*b*) person has been driving or attempting to drive or been in charge of a vehicle with alcohol in body and still has alcohol in body, or
(*c*) person has been driving or attempting to drive or been in charge of vehicle and has committed traffic offence while vehicle in motion.
Section 6(2) After accident constable may require any person who he has **reasonable cause to believe** was driving or attempting to drive or in charge of the vehicle at the time of the accident to provide a specimen of breath for breath test.
Section 6(3) Specimen of breath must be given at or near the place where the requirement is made.
Section 6(4) Failure to provide specimen **without reasonable excuse** constitutes offence.
Section 6(5) Constable may arrest without warrant if
(*a*) as a result of breath test he has reasonable cause to suspect that proportion of alcohol in person's breath or blood exceeds prescribed limit, or
(*b*) person has failed to provide specimen of breath and constable has reasonable cause to suspect that person had alcohol in body.

COMMENTARY	CASE LAW	STATUTE LAW
Reasonable cause to suspect		
	Copeland v Macpherson 1970 SLT 87 Suspicion arose out of information given to constable by another officer. *Held* to be reasonable.	Section 6(1)
Wide powers to stop vehicles, but these must not be exercised oppressively.	*Chief Constable of Gwent v Dash* [1985] Crim L R 674 Constable may stop a motorist with sole intention of seeing whether or not he has been drinking.	
Public place	*Alston v O'Brien* 1992 SCCR 238 Breath test, 'public place', car on farm drive. *Held* on appeal that the public were not expected to be there so not a public place.	
	See also: *Thomson v MacPhail* 1992 SCCR 513	
Reasonable cause to believe		
	Merry v Doherty 1977 JC 34 Police officers found D alone in car at roadside. Engine was hot, there was damage to front of car, and D had fresh injuries on forehead and nose. No evidence to indicate where accident had happened. D found not guilty of driving with alcohol above prescribed limit as no evidence of reasonable cause to believe that accident had occurred on public highway.	Section 6(2)
	Topping v Scott 1979 SLT (Notes) 21 Police received anonymous phone call informing them that white van involved in accicent with blue car. Police found white van with traces of blue paint parked outside accused's house. Accused gave positive breath test. *Held* that sheriff entitled to convict. Police had knowledge of accident although they had not witnessed it.	

Failure to provide specimen without reasonable excuse

R v Lennard [1973] RTR 252
Per Laxton LJ '[N]o excuse can be adjudged a reasonable one unless the person from whom the specimen is required is physically or mentally unable to provide it, or the provision of the specimen would entail a substantial risk to his health'.

Once issue of reasonable excuse sufficiently raised, it is for prosecution to rebut it.

Earnshaw v HMA 1982 JC 11.

Reasonable excuse relates to taking of test only.

McNicol v Peters 1969 SLT 261
Not a reasonable excuse for driver to maintain he had not consumed alcohol.

McGrath v Vipas [1984] RTR 58
Not a reasonable excuse that accused not driver at material time.

McLaren v MacLeod 1994 SCCR 478
Constable requiring a specimen under s 7 does not require to ask the person if there are medical reasons why blood should not be taken although the suspect should be told that not giving the specimen without reasonable excuse is an offence.

Provision of specimens for analysis

Road Traffic Act 1988, ss 7, 8.

Section 7(1) Constable may require person suspected of offence under s 4 or s 5
(*a*) to provide two specimens of breath for **analysis by means of a device of type approved by Secretary of State** or
(*b*) to provide a specimen of blood or urine for a laboratory test.
Section 7(2) Requirement to provide specimens of breath under s 7(1)(*a*) can only be made at a police station.
Section 7(3) Requirement to provide specimen of **blood or urine** under s 7(1)(*b*) can only be made at police station or hospital, and cannot be made at police station unless
(*a*) constable has reasonable cause to believe that for **medical reasons** breath specimen cannot be provided or should not be required, or
(*b*) **no device or reliable device available**, or
(*c*) suspected offence is under s 4 and medical advice suggests conditions may be due to drugs.
Section 7(4) If specimen other than breath required, constable decides whether blood or urine is required, unless medical practitioner advises blood cannot or should not be taken.
Section 7(5) Specimen of urine shall be provided within one hour of its requirement, and after provision of previous specimen.
Section 7(6) Failure to provide specimen, without **reasonable excuse**, is an offence.
Section 7(7) Constable must warn that failure to provide specimen may lead to prosecution.
Section 8(1) Where two breath specimens have been provided in pursuance of section 7, the one with the lower proportion of alcohol in the breath shall be used, and the other disregarded.
Section 8(2) If the specimen with the lower proportion of alcohol contains no more than 50 mg of alcohol in 100 ml of breath, the person who provided it may elect to replace it with a specimen of blood or urine, under s 7(4).

COMMENTARY	CASE LAW	STATUTE LAW
Requirement to provide specimen must be corroborated.	*Carmichael v Gillooly* 1982 SCCR 119.	
Analysis by means of a device of type approved by Secretary of State.	*Knox v Lockhart* 1984 SCCR 463 Crown failed to present in evidence at trial that device used was of type approved by Secretary of State. *Held*, on appeal, Crown must prove in evidence that device used is of approved type.	
Specimen of blood.		Road Traffic Act 1988, s 11(4). Person must consent to blood being taken by medical practitioner.
Only one breath specimen provided.	*Reid v Tudhope* 1985 SCCR 268 Conviction upheld where R in attempt to frustrate procedure failed to provide second specimen. But compare: *Douglas v Stevenson* 1986 SCCR 519 Accused gave one specimen. After genuine failure to provide second specimen, he was refused opportunity to try again. *Held* that police had not given him fair opportunity for provision of second specimen.	Section 7(1)(*a*)

Medical reasons.	*Dempsey v Catton* [1986] RTR 194 Decision of constable is subjective, and he is not required to obtain medical advice. Defendant refused to give specimen claiming he suffered from agoraphobia, and phobia of machines. Constable accepted the latter and required blood specimen.	Section 7(3)(*a*)
No device or reliable device available.	*Gilligan v Tudhope* 1985 SCCR 434 G charged with driving with excess alcohol on basis of blood sample. He had earlier provided two breath specimens. Readings on the visual display showed that it was in working order, but device then produced printout giving nonsensical dates and times. *Held* that analytical function of device working and no justification for requiring blood test. Conviction quashed. See also: *Walker v Walkingshaw* 1991 SCCR 358 *Ramage v Walkingshaw* 1992 SCCR 82 *Carson v Orr* 1992 SCCR 260	
Test is subjective.	*Burnett v Smith* 1989 SCCR 628 B had provided two breath specimens but police concluded device unreliable and required blood specimen. On appeal *held* that proper test is subjective and police entitled to require blood specimen if they concluded on reasonable grounds that device unreliable, even if it was reliable, and appeal refused.	
Blood or urine: constable decides.	*Bain v Tudhope* 1985 SCCR 412 B gave positive breath specimen and elected to exercise right to provide alternative specimen. Required to provide urine, but failed, and convicted on breath specimen. *Held* that decision to require blood or urine was to be left wholly to discretion of constable. See also: *MacLeod v MacFarlane* 1992 SCCR 178 *Simpson v McClory* 1993 SCCR 402	Section 7(4)
Failure to provide specimen without **reasonable excuse.**	See p 61 *McLeod v Murray* 1986 SCCR 369 M, lorry driver, gave evidence that he had been assaulted by police officers who required specimens, and he refused to give specimens because he did not trust officers not to tamper with them. *Held* (1) that accused's evidence, if believed, would constitute reasonable excuse; and (2) onus of proof that there was no reasonable excuse lay on the Crown, and accused had raised reasonable doubt on the matter: accused acquitted. See also: *McIntosh v Lowe* 1991 SCCR 154	Section 7(6)
Accused must raise reasonable excuse at time of requirement if asked why he cannot provide specimen,	*Singh v McLeod* 1986 SCCR 656 At trial S claimed that asthmatic attack prevented him from providing breath specimen. S's doctor gave evidence that any asthmatic attack would have been obvious to anyone. S had not mentioned asthma at time of requirement to provide specimen. *Held* to be sufficient evidence of no reasonable excuse.	

but if not asked no obligation to volunteer information.

Pringle v Annan 1988 SCCR 423
P unable to provide breath specimen as result of injuries suffered.
Held that physical inability constituted reasonable excuse, and there is no general duty on motorist to inform police of the reason for his inability to provide specimen.

McClory v Owen-Thomas 1989 SCCR 402
O-T required to give specimen of blood and refused to do so saying 'There's no way I want to give blood. I tend to get faint . . .'. At trial evidence led of O-T's suffering from phobic fear of needles. Sheriff acquitted. On appeal *held* onus of establishing absence of reasonable excuse lies on Crown; no onus on motorist to disclose anything to police; appeal refused.

But compare:
Milne v Westwater 1990 SCCR 46
M gave evidence that because of earlier amputations he was terrified of doctor putting needles in his arm. Sheriff disbelieved him and convicted. On appeal *held* that onus of proving absence of reasonable excuse was on Crown, but that as sheriff disbelieved him and no rational explanation provided, no merit in appeal.

Manual v Steward 1986 SCCR 121
It is not a reasonable excuse to refuse to give specimen until solicitor arrives.

Accused must **unequivocally** agree to provide specimen,

Beveridge v Allan 1986 SCCR 542
On being required to provide specimen, B replied 'Yes, I refuse'. Officer asked him why and B said 'Oh well, I'll blow the thing'. Officer did not allow him to give specimen, but charged B with failure to provide breath.
Held that sheriff entitled to treat B's initial response as a refusal. Not open to B to change his mind.

and cannot specify part of body from which sample to be taken.

Salesbury v Pugh [1969] 2 All ER 1171
Driver insisted on samples being taken from big toe. Convicted of failure to provide.

Friel v Dickson 1992 SCCR 513
Blood specimen, s 11(4). Accused under the influence of medication. Sheriff said that the Crown had failed to show consent and exclude the possibility of less than complete consciousness. Appeal.
Held that the Crown must show consent which it had not but need not exclude the possibility of less than complete consciousness. Not convinced here that T knew what was being asked of him.

Police must not exert pressure on driver to provide blood or urine,

Green v Lockhart 1985 SCCR 257

and must inform driver fully of his rights.

Pelosi v Jessop 1990 SCCR 175
Police told P that he could give specimen of blood, without mentioning urine.
Held proper procedure not carried through and conviction quashed.

Police decide whether to require blood or urine.

Bain v Tudhope supra at p 64.

See further, Wheatley *Road Traffic Law in Scotland* (2nd edn).

Mitigating circumstances; special reasons

Mitigating circumstances may avoid disqualification which normally results from the 'totting up' of a total of twelve penalty points incurred over a period of three years. **Special reasons** for not ordering obligatory endorsement or disqualification.

COMMENTARY	CASE LAW	STATUTE LAW
Mitigating circumstances: all the circumstances both in relation to the offence and the offender, including all previous offences.		Road Traffic Offenders Act 1988 Section 35. Where a driver has incurred twelve points within a three-year period, he must be disqualified for at least six months unless the court is satisfied, having regard to all the circumstances, that there are grounds for mitigation and thinks fit to order a shorter period of disqualification or none at all.
	Smith v Craddock 1979 JC 66 Speeding. Driver by trade and would lose employment if disqualified. Wife and children relied totally on accused for income. Sheriff refrained from disqualification and imposed a fine. *Held*, on appeal by Crown, that sheriff entitled to take such factors into consideration in his exercise of discretion.	Section 35(4). The court, in considering whether such mitigating circumstances exist, may not take account of (*a*) triviality of the offence; (*b*) hardship, other than exceptional hardship; (*c*) circumstances previously taken into account by any court within the previous three years.
Exceptional hardship—loss of licence involving loss of employment and house.	*Stephens v Gibb* 1984 SCCR 195 S convicted of offence involving discretionary disqualification. S's driving licence contained endorsements showing that the number of penalty points to be taken into account was such as to involve disqualifiation. Appealed. *Held* that '. . . by reason of a combination of factors special and peculiar to this particular appellant, disqualification would result in exceptional hardship. . .'. Appeal allowed; disqualification quashed. But compare: *Holden v McPhail* 1988 SCCR 486 Observed that court should examine very carefully any suggestion of exceptional hardship and hold it established only on clearest possible evidence. *Stephens v Gibb* was a very special case and was not authority for proposition that in every case loss of job and inability to pay mortgage constituted exceptional hardship. *Mowbray v Guild* 1989 SCCR 535 *Held* to be exceptional hardship in that loss of licence would lead to loss of business, affect M and his wife's health, and interfere with child's education. See also cases under Sentencing, Totting Up.	Road Traffic Offenders Act 1988, s 28 provides for award of penalty points on conviction of contraventions of Road Traffic Act 1988. Section 35(4): 'No account is to be taken under subsection (1) of . . . (*b*) hardship, other than exceptional hardship.'
Special reasons Question of whether a special reason exists is one of law.	*Muir v Sutherland* 1940 JC 66 Speeding charge. *Held* that question whether a special reason existed was one of law and not of discretion.	Road Traffic Offenders Act 1988, s 34 and Sched 2. Certain offences carry obligatory disqualification. In all these instances disqualification can only be avoided if offending motorist successfully pleads special reasons for not being disqualified.

Special reasons for reducing period of disqualification or ordering not to be disqualified.	*Orttewell v Allan* 1984 SCCR 208 Disqualified driver pushed broken down car off busy main street and then got into driving seat and was pushed into car park where it collided with another vehicle. *Held* to be sufficient grounds to reduce period of disqualification from three years to one year.
Reason must be special to the facts of the offence and not to the peculiar circumstances of the offender.	*Adair v Munn* 1940 JC 69 Drunk driving charge. *Held* that considerations of hardship and similar mitigating circumstances personal to the convicted person were not 'special reasons' entitling the court to reduce or remit the sentence. *Carnegie v Clark* 1947 JC 74 Charge of driving while disqualified. Fact that sentence might lead to expulsion from university not a special reason. *Muir v M'Pherson* 1953 SLT 307 Charge of drunk in charge of a motor vehicle under Road Traffic Act 1930, s 15(2). Accused was a taxi driver. Fact that disqualification would cause considerable personal hardship held not to constitute a special reason. *Robertson v M'Ginn* 1955 JC 57 Insurance. Submitted as special reasons that offender was a 'man of substance' and required to drive for business as a farmer and for local government affairs. *Held*, no special reason. *Norman v Cameron* 1992 SCCR 390 Section 5(1)(*a*) of the 1988 Act disqualification. Accused said that he had waited until he should have been fit to drive. Accepted by sheriff as a special reason. Overturned on appeal, special reasons must relate to the facts which constitute the offence. See also: *McClelland v Whitelaw* 1993 SCCR 1113
Medical condition.	*Scott v Hamilton* 1988 SCCR 262 Lady motorist pled guilty to failure to provide specimen but claimed she had been suffering from pre-menstrual tension, and was not amenable to reason. *Held* that this was not special reason for not disqualifying.
Accused's mistaken belief.	*Robertson v McNaughtan* 1993 SCCR 226 Driving while disqualified, special reasons. R thought his disqualification was suspended pending an appeal but it had revived when his solicitor failed to lodge the appeal timeously. Sheriff imposing penalty points but not disqualifying on the grounds that there were special reasons. Appeal. *Held* that there were special reasons and licence should not even have been endorsed. See also: *Carmichael v Shelvin* 1991 SCCR 247
The safety of the public in their use of the roads must be viewed as the vital consideration.	*Adair v Munn*, supra Considerations tending to show that the safety of the public on the roads would not be prejudiced by a reduction or remission were special reasons. *Fairlie v Hill* 1944 JC 53 Insurance contravention under Road Traffic Act 1930, s 35(2).

Held that in considering a remission or reduction in relation to disqualification the protection of the public is the chief criterion. If reasons adduced by offender tend to show public protection will not be prejudiced, the court has a discretion and may have regard to personal hardship.

Lowe v Mulligan 1991 SCCR 551
Driving with excess alcohol. M had moved car a short distance to prevent it being a hazard. The road on which he had originally parked prior to going into the pub was due to become one-way in the morning due to road works.
Held that it was a special reason.

Performance of public duties cannot in itself be a special reason. Exceptions made to this rule during wartime.

Murray v Macmillan 1942 JC 10
Insurance contravention under s 35(2) of Road Traffic Act 1930. Convicted person was a doctor with a number of emergency posts in relation to colliery and aerodrome for which a car was essential.

Compare with:

M'Fadyean v Burton 1954 JC 18
Charge of drunk driving. Officer in Territorial Army used car for related duties.
Held did not constitute special reason.

Triviality of the circumstances of the offence not a special reason.

Tudhope v Birbeck 1979 SLT (Notes) 47
Pedestrian crossing. Fact that circumstances of offence trivial and that no danger caused to anyone did not constitute a special reason.

Circumstances held to have established special reasons include emergencies: accused must prove there was a genuine emergency

Graham v Annan 1980 SLT 28
Driving while disqualified and without insurance. Pregnant woman who was driving car became ill and husband, who was disqualified, took over.
Held, on appeal, that circumstances disclosed a special reason for not ordering further disqualification or endorsement.

and offence must have been committed out of circumstances of real necessity.

Copeland v Sweeney 1977 SLT (Sh Ct) 28
Drunk driving charge. Daughter who suffered from unusual medical condition was stung by wasp. Father drove to his daughter collecting medicine on the way.
Held no special reason. 'Must show not only that the circumstances amounted to a medical emergency but also that the driver had a compelling reason and no alternative in the circumstances but to drive.'

Where driver breaks the law only because he is ordered to do a certain act by a police officer.

Farrell v Moir 1974 SLT (Sh Ct) 89
Refusal to give sample. Convicted. Argued that he should not be disqualified in that he had driven only because police had ordered him to move his car. On appeal, disqualification quashed and admonition substituted.

Onus lies on accused to establish special reasons,

McLeod v Scoular 1974 SLT (Notes) 44
Drugs and driving. Observations made by Lord Justice-Clerk on proper procedure for determining whether special reasons have been established. Onus on accused to satisfy the court that there are special reasons and prosecution should have opportunity to contradict or qualify that evidence.

although such reasons may be established without specific reference to their 'special' quality.

Keane v Perrie 1982 SCCR 377
Careless driving. Plea of guilty by letter. No reference in letter to special reasons as such but referred to certain mitigating factors and his driving record.
Held, on appeal by Crown, that sheriff entitled to refrain from ordering endorsement and not necessary for circumstances to be expressly described as special reasons in the letter.

See also:

Trotter v Burnet 1947 JC 151
Plea of guilty by letter. Where reasons purporting to prejudice the public interest are raised, the court should be slow to pronounce sentence in accused's absence.

Herron v Sharif 1974 SLT (Notes) 63
Small excess of alcohol in blood. Not a special reason.

Keane v Savage, Crown Office Circular A26/82
Accused found guilty after trial of offence of speeding at 44 mph. On conviction fined £15 but sheriff *ex proprio motu* declined to order endorsement. Sheriff was not moved to hold that there were special reasons why he should not endorse. Crown appeal successful.
Held, in absence of special reasons, sheriff should have ordered endorsement.

See also Sentencing Policy, Totting Up, infra.

ROAD TRAFFIC

SENTENCING POLICY

Careless Driving

Sharp v HMA 1987 SCCR 179—S charged with causing death by reckless driving and alternately with careless driving. Convicted of careless driving. Sheriff imposed fine of £250 and one year's disqualification, having regard to consequences. S appealed on grounds that sheriff had wrongly taken consequences into account.
Held that grounds of appeal sound. Period of disqualification reduced to six months.

McLean v Annan 1986 SCCR 52—M convicted of careless driving, offence committed ten days after passing driving test. Sheriff disqualified for a month and ordered her to resit test.
Held sentence inappropriate, order to resit test not being penalty, but for case in which driving skills lost through disqualification. Sentence quashed.

McCrone v Normand 1988 SCCR 551—M, driver of mobile shop, reversed in area known by him to be used as children's playground. Collided with and killed sixteen-month-old child. Fined £400 and licence endorsed. On appeal *held* that fine excessive, fine of £100 substituted.

Malpas v Hamilton 1988 SCCR 546—M, first offender, convicted of careless driving after hitting pedestrian with car. Fined £200 and disqualified for six months. On appeal against disqualification, *held* that disqualification should be imposed for careless driving only in more than usually serious cases. Disqualification quashed and five penalty points imposed.

Buchan v McNaughtan 1990 SCCR 13—B, in receipt of £47 per week invalidity benefit, pleaded guilty to careless driving and driving with excess alcohol in blood. Fined £75 on first charge and £150 on second charge.
Held fine not excessive.

Owens v McNaughtan 1990 SCCR 355—Careless driving conviction, O had a clean licence previously. £500 fine upheld on appeal but nine penalty points reduced to seven.

Neill v Ingram 1990 SCCR 454—Twenty-one-year-old convicted of careless driving, wheelspinning U-turn from parked position.
Held on appeal, six months' disqualification under totting up and a requirement to resit driving test appropriate given that the accused lacked discipline and responsibility.

Ross v Houston 1991 SCCR 102—Lorry driver convicted of careless driving, nine points awarded as he was a professional driver.
Held on appeal, approach incorrect and six points substituted.

Thomas v Lowe 1991 SCCR 943—Careless driving, failing to stop. T alleging pre-menstrual tension. Sentenced to six months disqualification. Appeal.
Held that given PMT, ten penalty points appropriate. PMT 'bad' or 'severe' but mitigation only.

Excess Alcohol

Weddle v Carmichael 1991 SCCR 64—Family man earning £23,000 a year, 128 µg of alcohol in 100 ml of breath. Sentenced to three months' imprisonment and six years' disqualification. Upheld on appeal, clear that the courts must take a strong and firm view.

Hawthorne v Jessop 1991 SCCR 674—Charge not averring but evidence showing that H very drunk. Disqualified for three years.
Held on appeal that sentence severe but not excessive. Sheriff entitled to take unfitness to drive into account. Court following *Jamsheed v Walkingshaw* 1989 SCCR 75 and disapproving *McParland v Wilson* 1988 SCCR 15.

Cairns v McLeod 1992 SCCR 787—Excess alcohol, third analogous offence, two months' imprisonment. Appeal.
Held that 200 hours community service appropriate, 'marginal case'.

Brown v McNaughtan 1993 SCCR 399—Excess alcohol, three years' disqualification on the ground that B aware that he had a similar charge outstanding at the time. Upheld on appeal.

Alexander v Hingston 1993 SCCR 431—Excess alcohol, specimen taken six hours after the accident. Sheriff on the basis of a formula to calculate alcohol level at the time of the accident disqualified for eighteen months. *Held* on appeal that without specific evidence sheriff not entitled to use the formula. Twelve months' disqualification substituted.

Stirling v Wilson 1988 SCCR 225—S pleaded guilty to driving with breath-alcohol level of 120 µg. Sheriff sentenced S to three months' imprisonment despite favourable social enquiry report. Disqualified for four years.
Held that in all the circumstances, including fact that S would lose job he had held for eight years, fine would meet case. Fine of £750 and three years' disqualification substituted.

McLean v MacDougall 1989 SCCR 625—M pleaded guilty to driving with excess alcohol and admitted recent similar conviction. Unemployed at time and sentenced to sixty days' imprisonment and disqualified for six years. Appealed against sentence of imprisonment. At date of appeal had obtained employment at salary of £10,000 which he would lose if imprisoned.
Held appropriate to replace imprisonment with fine of £1,000.

Marshall v Carmichael 1990 SCCR 58—M pleaded guilty to driving van with excess alcohol in breath. Two previous analogous convictions. Only drove van short distance as window broken and he was afraid it was vulnerable to theft. Sheriff sentenced M to six months' imprisonment and disqualified for ten years.
Held sentence excessive, sentence of imprisonment quashed and 150 hours' community service substituted.

Giordano v Carmichael 1990 SCCR 61—G pleaded guilty to driving with blood alcohol level of 220 mg per 100 ml. Two previous convictions in 1981 and 1983. Attending doctor and psychiatrist in connection with alcohol problem and agreed to attend alcohol advice centre. Sentenced to sixty days imprisonment. Upheld on appeal.

McGrory v Jessop 1990 SCCR 222—M pleaded guilty to driving with excess alcohol and driving while disqualified and to another offence. Sentences to run consecutively.
Held that as the driving offences had all occurred on same occasion, it was excessive to order sentences to run consecutively. Sentences ordered to be served concurrently.

Failure to provide specimen
Aird v Valentine 1986 SCCR 353—A pleaded guilty to failure to provide specimen but evidence led that it had not been proved that A was driving at relevant time. Sheriff took view that obligatory disqualification applied and disqualified him for three years. *Held* that obligatory disqualification arises only when proved that accused driving or attempting to drive; disqualification quashed and case remitted to sheriff.

Tudhope v O'Kane 1986 SCCR 538—O convicted. Sheriff found O was teetotaller and for that reason refrained from imposing obligatory disqualification. On appeal, *held* that present case special and public safety would not be prejudiced by refraining from disqualification.

Goldie v Tudhope 1986 SCCR 414—G had large number of previous convictions, many leading to custodial sentences, but no previous road traffic offences. Sheriff took view that he was committed to life of law breaking and imposed maximum sentence of six months.
Held that sheriff entitled to look at appellant's record; but that six months was too severe; sentence of three months substituted.

Reynolds v Tudhope 1987 SCCR 340—R pleaded guilty to failing to provide specimens of breath, offence carrying minimum disqualification for one year. Magistrate disqualified her for eighteen months on ground that 'this type of quite deliberate action is heard about far too often'. On appeal *held* that magistrate entitled to take the view he did.

McMillan v Scott 1988 SCCR 219—M pleaded guilty to failure to provide roadside test. Fined £100 and disqualified for six months. On appeal against disqualification held to be no reason for sheriff to deviate from normal practice of imposing penalty points. Disqualification quashed, endorsement with four points substituted.

McParland v Wilson 1988 SCCR 158—M first offender, pleaded guilty to failing to provide specimen, careless driving and failure to stay after, or to report an accident. M had had considerable amount to drink. Sheriff sentenced M to three months' imprisonment and referred to public interest in deterring people from driving under influence of drink. On appeal *held* (1) sheriff had wrongly referred to unfitness to drink as no charge under that head and (2) imprisonment inappropriate for first offender, fine of £100 substituted.

Jamsheed v Walkingshaw 1989 SCCR 75—J pleaded guilty to failure to provide specimen, reckless driving and resisting police. Appearance indicated he was heavily intoxicated. Fined £500 and disqualified for three years. On appeal *held* that sheriff entitled to impose substantial period of disqualification, and fine not excessive.

McGuinness v Jessop 1989 SCCR 349—Failure to provide breath a deliberate attempt to avoid providing evidence of how much M had drunk, disqualified for three years.
Held that disqualification not excessive.

Totting Up
McLaughlin v Docherty 1991 SCCR 227—Exceptional hardship. Loss of licence would prevent work being found for three contractors. Disqualification overturned on appeal, hardship made out.

Marshall v MacDougall 1991 SCCR 231—Exceptional hardship, risk of heating business collapsing. Disqualified.
Held on appeal that there was exceptional hardship in the real possibility of the business collapsing.

Edmonds v Buchanan 1993 SCCR 1048
Held on appeal that exceptional hardship made out where there was a possible need to seek urgent medical attention for a newly-born baby, given that there had been one cot death in the family previously.

Bibby v MacDougall 1990 SCCR 121—Not exceptional hardship that B would lose his job as would the employees of the company he managed. Upheld on appeal.

ROBBERY

Robbery is **theft achieved by means** of **personal violence** or **intimidation**. Robbery may be further aggravated where it is preceded by a distinct **assault**.

COMMENTARY	CASE LAW	STATUTE LAW
Theft Must be completed for conviction of robbery. See Theft, p 77.	*O'Neill v HMA* 1934 JC 98 Knocked woman against a wall and took her handbag. *Purves & McIntosh* 1846 Ark 178 Pulled watch out of victim's pocket and then dropped it. *Held* amotio completed when watch taken out of pocket. Convicted of robbery.	
Achieved by means Violence used must precede or be contemporaneous with theft and be for the purpose of the theft.	*Reid and Barnet* (1844) 2 Broun 116 *Held* that it is not robbery to use force against an owner so as to retain an article one has just snatched from him. *A McGinnes* (1842) 1 Broun 231 Accused, who had been charged with assault and robbery, was found guilty of robbery alone since the assault had been committed 'entirely for the purpose of the plunder' and was held not to constitute a distinct assault.	
Personal violence Degree of violence necessary may vary according to the circumstances but must be more than that required for 'theft by surprise'.	*Jas Fegen* (1838) 2 Swin 25 Pulled victim's watch out of pocket by grabbing at chain. Victim fell and while he was falling accused broke the chain by another pull. Convicted of robbery. *Givan* 1846 Ark 9 Accused put his arms round the victim and gripped him while other stole his watch. Convicted of robbery.	
The violence used need not constitute an actual physical assault.	*O'Neill v HMA*, supra Per L J-C Aitchison: 'It is enough if the degree of force used can reasonably be described as violence.' Convicted.	
Intimidation Consists of any threat of immediate injury which induces the victim to hand over the property (Gordon, p 556).	*Matthias Little* 1830 Alison I 231 Convicted of robbery. Robbed woman of valuable property by threats of instant death. Condemned and executed.	
Assault Where there is a distinct assault preceding the violence involved in the actual act of taking there may be a charge of assault and robbery.	*O'Neil v HMA* 1976 SLT (Notes) 7 Armed robbery of station booking office. Convicted of assault and robbery.	

References: Hume I, 104; Alison I, 227; Macdonald, 39; Gordon, 550; Gane and Stoddart, 572.

SENTENCING POLICY

Davidson and Anr v HMA 1981 SCCR 371—Armed robbery. D convicted. Used sawn-off shotguns (one of which was loaded and operative) and bayonet. £4,500 stolen. D had long criminal record. Sentence of fourteen years' imprisonment. Appealed. Sentence reduced to eleven years, but court upheld trial judge's view that in the public interest a very substantial sentence was merited.

McIntyre v HMA 1989 SCCR 34—Assault and robbery. M convicted of luring doctor to locus by making false telephone call, where he was threatened with sticks and forced to hand over his medical bags. Sentenced to seven years' imprisonment. On appeal *held* that sentence was the minimum which could properly be imposed.

SEXUAL OFFENCES

Homosexual offences

Homosexual offences are principally regulated by **statute** although they can also be dealt with at **common law**.

COMMENTARY	CASE LAW	STATUTE LAW
Statute		Criminal Justice (Scotland) Act 1980 Section 80(1) homosexual act not an offence if in private between two persons both over 21 years, both parties consent. Section 80(2) 'private'—not more than two people present and not in a public lavatory. Section 80(11) defence if accused less than twenty-four years old with no previous for like offence and had reasonable cause to believe other person over twenty-one years old.
Common law Charges may relate to sodomy or acts short of sodomy.	*M'Laughlan v Boyd* 1934 JC 19 Lewd, indecent and libidinous charge arising out of incident involving boys whose ages were not proved. *Held* on appeal, charge relevant even if boys not below the age of puberty.	

Incest

Under the Sexual Offences (Scotland) Act 1976, as amended by the Incest and Related Offences (Scotland) Act 1986, a person who has sexual intercourse with a person of the opposite sex who falls within one of the **specified categories** is guilty of an offence unless he can establish a relevant **defence. Step relations** are also covered.

COMMENTARY	CASE LAW	STATUTE LAW
Specified categories		Sexual Offences (Scotland) Act 1976 Section 2A: specified categories eg mother, sister, niece etc (or male equivalents if female charged). Half blood is treated as equivalent to full blood
Defence		—accused did not know and had no reason to suspect the person was related to him/her. —accused did not consent to the sexual intercourse. —accused married to the person within the specified category and the marriage is recognised as valid in Scotland.
Step relations		Section 2B: Offence for a step parent to have intercourse with a step child if the child under the age of twenty-one or at any time before eighteen years old the child lived in the parent's household and was treated as a child of the family.
	Note: *R v HMA* 1988 SCCR 254 Any sexual relationship between a parent and child may also constitute shameless indecency.	Defences: accused —did not know child was a step child —had reasonable cause to believe the child was over twenty-one years old —did not consent to the intercourse —was married to the child and the marriage was recognised as valid in Scotland.

Rape

Rape occurs when **a man** has **sexual intercourse** with **a woman** by **intentionally or recklessly overcoming her will**.

COMMENTARY	CASE LAW	STATUTE LAW
A man Above the age of eight, question of proof in each case (Macdonald, 121),		
'Sex change.'	*R v Tan* [1983] QB 1053 Charge of living on the earnings of a prostitute. *Held* that a person who is biologically male, despite a 'sex change', still a male in law.	
A woman may only be guilty of rape art and part.	*Walker and McPherson* 1976 (unreported)	
Sexual intercourse Penetration per vaginam by male genitals, extent of penetration unimportant.	*Alex Macrae* (1814) Bell's Notes 83	
No emission required.	*Arch Robertson* (1836) 1 Swin 93	
A woman A female of any age can be raped. Intercourse with a girl under twelve years of age is rape regardless of 'consent'.	*Jas Burtnay* (1822) Alison I, 214	
Mentally abnormal.	*Chas Sweenie* (1858) Alison I, 214 Charge of raping a sleeping woman. Charge held irrelevant. Dicta equating the position of the mentally abnormal with the position of children ie consent irrelevant.	
Wife.	*Stallard v HMA* 1989 SCCR 248 Husband charged with violent rape of wife while cohabiting with her in the matrimonial home. *Held* that Hume's statement of the husband's immunity (I, 306) no longer consistent with modern attitudes. Per LJ-G Hope, 'Nowadays it cannot be seriously maintained that by marriage a wife submits herself irrevocably to sexual intercourse in all circumstances.'	
Intentionally or recklessly Honest belief of consent may be a defence even if based on unreasonable grounds.	*Meek and Ors v HMA* 1982 SCCR 613 Gang rape. Trial judge refusing to give a direction that an honest belief even on unreasonable grounds would stop conviction. *Held* on appeal, absence of honest belief essential. Reasonableness of grounds will affect whether jury sees belief as honest. No direction necessary here where jury choosing between two completely contradictory accounts of the same incident. See also: *Jamieson v HMA* 1994 SCCR 181	
Overcoming her will Victim's physical resistance not a pre-requisite, matter of proof.	*Barbour v HMA* 1982 SCCR 195 Charge of abduction, rape and indecent assault. Victim not consenting but not physically resisting. *Held* that threats of violence may be enough to overcome will. Per Lord Stewart: 'The important matter is not the amount of resistance put up but whether the woman remained an unwilling party throughout'.	Sexual Offences (Scotland) Act 1976, s 2(1)(*a*)—procuring sex by threats an offence. Section 2(1)(*b*)—obtaining sex by false pretence an offence.

Fraud.	*Wm Fraser* (1847) Ark 280 Charge of rape held not to be relevant where F had pretended to be the victim's husband.	Section 2(2)—sex by pretending to be victim's husband is rape
	Sweenie, supra Sexual intercourse with a sleeping woman was a crime but not rape.	
Victim intoxicated.	*HMA v Grainger and Rae* 1932 JC 40 Supplying alcohol to make victim insensible so as to have intercourse may be rape but taking advantage of victim voluntarily incapacitated by alcohol held to be the crime of clandestine injury on a woman.	Section 2(1)(*c*) Offence to administer a drug or any other matter with intent to obtain sex
	See also: *Quinn v HMA* 1990 SCCR 254	

References: Hume I, 301; Alison I, 209; Macdonald, 119; Gordon, 883; Gane and Stoddart, 479; McCall Smith and Sheldon, 171.

Sexual offences against children

Sexual offences against children are regulated at **common law** and by **statute**.

COMMENTARY	CASE LAW	STATUTE LAW
Common law Girl below the age of twelve incapable of consent. (Macdonald, 112)	*C v HMA* 1987 SCCR 104 Indecent assault by fourteen-year-old boy on eleven-year-old girl. Defence that girl consented or that C believed that she consented. Conviction upheld on appeal. Girl below the age of twelve incapable of consenting so C's state of mind irrelevant. See also: Brothel keeping Shameless indecency Assault, indecency	
Statute Intercourse with: —girl under thirteen years, —girl thirteen to sixteen years.		Sexual Offences (Scotland) Act 1976 Section 3: Offence of strict liability Section 4(1) Offence Section 4(2) Defence if man has either: (*a*) reasonable cause to believe the girl was his wife. (*b*) man under twenty-four years, no previous analogous convictions, reasonable cause to believe girl above sixteen years.
Indecent behaviour to girl twelve to sixteen years.		Section 5: Offence if behaviour such as would be an offence if girl under twelve years ie lewd, indecent or libidinous practices.
Abduction of girl under eighteen.		Section 8: Offence to abduct girl from the possession of her parents for purpose of unlawful sexual intercourse.
Abuse of position of trust—any child under sixteen years, abuse by person over sixteen years.	*HMA v RK* 1994 SCCR 499 Shameless indecency. RK had sexual intercourse with a girl aged over sixteen years of age but who had been his foster daughter since the age of eight. Plea to the relevancy of the charge repelled. *Held* that the fact that under the Sexual Offences (Scotland) Act 1976, s 2C, a person is only guilty of an offence if the girl is under sixteen years of age or the accused has no reasonable belief that she is over that age does not mean that intercourse such as charged cannot be a crime. Society would regard RK's behaviour as repugnant certainly as long as the fostering relationship continued. See also: Incest Homosexual offences	Incest and Related Offences Act 1986, s 2C—person in the same house and in a position of trust and authority to the child. Defences—belief child over sixteen years— belief of marriage to the child and marriage recognised as valid in Scotland.

References: Hume I, 309; Macdonald, 119; Gordon, 901; Gane and Stoddart, 672; McCall Smith and Sheldon, 171.

THEFT

Definition

Theft is the **felonious taking** or **appropriation** of the **property of another** without the consent of the owner and **with intent to deprive** him of that property.

COMMENTARY	CASE LAW	STATUTE LAW
Felonious taking Amotio: taking property from its place. Place: (a) Container—property must be taken out of container before amotio occurs. Movement inside the container may be attempt to steal only. (b) Room, etc—amotio occurs if property taken out of room *or* moved in a way indicating intention to steal. (c) Open spaces—any movement of the property probably sufficient for amotio (Gordon, p 464).	*Peter Anderson* 1800 Hume I 72 Taking something out of a till. *Cornelius O'Neil* (1845) 2 Broun 394 O'N raised window from outside. With a stick he moved some clothing in the room from original position to a place nearer the window. *Held* theft completed.	
Appropriation By dealing with goods as if they were one's own property,	*Dewar v HMA* 1945 JC 5 Manager of crematorium convicted of theft of two coffins and the lids of others which had been received for cremation. Sold them for use as coffee tables. *Herron v Diack* 1973 SLT (Sh Ct) 27 Manager of firm of funeral directors convicted of theft for dishonest appropriation of a steel casket intended for sea burial. *Black v Carmichael* 1992 SCCR 709 Wheel clamping. Car clamped in a private car park, notice attached demanding payment for release. Sheriff said it could be theft but not extortion. Appeal. *Held* that it was theft and extortion. Extortion to seek to enforce a debt otherwise than by legal process even if legitimate. The appropriation necessary for theft existed in the immobilising of the car and the mens rea in deliberately so appropriating. Intention to deprive temporarily would suffice. Theft by appropriation in the car park, detaining the motor car against the owner's will. But see: *Mackenzie v Maclean* 1981 SLT (Sh Ct) 40 Bar manager told to dispose of damaged cans of beer. Sold cans to passers-by at rubbish tip. *Held* that abandoned cans were the property of the Crown, but found not guilty due to lack of intent to steal.	
or by finding. Finding property of another and appropriating it, is theft.	*John Smith* (1838) 2 Swin 28 Found a wallet and appropriated it. Convicted of theft. *Lawson v Heatley* 1962 SLT 53 L received £1 from son which she knew must have been lost. Made no attempt to find owner and appropriated it for her own use. Convicted of theft.	Burgh Police (Scotland) Act 1892, s 412. It is an offence for a finder of property to fail to hand it into a police station within 48 hours.

MacMillan v Lowe 1991 SCCR 113
M found with chequebooks, said he had found them four hours earlier. Convicted on the grounds that he had not tried to hand them in and tried to conceal them from the police. Upheld on appeal.

Repealed by Civic Government (Scotland) Act 1982, s 67. Duty of finder of property to take reasonable care of it and to hand it to a police constable or official mentioned in subsection (3).

Under s 134 of the 1982 Act the provisions of the Burgh Police (Scotland) Act 1892 remained in force until end of 1984. See also 1982 Act, s 137(3).

1982 Act, s 73: no right of ownership conferred by finding.

Property
Anything which is the subject of public or private ownership can be stolen.

A *res nullius*, eg, a wild animal, cannot be stolen until brought into ownership.

John Huie (1842) 1 Broun 383
Once fish are in a fisherman's net they are his property and can be stolen from him.

Animals which have escaped from captivity.

Valentine v Kennedy 1985 SCCR 89
Theft of rainbow trout which had escaped from 'stank' or enclosure.
Held that the enclosed trout were clearly owned by person who purchased them from fish farm and who subsequently enclosed them. If, despite adequate precautions, some trout escaped, they still were owned and could be stolen by another.
Per Sheriff Younger: '. . . if some of these rainbow trout escaped occasionally in spite of proper precautions from that enclosed water or stank I consider that they as escapers remain the property of that purchaser insofar as they can be identified as his property; accordingly, someone who catches trout which he knows to have escaped . . . is guilty of theft, if he does not return them to their rightful owner.'

Of another
A person cannot steal his own property (Hume I, 77).

Sandlan v HMA 1983 SCCR 71
S and K charged with theft of jewellery, money and sales records from company of which S was a director. K's defence was that he believed goods belonged to S personally. S convicted. K found not proven.

If a person takes, believing what he is taking is his own, or that he has the owner's concurrence, he is not guilty of theft, but his belief must be reasonable and he must prove it (Macdonald, p 18).

Dewar, supra
The belief in this case was totally unreasonable.

With intent to deprive
Generally, intention to deprive permanently required.

Kivlin v Milne 1979 SLT (Notes) 2
Theft of car. Abandoned where owner could not find it. Found by police.
Held, on appeal, that facts demonstrated that appellant had intention to deprive owner permanently of car.

Herron v Best 1976 SLT (Sh Ct) 80
Car mechanic removed van from its owner, without permission, in pursuit of unpaid repair bill. Intended to return it when bill was paid.

Hold conditional intention to appropriate van not sufficient for theft. (Disapproved in *Milne v Tudhope*, infra.)

Smith v Dewar 1977 SLT (Sh Ct) 75
Taking a moped with intention of having a 'shot'. Not guilty due to lack of theftuous intent.
Would, however, if charged be guilty of offence under Road Traffic Act 1988, s 178.

But in certain exceptional cases, intention to deprive temporarily may suffice where the accused's purpose is reprehensible.

Milne v Tudhope 1981 JC 53
Accused contracted to carry out work on cottage. Owner dissatisfied and accused refused to remedy work unless he received further payment. Removed and stripped house of various items to force owner to grant further payment. Convicted of theft.
Opinion of the court: 'We agree that in certain exceptional cases an intention to deprive temporarily will suffice and disagree that an intention to deprive permanently is essential.'

Sandlan v HMA, supra
Goods taken for a nefarious purpose with intention of returning them later sufficient for conviction of theft.

Kidston v Annan 1984 SCCR 20
K received goods from owner for the purpose of estimating cost of repairs. He refused to return the goods unless owner paid for repairs.
Held guilty of theft.

Fowler v O'Brien 1994 SCCR 112
Intention to deprive indefinitely. Bicycle taken without permission but openly and not returned. Conviction upheld on appeal.
Held that it could not be said that the intention was to deprive permanently or temporarily, most accurate to say indefinitely. No need for theft to be clandestine.

Aggravation of theft

Theft may be aggravated by certain factors; in particular, **by opening lockfast places, by housebreaking** or **by violence**.

COMMENTARY	CASE LAW	STATUTE LAW
By opening lockfast places Applies to anything secured by a lock apart from buildings.	*Jas Gray* 1824 Alison I 296 Breaking open a chest in a stable loft by staving in the lid. *McLeod v Mason & Ors* 1981 SCCR 75 Lockfast car. Unnecessary to prove whether intent to steal car or contents or both, since in the circumstances theftuous intent could be presumed from the facts.	
The effraction of the lockfast place must precede the theft and be for the purpose of the theft.	*Jas Stuart and Alex Low* (1842) 1 Broun 260 Accused of stealing a lockfast chest and then forcing it open and stealing its contents. *Held*, that removing a container meant removing its contents, and aggravation of opening lockfast place was not relevantly charged.	
By housebreaking 'House' covers any roofed building.	*John Fraser* 1831 Bell's Notes 41 A henhouse.	
'Breaking': any means of surmounting the security of the building or by unusual entry.	*Alston & Forrest* (1837) 1 Swin 433 Improper use of a key to enter. *Jas Davidson* (1841) 2 Swin 630 Entry through a window was normal mode of access and did not constitute the aggravation of housebreaking. *Burns v Allan* 1987 SCCR 449 B charged with attempted housebreaking with intent to steal in that he disconnected the external burglar alarm of premises in question. *Held* that an alarm system is an integral part of the security of a building and to disconnect it is plainly an attempt to overcome that security and therefore constitutes attempted housebreaking with intent to steal.	
Housebreaking must precede and be for purpose of theft.	*Cornelius O'Neil* (1845) 2 Broun 394 Standing outside window O'N used a stick to remove handkerchief and socks in room, having overcome security by pushing up window. *Donaghy v Normand* 1991 SCCR 877 D convicted of housebreaking with intent to steal. D had entered house to rescue an intruder who had been discovered by the houseowner. On appeal *held* that there was no need for D to give explanation for his presence in the house but if he did not, court entitled to draw its own inference.	
Crime completed by gaining entry and stealing. Actual bodily entry not required.	*McClung v McLeod* (1974) 38 JCL 221 Court held that the essential feature was the violation of the security of the premises, not the entry. Accused had broken the window of the premises but not actually entered them. Conviction of housebreaking with intent to steal upheld.	
Note: The act of housebreaking without intent to steal does not of itself constitute a nominate crime (but see Malicious Mischief, p 30, or could be Breach of the Peace, p 7).		

By violence
If theft is followed by violence it may constitute the aggravated offence of theft and assault.

See also: Robbery, p 71.

Associated crimes.
Clandestinely taking possession of property.

Reid and Barnet (1844) 2 Broun 116
Struggle to retain a purse by its owner after accused had snatched it from him. Not robbery to use force to retain a stolen article.

Strathern v Seaforth 1926 JC 100
'Clandestinely taking possession of a motor-car, property of another, in the knowledge that permission to do so would be refused.'
Defence objected to relevancy of complaint. Sustained by sheriff, but High Court held complaint relevant under law of Scotland.

Murray v Robertson 1927 JC 1
Fish merchant charged with clandestinely taking possession of a number of fish boxes belonging to other merchants and using them to transport his own fish. Conviction quashed on basis that accused had used boxes openly.

Road Traffic Act 1988, s 178(1)(*a*): taking and driving a motor vehicle without consent or lawful authority.

References: Hume I, 57; Alison I, 250; Macdonald, 16; Gordon, 449; Gane and Stoddart, 548.

Civic Government (Scotland) Act 1982, ss 57, 58

Civic Government (Scotland) Act 1982, ss 57, 58.
Section 57(1) **Any person** who without lawful authority **is found** in or on **any building, premises, vehicle or vessel** in circumstances from which it may be reasonably inferred that he intended to commit theft there, shall be guilty of an offence.
Section 57(2) 'Theft' includes any aggravation, including robbery.
Section 58(1), (4) Any person with **two or more convictions for theft which are 'not spent'**, who has or has **recently** had in his possession any tool or object from which it may be reasonably inferred that he intended to commit theft or has committed theft, and is unable to demonstrate satisfactorily that his possession was not for this purpose, shall be guilty of an offence.
The maximum penalty under each section is level 4 fine or three months' imprisonment or both.

COMMENTARY	CASE LAW	STATUTE LAW
Any person Person no longer requires to have been a 'known thief'.		Civic Government (Scotland) Act 1982, s 57, replaces the provisions of the Prevention of Crimes Act 1871, s 7, and also the Burgh Police (Scotland) Act 1892, s 409.
Is found Must be actually present on the building, etc. Not sufficient to prove that he had been there or might have been there.	*Maclean v Paterson* 1968 JC 67 Convicted of having been found in a goods yard. Ample circumstantial evidence but no direct eye-witness evidence. *Held* could not be held to have been found! (Prosecution under Prevention of Crimes Act 1871, s 7.)	
Any building, premises, vehicle or vessel Defines more clearly the locus compared to the old provision of 'certain places'.	*McIntyre v Morton* (1912) 6 Adam 634 Found in entrance of hotel. Convicted. (Prosecution under Prevention of Crimes Act 1871.) *Moran v Jessop* 1989 SCCR 205 M found on roof of office block undergoing renovation, which had been broken into by others. M argued that there was no case to answer as Crown had not proved that he had no lawful authority to be there. Defence evidence did not include any evidence of lawful authority and M convicted. *Held* on appeal that the circumstances were such as to support the inference of absence of lawful authority and appeal refused.	
Two or more convictions for theft which are 'not spent'		Re provision of Rehabilitation of Offenders Act 1974, s 1. After a set period certain convictions must be treated as 'spent' and convicted person treated as a rehabilitated person. Consult statute for definition of 'spent'. Civic Government (Scotland) Act 1982, s 58, replaces reference to known thief or reputed thief and the offence no longer extends to possession of unexplained sums of money or articles, nor does the offence apply to 'associates of known thieves'.

Recently
Within fourteen days before the
date of arrest without warrant, issue
of warrant, or service of complaint
against him alleging that he has
committed the offence.

Section 58(2)

THEFT

SENTENCING POLICY

Clark v Cardle 1989 SCCR 92—C, unemployed and dependent on state benefits, pleaded guilty to theft by housebreaking of nine jackets valued at over £4,000. Sentenced to six months' imprisonment and ordered to pay £500 compensation at £3 per week after release.
Held on appeal that in light of financial and family circumstances, it was unreasonable to impose order on top of maximum sentence and compensation order quashed.

Collins v Lowe 1990 SCCR 605—C convicted of theft by housebreaking, damage caused. Four months' imprisonment and compensation order to cover the damage, humiliation and distress. Upheld on appeal.

McQueeney v Carmichael 1991 SCCR 221—M and another caught stealing tiles worth £350. Fined £200 and van worth £1,500 used in theft ordered to be forfeited. Upheld on appeal. Criminals using vehicles do so at their own risk.

Downie v Normand 1992 SCCR 894—Security guard stealing £4,500 from employer, no money recovered. First offender. Three months' imprisonment upheld on appeal.

McCulloch v Friel 1993 SCCR 7—Plagium by fifty-three-year-old, first offender with alcohol problem. Three months' imprisonment reduced to 200 hours community service on appeal. Determination to beat the alcohol problem.

CONCEPTS

ART AND PART GUILT

All persons who **participate** in the commission of a crime **together** are **equally liable for the outcome** of that act irrespective of the particular role played by each individual in its commission.

COMMENTARY	CASE LAW	STATUTE LAW
Participate Before a person may be held so responsible, he must have actually participated in the crime. Mere presence at, or failure to prevent, the commission of an offence will not, in the absence of any 'special duty', impose guilt for that offence.	*HMA v Kerr & Ors* (1871) 2 Couper 334 Three accused charged with assault with intent to ravish. One of the accused, Donald, had taken no direct part in the attack but had only stood at the other side of a hedge watching the attack. Had not spoken to his friends or the girl during the attack. *Held* no art and part liability.	Criminal Procedure (Scotland) Act 1975. Sections 216 and 428 apply concept of art and part guilt to all statutory offences. Sections 46 and 312(*d*) provide that it is unnecessary to state in any charge that accused is 'guilty actor or art and part' as every charge now impliedly contains these words.
Dissociation must be explicit.	*MacNeil v HMA* 1986 SCCR 288 Per L J-G Emslie 'A person who is an instigator of a contemplated crime or a participator in preparation for it, may successfully dissociate himself from criminal responsibility in the crime, if it is committed by others, if he clearly intimates to them that he is withdrawing and seeks to discourage them from proceeding. . . . In such circumstances he cannot be guilty of the crime if it is nevertheless committed.'	
Special duty	*Bonar v McLeod* 1983 SCCR 161 Two police officers. One assaulted prisoner. Senior officer did nothing. *Held* art and part guilty as did not dissociate himself from actions; thus even stronger than position of official standing by and allowing offence; placed in active position as part of escort.	
A person may be held to have so participated and thus invoke art and part guilt by several methods: by 'serious, earnest and pointed' instigation or advice whose effect is to induce the commission of a crime (Hume I, 278). 'The instigation must be to such an act as was likely to result in the crime charged.' (Macdonald, p 4). 'The connection between the instigation or assistance and the act must continue to the last. If the instigator repent, he is not guilty if he genuinely attempts to dissuade the person whom he instigated. . . .' (Macdonald, pp 5–6).	*Spiers v HMA* 1980 JC 36 All accused charged with murder and attempted murder. S was not proven present at attack. Appeal court held S could only be liable art and part if he instigated the attack, this being antecedent concert. Conviction quashed.	
Advice of a general nature not directly connected with an imminent crime is not, however, sufficient for guilt.	*HMA v Johnstone & Stewart* 1926 JC 89; 1926 SLT 428 Two accused were charged with procuring an abortion. The accused were unknown to each other and the first accused had only given the name of the second accused to persons seeking an abortion and received no benefit from such a referral. Per Lord Moncrieff: 'It would be straining the law to hold that the mere communication of a name by a party, who was not in actual communication with the party named, was actual participation in the illegal act.' J found not guilty.	

By supplying material assistance prior to the commission of the crime, eg, supplying a car for a bank robbery where the supplier knows of the imminent plot to commit the crime, or through actual participation in the commission of the crime itself either

HMA v Semple 1937 JC 41; 1937 SLT 48
Charge of attempting to procure an abortion through instigation and supply of powders to a pregnant woman held relevant.

by a prior agreement to take part in the crime,

HMA v Fraser and Rollins 1920 JC 60; 1920 2 SLT 77
Robbery and murder. Woman lured victim to park where two men were waiting to rob him. Victim died of his injuries. The two male co-accused convicted of murder.

or by a concerted and spontaneous coming together at the time of the offence.

Gallacher v HMA 1951 JC 38; 1951 SLT 158
One of accused started a fight with the deceased and a number of men joined in. All stood round the victim and kicked him to death.
Per Lord Keith: 'If the accused were in a kicking crowd animated by a common purpose, joining in the attack, assisting and encouraging, each and all are responsible for the consequences.' Three of the accused convicted of murder.

But see:

Melvin v HMA 1984 SCCR 113
Held that a jury are entitled, in the absence of intent to kill or any antecedent concerted intention to carry out an assault and robbery, to assess the degree of recklessness displayed by each participant, and to return verdicts of murder or culpable homicide in accordance with that assessment.

Malone v HMA 1988 SCCR 498
Two appellants charged with murdering B after repeated kicks and blows to his face. First appellant found guilty of murder, second appellant who desisted from assault shortly before first appellant found guilty of culpable homicide. Convictions upheld but observed by LJ-G Emslie 'If a distinction is to be made in a case involving a joint assault causing deaths it could normally only be justified if there were striking differences in the relevant conduct of each of the assailants.'

Where accused knew or should have known that a weapon was being used by co-accused,

Walker v HMA 1985 SCCR 150
W and R involved in fight with deceased in discothèque. R's conviction of murdering victim by stabbing him upheld on appeal. W convicted art and part on the basis that he knew or should have known of knife attack but still continued with his own assault. Conviction against W quashed on appeal.
Per LJ-C Wheatley: '. . . it would be reasonable to infer that, if [W] should have known that [R] was using a knife he still persisted in his attack on the victim [then this] would bring into operation the law of art and part and warrant the conviction. But insofar as it has never been established at what point of time the fatal blow was struck it is quite impossible to affirm that the appellant can be involved. . . .'

or if weapon used sufficiently similar to those contemplated.

O'Connell v HMA 1987 SCCR 459
O and three others charged with murder. They had formed common plan to assault deceased with sticks, one of which was three or four feet long. Deceased killed by blow from his own hammer and no evidence as to which accused had wielded it. Trial judge directed jury that where the weapons used were of a broadly similar nature it was for them to decide whether the assailants should have anticipated the use of a broadly similar weapon. Appellant was convicted and his appeal refused.

Art and part guilt applies even where a person could not be convicted as the principal.

Vaughan v HMA 1979 SLT 49
V accused that, acting along with the mother of a small boy, he forced the boy to have intercourse with the mother, contrary to Incest Act 1567. The accused was not related to either the mother or the son and argued that he could not be found guilty since not within the forbidden degrees.
Held, on appeal, that Act did not exclude its application to those art and part in commission of offence. Convicted.

Criminal Justice (Scotland) Act 1987, s 64 adds a subsection (2) to ss 216 and 248 of the 1975 Act: 'Any person who aids, abets, counsels, procures or incites any other person to commit an offence against the provisions of any enactment shall be guilty of an offence.'

Together
The essence of art and part guilt is that the accused execute a common plan or, if acting in concert, a spontaneous common purpose.

HMA v Lappen 1956 SLT 109
L charged along with five others with assault and robbery. Convicted.
Per Lord Patrick: 'If a number of men form a common plan whereby some are to commit the actual seizure of the property and some, according to the plan, are to keep watch and some, according to the plan, are to help carry away the loot . . . then, although the actual robbery may only have been committed by one or two of them, every one is guilty of the robbery because they joined together in a common plan to commit the robbery . . . if it has not been proved that there was such a common plan or if it has not been proved that the accused were parties to this previously conceived common plan then in law each is only responsible for what he himself did.'

If the prosecutor cannot prove concert each individual accused is judged only by his own proved actings.

Docherty v HMA 1945 JC 89; 1945 SLT 247
D was charged that, along with another unknown man, he murdered a man in a room of a flat. When blow was struck the other person was in the room and there was no direct evidence to show who in fact struck the blow. Concert was therefore essential to conviction, and D's conviction of murder was quashed because the jury were not explicitly told they must acquit unless concert proved.

Low v HMA 1993 SCCR 493
Trial judge entitled to direct that the first accused did not act in concert but the second accused did act in concert with the first accused, given that each accused treated separately and different evidence admissible for each.

A party cannot 'dissociate' himself from a crime once it has been perpetrated.

MacNeil v HMA 1986 SCCR 288
Appellant (S) and seven others charged with importing cannabis into UK. S engaged as engineer on vessel which sailed from Oban to West Africa and helped to store cannabis in fuel tank. His defence was that he only became aware that cargo was cannabis after loading it, and thereafter left ship at first opportunity.
Held that there is no defence of dissociation. But compare the case of dissociation *before* perpetration of the offence, supra, p 85.

Equally liable for the outcome
Where the common plan or purpose is proved, the accused will be held responsible for any foreseeable consequences of the crime whether or not it was intended.

HMA v Welsh & McLachlan (1897) 5 SLT (Reports) 137

Docherty v HMA, supra

But not for any action of another which goes unforeseeably outwith the common plan or purpose.

HMA v Welsh & McLachlan, supra
Two accused charged with murder of old woman having broken into her house and stolen certain articles. Failure by Crown to prove common plan went beyond theft by housebreaking and who in fact murdered the woman. Found not proven.

Concepts

Boyne v HMA 1980 JC 47; 1980 SLT 56
Three men convicted of murder during assault and robbery. Conviction of murder against two accused quashed since there was no evidence to show that they either knew or had reason to anticipate the use of a knife, or that they continued the attack once the knife was produced.

McLaughlan v HMA 1991 SCCR 733
M joining in serious assault in which one life-threatening blow inflicted. Whether sheriff wrong to direct that M, by joining in, responsible for 'all that has taken place'?
Held on appeal that M only responsible for everything that happened after she joined in, important to know when the life-threatening blow took place.

Brown v HMA 1993 SCCR 382
Homicide. Two accused attacking victim with knife and iron bar, both denied inflicting the fatal wound. Culpable homicide withdrawn, convicted of murder. Appeal.
Held that for murder both accused would require the necessary degree of wicked recklessness, if either of their intentions was only to inflict serious injury the culpable homicide open. Culpable homicide convictions substituted.

References: Hume I, 264; Macdonald, 2; Gordon, 129; Gane and Stoddart, 243.

ATTEMPT

A person may be convicted of attempting a crime where he has taken an overt step in pursuance of his criminal intention and has passed from the stage of **preparation** to the stage of **perpetration** but has not completed the crime.

COMMENTARY	CASE LAW	STATUTE LAW
Under statute any person charged with a crime may also be convicted of attempt.		Criminal Procedure (Scotland) Act 1975, s 63: 'Attempt to commit any indictable crime shall itself be an indictable crime, and under an indictment which charges a completed crime, the accused may be lawfully convicted of an attempt to commit such crime.' See also: s 312(*o*) for **summary** prosecution.
The mens rea for an attempted crime is the same as for the completed crime.	*Cawthorne v HMA* 1968 JC 32; 1968 SLT 330 *Held* that attempted murder may be committed either intentionally or recklessly.	
Mere **preparation** shall not suffice. An attempted crime is where the accused failed to complete the crime but had actually taken overt steps in the **perpetration** of it.	*R v John Eagleton* 1855 Dears 376, 515 Parke said: 'The mere intention to commit a misdemeanour is not criminal. Some act is required, and we do not think that all acts towards committing a misdemeanour are indictable. Acts remotely leading towards the commission of the offence are not to be considered as attempts to commit it but acts immediately connected with it are.'	
	HMA v Mackenzie 1913 SC(J) 107; 1913, 2 SLT 48 'The law does not strike at preparation to commit a crime . . . the overt act . . . is essential to a conviction.' Per LJ-C Macdonald: '. . . the preparation of a fraudulent document, or a document intended to be fraudulently used is not in itself a punishable crime . . . it requires an overt act of use to constitute an indictable offence.'	
	HMA v Tannahill and Neilson 1943 JC 150 Per Lord Wark: 'I think you would require some overt act, the consequences of which cannot be recalled by the accused, which goes towards the commission of the crime, before you can convict even of attempt.'	
	(But in certain cases where two or more persons are involved this could be conspiracy—see Conspiracy, p 93.)	
'But the vicious will is not sufficient, unless it is coupled to a wrongful act. And here the question arises, how far must the culprit have proceeded in the prosecution of his wicked purpose, to make him answerable in the tribunals of this world?' (Hume I, 26).	*HMA v Camerons* (1911) 6 Adam 456 Where deciding whether what accused had done amounted to attempted fraud, Lord Dunedin charged the jury that 'the root of the whole matter' was 'to discover where preparation ends and where perpetration begins. In other words, it is a question of degree, it is a jury question'.	
The fact that it was impossible for the accused to complete the crime is no defence against attempt.	*Lamont v Strathern* 1933 JC 33; 1933 SLT 118 Attempted to steal from an empty pocket. Per Lord Sands: 'I am not, I confess, impressed by the metaphysical argument that, whereas one cannot take what is not there, therefore one cannot attempt to take what is not there.' Convicted of attempted theft.	

However, impossibility may be a defence to certain attempts of abortion.	*HMA v Anderson* 1928 JC 1; 1928 SLT 651 Court held that it was not attempted abortion to try to abort a woman who was not pregnant. Per Lord Anderson: 'To attempt to do what is physically impossible can never, in my opinion, be a crime.'
A criminal act may be charged with intent to commit a further crime.	
Where murder or culpable homicide is charged and it is not proved that death resulted from the assault, convictions may be assault with intention to murder or kill. Similarly, in assault to danger of life, where it is not proved life was endangered the conviction may be for assault with intent to endanger life.	

References: Hume I, 26; Alison I, 163; Macdonald, 254; Gordon, 163; Gane and Stoddart, 211.

SENTENCING POLICY

Moore v HMA 1984 SCCR 25. Attempted robbery by threats. Attempt to rob a post office by handing employees a note asking for money and adopting a menacing attitude to them. Four years' imprisonment. Appeal dismissed.
Per LJ-G Emslie: '. . . one could hardly have quarrelled with a longer sentence.'

COERCION

The plea of **coercion** may operate as a defence to a criminal act or as plea in mitigation. Similarly, where such coercion takes the form of **superior orders** such a plea will have the same effect.

COMMENTARY	CASE LAW	STATUTE LAW

Coercion

'Crime consists in the intentional violation of the rights of others; it follows it cannot be visited with punishment where it has arisen not from intention or voluntary depravity but such coercion as has deprived the party of the free exercise of his will' (Alison I, 668).

Thomson v HMA 1983 SCCR 368
Threat must be of immediate harm in circumstances where resort to protection of authorities impossible, and it is impossible to resist or avoid participation. The defence of coercion can extend even to a person playing a principal part, and the question whether the gain, etc, was disclosed to the authorities matters only as regards the credibility of the accused.

Coercion may take different forms.

It may be of a public nature,

James Purdie 1720 Hume I 52
Charge of mobbing. Acquitted on basis that he was forced and compelled to participate by the mob.

or be issued by one individual to another, the essence of the plea being the existence of such coercion that the accused 'could not resist without manifest peril to his life or property' (Alison I, 672).

Docherty & Others (1976) SCCR Supp 146
Three men charged with armed robbery. Two of them pleaded that they had been coerced by the third who had threatened them and their mothers. Issue of coercion left to jury to decide.
Per Lord Keith: 'In order that coercion may be a defence the position must be that the accused acted in a situation created by a threat to him which he had reason to believe would be carried out.'

The threat must be imminent.

HMA v McCallum (1977) SCCR Supp 169.

Fear of imminent death or serious injury may operate as a defence even to a serious crime.

Gordon, p 429, for position re murder in England.

Sayers & Ors v HMA 1981 SCCR 312
Jury directed that where a person's will is overborne by the will of another so that he is not acting of his own free will, that might be a defence to a criminal charge, but that matter be approached with some caution lest it become an easy answer for those that could not otherwise explain their conduct.

But see:

Thomson v HMA, supra
Cast doubt as to whether coercion could be a defence to murder in Scotland.
Per Lord Hunter: '. . . I would, until the question arises for decision, wish distinctly to reserve my opinion as to whether coercion could ever or in any circumstances affect the verdict in a case of murder.'

DPP (NI) v Lynch [1975] AC 653
Abbott v Queen, The [1977] AC 755

However, Sheriff Gordon suggests (1983 SCCR 383 and 384) that there is a difference in the English approach, as stated in *DPP v Lynch*, where the emphasis is concentrated on the overcoming of the accused's will by the force of the threat; whereas in Scotland the concentration is on the requirement that the commission of the crime should be the *only* way to avoid the threatened danger. This is in keeping with Hume's definition and the terms of *Thomson v HMA*.

Superior orders

may form the basis of a plea of coercion where a soldier acts under a lawful order or believes that he is so acting.

HMA v Sheppard 1941 JC 67; 1941 SLT 404
Charge of culpable homicide. Private in army part of escort to return a deserter to the regiment. Accused left alone with deserter for a few minutes and deserter attempted to escape. Accused shot and killed him. No clear orders but told by superior officer to 'stand no nonsense and shoot if necessary'. Found not guilty.

Per Lord Robertson: 'It would be altogether wrong to judge his actings so placed too meticulously— to weigh them in fine scales. If that were to be done it seems to me that the actings of soldiers on duty might well be paralysed by fear of consequences with great prejudice to national interests.'

See also:

HMA v Hawton and Parker (1861) 4 Irv 58
Marine firing at boat illegally fishing. Killed fisherman.
Held not guilty of culpable homicide.

References: Hume I, 47–56; Alison I, 668; Macdonald, 11; Gordon 429; Gane and Stoddart, 320.

CONSPIRACY

Conspiracy is complete as soon as two or more persons **have agreed** together to commit a **crime.**

COMMENTARY	CASE LAW	STATUTE LAW
Conspiracy '. . . process is properly brought under this generic name, for any sort of conspiracy or machination, directed against the fame, safety, or state of another, and meant to be accomplished by the aid of subdolous and deceitful contrivances, to the disguise or suppression of the truth . . .' (Hume I, 170).	*Elliot & Nicolson* 1694 Hume I 170, 181 N induced physician to provide poison with which to murder wife. Changed plan to one whereby they conspired to fix on N's wife a false charge of attempting to poison N himself. Conviction for conspiracy and other charges.	
Most recent definition of conspiracy is that made by Viscount Simon in a House of Lords civil appeal case which has subsequently been adopted by the Scottish criminal courts.	*Muschet & Campbell* 1721 Hume I 170 *Crofter Hand-Woven Harris Tweed Co v Veitch* 1942 SC (HL) 1 Per Viscount Simon LC: 'Conspiracy . . . is the agreement of two or more persons to effect any unlawful purpose whether as their ultimate aim or only as a means to it, and the crime is complete if there is such agreement even though nothing is done in pursuance of it.' *HMA v Wilson, Latta & Rooney* 1968, High Court, unreported: Gordon 200 Charge of conspiring to have false evidence led and thus defeat the ends of justice. Viscount Simon's statement adopted by LJ-C Grant. *HMA v Carberry & Ors* 1974, High Court, unreported; Gordon 198 LJ-C Wheatley approves Viscount Simon's definition.	
Sheriff Gordon refers to three possible categories of conspiracy:		
(1) Conspiracy where a specific crime has been carried out in pursuance of that conspiracy.	*Wilson, Latta & Rooney*, supra Charge was a conspiracy to pervert the course of justice and the commission of subornation and attempted subornation in pursuance thereof. LJ-C Grant directed jury that they could acquit in the conspiracy and convict on the subornation. *HMA v Milnes & Ors*, January 1971, High Court, Glasgow, unreported; Gordon 201 Per Lord Avonside: 'If . . . conspiracy has not been proved, your verdict will be not guilty or not proven as regards the conspiracy . . . if you find the heads . . . not proved you will find . . . not guilty . . . but guilty on those which are [proved].'	
However, a conspiracy to do something by criminal means is not a crime unless the criminal means are proved.	*Sayers v HMA* 1982 SLT 220 Charged with conspiring to aid the UVF by criminal means and by contravention of Prevention of Terrorism (Temporary Provisions) Act 1976. Jury found accused guilty of conspiracy but deleted specification of criminal means libelled. Appeal against conviction allowed; charge was irrelevant because of lack of specification and was not a crime known to the law of Scotland.	
(2) Conspiracy where no specified crime is charged in pursuance of the conspiracy, where charge does not set out specified crime by which conspiracy to be effected.	*HMA v Walsh & Ors* 1922 JC 82; Gordon 204 Conspiracy to further the purposes of the IRA by the unlawful use of force and violence by the use of explosive substances to be used to endanger the lives and persons and property of the lieges.	

(3) Conspiracy may often be charged as a substitute for attempt. There is an attempt where the person involved goes beyond the stage of preparation for the crime into perpetration. Thus there may be a conspiracy charge where accused person does not move into perpetration but has agreed with another to commit the crime.

See *Elliot & Nicolson*, supra

West v HMA 1985 SCCR 248
W and another charged with conspiracy to assault and rob persons employed in named premises. They loitered suspiciously outside these premises and were in possession of blade from pair of scissors and open razor, respectively. Conviction for conspiracy upheld on appeal.
Per LJ-G Emslie: 'Taking all the evidence together . . . we are of the opinion that there was sufficient. . . .'

Have agreed
As soon as two or more persons have agreed to commit a crime they are guilty of a complete crime of conspiracy. The mens rea of the offence is the intention to commit the crime libelled.

Smith & Ors 1975, High Court, Gordon 198
Lord Keith directed the jury that to 'find a conspiracy they would have to be satisfied that matters went beyond the putting forward by one man of his ideas to another with a view to the matter being discussed and possibly agreed upon at another date. There must be actual agreement.'

Crime
Only conspiracies to do what would be criminal if done by one person are criminal conspiracies (Macdonald, p 185).

Smith & Ors, supra

Factual impossibility of achievement of the ultimate object of the conspiracy does not act as a defence to the charge.

Maxwell v HMA 1980 JC 40; 1980 SLT 241
Three accused convicted of conspiracy to bribe licensing board to approve transfer of gaming licences. At dates of offence, board did not have legal power to approve transfer since the matter of the issue of the licence was at the time under appeal to sheriff. Conviction sustained on appeal. It is the criminality of purpose and not the result which may or may not follow from the execution of the purpose which makes the crime a criminal conspiracy.

References: Hume I, 170; Alison I, 369; Macdonald, 185; Gordon, 198; Gane and Stoddart, 202.

ERROR

Error of law does not affect criminal responsibility. An **error of fact** may affect responsibility where it is **genuine and reasonable** and where the accused's responsibility would have been affected had the circumstances been as he thought them to be.

COMMENTARY	CASE LAW	STATUTE LAW
Error of law Every man is presumed to know the law—*ignoratia juris neminem excusat*.	*Clark v Syme* 1957 JC 1; 1957 SLT 32 C, charged with maliciously killing a neighbouring farmer's sheep, pleaded that he thought he had a legal right to do so after giving due warning to his neighbour about sheep damaging his crops. Acquitted by sheriff on ground that he had acted under a misconception of his legal rights; but appeal court rejected this defence. Per LJ-G Clyde: 'The mere fact that his criminal act was performed under a misconception of what legal remedies he might otherwise have had, does not make it any the less criminal.'	
Error of fact Must affect mens rea: a mistake as to identity of the victim is irrelevant unless the mens rea of the particular crime (eg, incest) requires knowledge as to the identity of the victim.	*Matthew Hay* 1780 Hume I 22 H put poison in a family's breakfast with the intention of killing his girlfriend. She survived but her parents died. H convicted of murder. *HMA v Brown* (1907) 5 Adam 312 B sent poisoned shortbread through the post, which was eaten by a servant of his intended victim. Murder indictment held relevant, but B found unfit to plead.	
Error must be **genuine and reasonable**.	*Dewar v HMA* 1945 JC 5; 1945 SLT 114 D, the manager of a crematorium, was convicted of theft of over one thousand coffin lids and some coffins. In defence he claimed to believe that it was the general and accepted practice in crematoria for the manager to remove lids at the time of cremation and keep them or use them as he saw fit; in effect to treat them as 'scrap'. Conviction upheld on appeal. Per LJ-C Cooper: '. . . if his beliefs were . . . not founded on rational grounds but founded only on the singular idea of the man himself . . . then . . . you . . . are bound to return a verdict of guilty.' *Crawford v HMA* 1950 JC 67; 1950 SLT 279 C stabbed his father five times after a verbal quarrel in which his father swore at him and made threatening gestures but with no indication of imminent violence. Appeal court upheld the trial judge's withdrawal of self-defence plea. Per LJ-G Cooper: '. . . when self-defence is supported by a mistaken belief rested on reasonable grounds, that mistaken belief must have an objective background and must not be purely subjective or of the nature of a hallucination.'	

If the error is found to be genuine and reasonable the accused is judged as if the facts were as he believed them to be.	*Owens v HMA* 1946 JC 119; 1946 SLT 227 O, charged with murder, claimed that after seeing what he thought was a knife in the deceased's hand, he had used his own knife in self-defence in the ensuing struggle. The trial judge told the jury that if O was 'completely wrong' in thinking the other man had a knife, his own use of a knife could not be justified. The appeal court held this to be a mis-direction and quashed the conviction. Opinion of the court: '. . . self-defence is made out when it is established . . . that the panel believed that he was in imminent danger and that he held that belief on reasonable grounds. Grounds for such belief may exist though they are founded on a genuine mistake of fact.'	
The defence of error may apply in rape cases.	*Meek & Others v HMA* 1982 SCCR 613 Honest belief that woman consenting is a defence of rape even if not based on reasonable grounds. Quaere whether the decision applies to all common law crime (see commentary by Sheriff Gordon, 1982 SCCR 620).	
There may be a statutory defence of mistake.		Trade Descriptions Act 1968, s 24(1). In any proceedings for an offence under this Act it shall be a defence for the person charged to prove (*a*) that the commission of the offence was due to a mistake or to reliance on information supplied to him or to the act or default of another person, an accident, or some other cause beyond his control.

References: Hume I, 73; Macdonald, 11; Gordon, 326; Gane and Stoddart, 107.

NECESSITY

Plea of **necessity** may be submitted in **certain limited circumstances** and according to these circumstances may be regarded as a **defence** or merely as a **plea in mitigation.**

COMMENTARY	CASE LAW	STATUTE LAW
Necessity Plea remains of slightly ambiguous quality due to lack of direct Scottish authority. Both Macdonald and Alison make slight reference to the plea in conjunction with compulsion.		
Certain limited circumstances Exact circumstances and actions which form foundation of a plea of necessity have been narrowly interpreted.	*HMA v Graham* (1897) 2 Adam 412 Drugs administered to cause an abortion. Convicted. *R v Dudley and Stephens* (1884) 14 QB 273 Two men and a boy cast adrift in open boat. The two men killed the boy, who was ill, after eight days without food and six without water. Fed on flesh of boy. Convicted of murder. Per Lord Coleridge: 'It is not correct to say that there is any absolute or unqualified necessity to preserve one's life.'	Abortion Act 1967, s 5(2), excludes defence of necessity by providing that anything done with intent to procure a miscarriage, unless authorised by the Act, is unlawful.
Defence Where, in order to preserve a greater value, there is the commission of a crime, eg, stealing a fire extinguisher to save a burning building (Williams, p 737).		
Where to ensure personal safety there is the commission of a crime.	*Tudhope v Grubb* 1983 SCCR 350 (Sh Ct) Accused charged under s 6(1) of Road Traffic Act 1972. *Held*, that as accused had attempted to drive so as to avoid further injury following an assault, he had established defence of necessity. Acquitted.	
Plea in mitigation Hume and Alison refer to old law of 'burthensack' as a form of necessity which was regarded as a plea in mitigation, where extreme hunger and want made the theft of a limited amount of food a non-capital offence.	*R v Dudley and Stephens*, supra Sentence of death for murder commuted to six months' imprisonment.	
	Graham v Annan 1980 SLT 28 Driving while disqualified and without insurance. Wife, who was pregnant, was driving car. Became ill and husband, who was disqualified from driving and uninsured, took over. *Held*, on appeal, that circumstances disclosed special reasons to mitigate penalty by avoiding a further period of disqualification or endorsement.	Road Traffic Offenders Act 1988, s 34, where special reasons established why an otherwise obligatory disqualification or endorsement should not be enforced.

References: Hume I, 55; Alison I, 674; Gordon, 420; Gane and Stoddart, 341; Williams, 722.

PROCEDURE

BAIL

Admission to bail is competent for all crimes and offences. In cases of **murder and treason**, only the Lord Advocate or the High Court may admit to bail. There are **standard conditions**, and there may be **special conditions**. The public interest may require the **refusal of bail**. Bail may be allowed where **reports** are **called for**.

COMMENTARY	CASE LAW	STATUTE LAW
Admission to bail		
		Criminal Procedure (Scotland) Act 1975
		Bail etc (Scotland) Act 1980
		Criminal Procedure (Scotland) Act 1975
		Solemn procedure:
		Section 26(1). All crimes and offences except murder and treason are bailable.
		Section 26(2). Accused person entitled to apply for bail when brought for examination on declaration. Prosecutor may object.
		Section 26(3). Discretionary to refuse application until committal stage.
		Section 27. Application, if refused, may be renewed at committal stage.
		Section 28(1). Grant or refusal of bail within sheriff's discretion.
	Lau, Petitioner 1986 SCCR 140	Section 28(2). Application to be dealt with within twenty-four hours of its presentation to the sheriff, which failing liberation forthwith.
	Per Lord Justice-Clerk 'Presentation can only occur when the application has been transmitted to the sheriff.'	
	Gibbons, Petitioner 1988 SCCR 270	Section 30(2). A court may review its decision to refuse bail.
	Petitioner fully committed for trial on 18.4.88 at 11.30 am and immediately applied for bail. Sheriff adjourned application till 9.45 am the next day. Case not heard till 11.50 am owing to delay in bringing peititioner from prison. Sheriff refused bail and petitioner appealed to High Court.	Section 30(3). Not before the fifth day after a first decision, and not before the fifteenth day after a subsequent decision.
	Held that requirement of s 28(2) was mandatory and petitioner entitled to be liberated.	Section 31(1). If bail application after committal is refused, or if applicant dissatisfied with amount of bail fixed, the applicant may appeal to the High Court.
		Section 31(2). Where bail application is granted at any stage, the prosecutor may appeal to the High Court; if he does, the applicant is not liberated.
		Section 33(1). Applicant shall be liberated after seventy-two hours (ninety-six for Outer Hebrides, Orkney or Zetland) where appeal is by public prosecutor, whether appeal is disposed of or not.

Murder and treason

McLaren v HMA 1967 SLT (Notes) 43
Murder. Petition to the High Court to exercise
discretionary power refused.
Opinion of the court: 'The fact that there are these
discretionary powers in the court is recognised by
our standard writers on criminal law (see Hume on
Crimes, II, p 90) and they are only exercised when
the Court sees reason for such an indulgence in the
whole circumstances of the case.'

Milne v McNicol 1944 JC 151
Theft. M not asked to plead. Bail refused. Appeal to
the High Court refused as incompetent because M
not committed.
Per LJ-C Cooper: 'It is true that . . . the powers of the
High Court of Justiciary to admit to bail any person
charged with any crime or offence are preserved,
but that section I read as referable to the paramount
and overriding authority of the High Court, which
has been described as equivalent or similar to the
nobile officium of the Court of Session; and that is an
authority which, as a single judge, I am unable to
exercise. . . .'

Standard conditions

MacNeill v Milne 1984 SCCR 427
M pled guilty to some, not guilty to other, charges on
summary complaint. Bail allowed on sole condition
that M attend all subsequent diets. Appeal by prosecutor against omission of other standard conditions upheld.
Held mandatory to impose standard conditions.
Per LJ-C Wheatley's interlocutor: '. . . finds that the
sheriff was wrong in forming the view that the imposition of the standard conditions or any of them was
a matter for his discretion.'

Summary procedure:
Section 298(1). All offences
bailable and discretionary to
grant or refuse bail (prosecutor
entitled to be heard).
Section 298(2). Application to
be disposed of within twenty-
four hours, which failing
liberation forthwith.
Section 299(2). A court may
review its decision to refuse
bail.
Section 299(3). Not before the
fifth day after a first decision,
and not before the fifteenth day
after a subsequent decision.
Section 300(1). The refusal of
or admission to bail may be
appealed; if admission to bail is
appealed, the applicant is not
liberated.
Section 300(4). Applicant shall
be liberated after seventy-two
hours (ninety-six for Outer
Hebrides, Orkney or Zetland)
where appeal is by public
prosecutor, whether appeal
disposed of or not.

Solemn procedure:
Section 35. Lord Advocate or
the High Court may admit to bail
person charged with any crime
or offence.

Bail etc (Scotland) Act 1980
section 1(1)(*a*). Release on bail
may be granted only on
conditions.
Section 1(2). Conditions such
as considered necessary to
secure that accused
(*a*) appears at diets in case;
(*b*) does not commit offence on
    bail;
(*c*) does not interfere with
    witnesses, nor obstruct
    course of justice;
(*d*) makes himself available for
    enquiries or report to assist
    court to deal with him.

Bail

Lockhart v Stokes 1981 SLT (Sh Ct) 71
Assault. S, on petition, granted bail. Address given was a fairground site. Attempts to serve indictment unsuccessful because site not in use. Warrant to arrest granted.
Per Sheriff Gow: '. . . a showground which is occupied on a seasonal basis only, and is simply a piece of waste ground at a time when citation is to be effected, is not a "proper domicile of citation" under the Bail Act.'

Section 2(1)(*b*). Address of accused to be specified by the court as domicile of citation.

Special conditions

Section 1(3). Court or Lord Advocate may impose requirement that accused or cautioner deposits a sum of money in court where satisfied that such imposition is appropriate to special circumstances of the case.

Note: Bail cannot normally be applied for while a sentence is being served.

Currie v HMA 1980 SLT (News) 187, (1980) SCCR Supp 248.

Refusal of bail

Smith v McC 1982 SCCR 115
McC, with numerous convictions for theft, on probation for theft, and awaiting trial on three charges of dishonesty, for one of which he was on bail, granted bail on further charge of theft by housebreaking. Appeal by prosecutor upheld.
Per LJ-C Wheatley: '. . . there are certain considerations which should generally regulate the decision on allowance of bail and adherence to such general considerations while having regard to the facts of the individual case could, I am sure, save a lot of needless appeals. . . . There is, however, the consideration of the public interest. An accused should be granted a bail order unless it can be shown that there are good grounds for not granting it. A complete catalogue of such grounds cannot be compiled. Generally, however, they can fall into two broad categories: (1) the protection of the public and (2) the administration of justice. Previous convictions per se should not be regarded as an automatic reason for refusal of bail, but if there is a significance in the record and the nature of the charge(s) then being preferred against an accused, the consideration of the protection of the public arises. . . . One of the factors which in my view is of importance is the allegation that at the time when the alleged offence (or offences) was (or were) committed the accused was in a position of trust to behave as a good citizen and not to breach the law. . . . the list which follows is merely illustrative of the more common examples and not exhaustive. . . . (1) . . . already on bail . . .; (2) . . . ordained to appear . . . for trial on another offence; (3) . . . on probation, or undergoing community service order; (4) . . . on licence or parole; (5) . . . on deferred sentence. In such circumstances I take the view that unless there are cogent reasons for deciding otherwise bail should be refused. Other circumstances which warrant refusal of bail are the nature of the offence in very special circumstances, alleged intimidation of witnesses by assaults or threats, absence of a fixed abode, or reasonable grounds for suspecting that the accused will not turn up for his trial.'

G v Speirs 1988 SCCR 517

G charged on petition with assault and robbery and breach of s 3(1)(*b*) of the Bail Act 1980. Prosecutor did not oppose bail and did not give sheriff any information relevant to bail. Sheriff refused bail and accused appealed.

Held that an accused ought to be granted bail unless a sufficient ground produced to justify its refusal; and that as no such grounds were advanced, bail ought to have been allowed. Bail granted.

Maxwell v McGlennan 1989 SCCR 117

Per Lord Brand 'If the Crown does not oppose bail, grant it'.

Note: These guidelines were reinforced by the Justiciary Office in 1984 SLT (Notes) 271.

Reports called for

Long v HMA 1984 SCCR 161

Fraud. L pled guilty on indictment. Case continued for social enquiry report. Bail refused. Application for review held competent but bail again refused.

Held, on appeal, review procedure incompetent *quoad* s 179.

Per LJ-C Wheatley: 'Manifestly, then, the provisions of section 30 have no application to a point in the procedure after the accused has pled guilty and his plea has been accepted.'

Thus review of bail decision under s 30 of 1975 Act inappropriate at, for example, the stage of remand awaiting best method of disposal or inquiries as to physical or mental condition. At such stage appeal to High Court under s 179 is the correct procedure.

McGoldrick v Normand 1988 SCCR 83

Appellants, aged twenty and twenty-two and not previously sentenced to detention, convicted of attempted theft. Sheriff continued case for social enquiry reports and remanded in custody, having refused bail. On appeal *held* that where court has to be satisfied after considering reports that custodial sentence is appropriate, very good reasons are required to justify refusal of bail. Bail granted.

Criminal Procedure (Scotland) Act 1975, as amended by Bail etc (Scotland) Act 1980, ss 5 and 6

Solemn procedure:

Section 179(1). Bail allowable where enquiries as to disposal to be made.

Section 179(2). Appeal may be made against refusal of bail within twenty-four hours of remand.

Section 180(1). Bail allowable where enquiry to be made into physical or mental condition of accused.

Section 180(5). Appeal may be made against refusal of bail within twenty-four hours of remand.

Summary procedure:

Section 380(1). Bail allowable where enquiries as to disposal to be made.

Section 380(2). Appeal may be made against refusal of bail within twenty-four hours of remand.

Section 381(1). Bail allowable where enquiry to be made into physical or mental condition of accused.

Section 381(5). Appeal may be made against refusal of bail within twenty-four hours of remand.

JUDICIAL EXAMINATION

When an accused appears on petition he may intimate his wish either to emit or not emit a **declaration.** Whether he does so or not, the prosecutor may then **examine** the accused with a view to eliciting any denial, admission, explanation or justification. The prosecutor may also question the accused on any alleged **confession.**

COMMENTARY	CASE LAW	STATUTE LAW
Declaration Must be entirely the composition of the accused.	*Carmichael v Armitage* 1982 SCCR 475 Accused read a declaration prepared by his solicitor on his instructions. *Held* that declaration was inadmissible, as being more of the nature of a precognition.	Judicial examinations are held in terms of the Criminal Procedure (Scotland) Act 1975, ss 19, 20, 20A and 20B, as amended and added to by the Criminal Justice (Scotland) Act 1980, s 6 and the Prisoners and Criminal Proceedings (Scotland) Act 1993, Sch 5. For detailed procedures consult Acts.
Examine The prosecutor may put certain questions to the accused.		Section 20A(2). Questions put by the prosecutor should not be designed to challenge the truth of anything said by the accused; there should be no reiteration of a question which the accused has refused to answer; and there should be no leading questions. The sheriff has the duty to ensure that questions are fairly put to and understood by the accused.
Where the accused declines to answer a question put to him in the examination, his having so declined may be commented on by the prosecutor, judge or any co-accused at subsequent trial even if he declines to answer on the advice of his solicitor.	*McEwan v HMA* 1990 SCCR 401 M giving no response to questions at examination on the advice of his solicitor, gave evidence of an alibi at trial. *Held* on appeal that the judge was allowed to comment on M's silence notwithstanding the legal advice. *McGhee v HMA* 1991 SCCR 510 Murder. At examination M not answering questions regarding an admission he was alleged to have made to the police, on legal advice. Judge commenting that such advice would have been extraordinary if lawyer had known of the proposed alibi defence. *Held* that the judge had gone too far, making comment as to his view of the facts and not relating to the jury M's explanation for not answering. See also: *Moran v HMA* 1990 SCCR 40	
With sheriff's permission, the solicitor for the accused may ask the accused any questions in order to clarify any ambiguity in an answer given by the accused to the prosecutor or to give him an opportunity to answer a question which he has previously refused to answer.		Section 20A(4)
Confession A statement clearly susceptible of being regarded as incriminating.	*McKenzie v HMA* 1982 SCCR 545 *Held* that the statement 'Just my luck, I knew I'd be picked out' was clearly a statement susceptible of being regarded as incriminating and thus constituted a 'confession' within the terms of the Act.	

Reference: Renton & Brown, 5–54.

A useful pamphlet on judicial examination was produced in 1981 by the then Convener of the Criminal Law Committee of the Law Society of Scotland. Copies may be obtained from the Society.

STATUTORY TIME LIMITS

Imposed to prevent undue delay in the commencement of trials.

Solemn procedure: If accused not detained in custody, trial must commence within **twelve months** of first appearance on petition. If detained pending liberation in due course of law, indictment must be served within **eighty days** of full committal and trial must commence within **110 days** of such full committal.

Summary procedure: If accused detained, trial must commence within **forty days** of bringing of complaint in court. For **statutory offences**, unless otherwise provided, proceedings must commence within **six months** of contravention.

COMMENTARY	CASE LAW	STATUTE LAW
		The question of time limits for the bringing of a person to trial is essentially regulated by Criminal Procedure (Scotland) Act 1975, s 101 (solemn) and s 331 (summary), as substituted by Criminal Justice (Scotland) Act 1980, s 14.
Solemn procedure **Twelve-month** rule. Where accused not detained in custody, trial must commence within twelve months of his first appearance on petition.		**Solemn procedure:** Twelve-month rule regulated by 1975 Act, s 101(1), as substituted by 1980 Act, s 14(1), which provides that 'An accused shall not be tried on indictment for any offence unless such trial is commenced within a period of twelve months of the first appearance of that accused on petition in respect of that offence; and, failing such commencement within that period, the accused shall be discharged forthwith and thereafter he shall be for ever free from all question or process for that offence'.
The twelve-month period will be extended where the delay is due to the non-appearance of the accused at a diet where a warrant for his arrest has been granted, and the period may also be extended on cause shown.	*McGinty v HMA* 1984 SCCR 176 McG and another first appeared on petition on 20.5.83. Trial arranged for 14.5.84. Last date for service of indictment was 14.4.84. Indictments not served by police. Crown applied for extension of twelve-month period. Application granted by sheriff. Appeals dismissed. *Held*, with some hesitation, that sheriff entitled to treat unforeseen illness of policeman responsible for serving indictment as adequate cause for extension. *Observer*, per LJ-G Emslie: '. . . it will not do for the Crown to say that there has not been time to serve an indictment . . . as the result of mere pressure of business.' *Dobbie v HMA* 1986 SCCR 72 An unexpected extra High Court sitting resulted in lack of accommodation for sheriff and guilty trial. *Held* that this was not a case of mere pressure of business (see *McGinty v HMA* supra) and sheriff entitled to grant extension. See also: *Fleming v HMA* 1992 SCCR 575	For extension of twelve-month rule 1975 Act, s 101(1) provides: '(i) Nothing . . . shall bar the trial of an accused for whose arrest a warrant has been granted for failure to appear at a diet in the case; (ii) on application . . . the sheriff or . . . in respect of the High Court, a single judge . . . may on cause shown extend the said period of twelve months.'

Rudge v HMA 1989 SCCR 105
R appeared on petition on 14.12.87 and indicted for trial on 1.11.88. On 3.11.88 Crown applied for three month extension on ground of volume of business. Sheriff granted extension.
Held that sheriff entitled to hold that pressure on accommodation could be sufficient reason for extension.
Per LJ-C Ross: '. . . the pressure of business referred to in *McGinty* [supra] was pressure of business on the Crown. In the present case the pressure of business is that on accommodation available for holding trials. . . .'

HMA v Swift; Allen v HMA 1984 SCCR 216
S arrested on petition. Indictment prepared. Crown repeatedly failed to serve S with indictment at his domicile of citation. Crown applied for extension of twelve-month period. Refused. Crown appealed to High Court. Appeal dismissed.
Held (1)(*a*) Section 101 rule is to be departed from only if sufficient reason is shown.
(*b*) Nature and degree of fault on Crown's part are relevant.
(*c*) That charges are serious is insufficient reason.
(*d*) Sheriff correct to refuse, as only reason offered by Crown was commission of a major error by them.
(2) Shortness of extension requested and little risk of prejudice to the accused are not relevant to consideration of whether sufficient reason shown, but may be relevant to consideration of whether judge should exercise discretion.

Lyle v HMA 1991 SCCR 458
Twelve-month rule. Extension sought and granted. Crown had made a mistake in calculating the date. Overruled on appeal. Rule to be applied except in exceptional circumstances. Mistake in this case inexcusable.

Mejka v HMA 1993 SCCR 978
Twelve-month rule. Crown seeking extension to allow it to try M and his co-accused, who was ill, together. *Held* that mere convenience would not justify extension, absence of fault of the Crown not conclusive.

HMA v Davies 1993 SCCR 645
Twelve-month rule. Metropolitan police failed to serve indictment and failed to inform the prosecutor as requested. Extension granted on appeal, prosecutor had no reason to foresee that the police would not comply with his request.

HMA v Brown 1984 SCCR 347
Accused had moved house but had given no notice of this to court. Consequently, they had not received their indictments until shortly before trial, which prejudiced defence preparation. Adjournment granted. Sheriff held that case still to proceed within twelve-month period. However, on Crown appeal, extension of three months granted.

Twelve-month rule does not prevent subsequent summary proceedings on same charge outwith twelve-month period.

MacDougall v Russell 1985 SCCR 441
R appeared on petition on 9.5.84, was committed for trial and liberated on bail. On 13.3.85 a complaint containing the same charges was called against him in sheriff court. Trial called for 17.6.85 and R tendered plea to competency on ground that trial not brought within one year of appearance on petition. *Held* that s 101(1) of the 1975 Act should be read as if the words 'on indictment' were added to it, and complaint therefore competent.

Concepts

Twelve-month rule can be retrospectively extended.

HMA v M 1986 SCCR 624
M appeared on petition on 26.9.85. Second indictment served for trial on 22.9.86. On 15.9.86 indictment dismissed as irrelevant. Crown appealed and appeal upheld on 24.10.86.
Held that it was competent to extend twelve-month period retrospectively and trial diet postponed for three months. Reasoning in *Farrell v HMA*, infra, followed.

Eighty-day rule.
If an accused is detained in custody being committed for trial until liberated in courts of law, the indictment must be served upon him within eighty days of such committal, otherwise he has to be released, although the Crown can still proceed against him on the charges.

HMA v Walker and Ors 1981 SCCR 154
Accused committed for trial. Indictment which was served within the eighty-day period was not called for trial. A second indictment in the same terms as the first was served outwith the eighty-day period.
Held, on appeal, that since the original indictment had fallen, there was no valid indictment served within the eighty-day period and accused must be liberated.

Eighty-day rule regulated by 1975 Act, s 101(2)(*a*), as substituted by 1980 Act, s 14(1), which provides that 'an accused who is committed for any offence until liberated in due course of law shall not be detained . . . for a total period of more than (*a*) eighty days, unless within that period the indictment is served on him, which failing he shall be liberated forthwith. . . .'

The eighty-day rule may be extended for any sufficient cause; however, not if the delay is due to some fault by the prosecution.

Farrell v HMA 1984 SCCR 301
Indictments served within eighty days and trial commenced within 110 days. However, due to illness of prosecution witness, trial abandoned. Crown petition for extension of both periods granted by Lord Justice-Clerk and, on appeal, decision upheld by High Court. Notable in that extension of eighty-day period granted retrospectively.

McCluskey v HMA 1992 SCCR 920
Eighty-day rule. First indictment within eighty days but not called, second indictment outwith eighty days. Conviction upheld on appeal. Section 101 deals only with detention, not with the validity of indictment.

Exception that (s 101(3)): 'A single judge of the High Court may . . . for any sufficient cause extend the period. . . . Provided that he shall not extend the said period if he is satisfied that, but for some fault on the part of the prosecution, the indictment could have been served within that period.'

110-day rule.
Where an accused is detained in custody having been fully committed for trial, the trial must actually commence within 110 days of such committal, and if it does not the accused has to be released and the Crown cannot proceed against him any further on these charges.

110-day rule regulated by 1975 Act, s 101(2)(*b*), as substituted by 1980 Act, s 14(1), which provides that '. . . an accused who is committed . . . until liberated in due course of law shall not be detained . . . for a total period of more than . . . (*b*) 110 days, unless the trial of the case is commenced within that period, which failing he shall be liberated forthwith and thereafter he shall be for ever free from all question or process for that offence'.

The 110-day rule can be extended if the delay is due to the illness or absence of certain vital personnel, or to any other sufficient cause not due to an error of the prosecution.

Gildea v HMA 1983 SCCR 114; 1983 SLT 458
Extension of 110-day period granted because of 'time-tabling, administrative difficulties and pressures'.
Held, on appeal, that extension justified.
Per LJ-G Emslie: 'The Crown undoubtedly took a calculated risk. . . . The question is whether the decision to take that risk was unreasonable. . . .'

See also:
Farrell v HMA, supra

Exception that (s 101(4)): 'A single judge of the High Court may . . . extend the period . . . where he is satisfied that delay in the commencement of the trial is due to:
(*a*) the illness of the accused or of a judge;
(*b*) the absence or illness of any necessary witness; or
(*c*) any other sufficient cause which is not attributable to any fault on the part of the prosecutor.'

HMA v Lewis 1992 SCCR 22

L convicted and sentenced in Scotland, transferred to England under s 26(1) of the Criminal Justice Act 1961, escaped and came back to Scotland where after more offences he was caught and committed. Detained beyond 110 days before trial. Crown argued he was being held under the sentence of imprisonment.

Held that the imprisonment to be treated as imposed by the English court, time exceeded and indictment dismissed.

See also:
HMA v Lang 1992 SCCR 642

Appeals for all solemn cases.

Appeal (s 101(5)): 'The grant or refusal of any application to extend the periods mentioned . . . may be appealed against by note of appeal presented to the High Court. . . .'

Commencement of trial.

Commencement of trial (s 101(6)): '. . . a trial shall be taken to commence when the oath is administered to the jury.'

If accused detained successively on full committal warrants, the 110 days run separately and in parallel.

Ross v HMA 1990 SCCR 182

R detained on 20.2.89 in respect of certain charges. Committed for certain other offences on 23.3.89. Indicted on all charges. Trial due to commence 18.6.89 being more than 110 days after 20.2.89. Charges in respect of 20.2.89 committal dismissed but March charges not time barred.

Summary procedure

Forty-day rule.

In the case of summary complaints where an accused is detained in custody his trial must commence within forty days of the bringing of the complaint in court, otherwise, as with the 110-day rule for solemn procedure, he must be set free and the Crown cannot proceed against him on those charges.

Brawls v Walkingshaw 1994 SCCR 7

Forty-day rule. B released on bail under the condition that he remain within the curtilage of his house. Took plea to the competency of proceedings on the basis that this was in effect detention and forty days exceeded. Sheriff repelled pleas.

Upheld on appeal. Condition did not involve an outside agency and relied on the accused's own willingness to abide by it. Such a condition should be used only exceptionally.

Forty-day rule regulated by 1975 Act, s 331A(1), as inserted by 1980 Act, s 14(2), which provides that 'a person charged with a summary offence shall not be detained in that respect for a total of more than forty days after the bringing of the complaint in court unless his trial is commenced within that period, failing which he shall be liberated forthwith and thereafter he shall be for ever free from all question or process for that offence.'

Again, as with the 110-day rule, the forty-day rule may be extended where the delay is due to illness or absence of vital personnel, or for any other sufficient cause not due to the fault of the prosecution.

Except that (s 331A(2)): 'The sheriff may [on application made to him] extend the period . . . for such period as he thinks fit where he is satisfied that delay in the commencement of the trial is due to
(*a*) the illness of the accused or of a judge;
(*b*) the absence or illness of any necessary witness; or
(*c*) any other sufficient cause which is not attributable to any fault on the part of the prosecutor.'

Appeals.		Appeals (s 331A(3)): 'The grant or refusal of any application to extend the period mentioned in subsection (1) may be appealed against by note of appeal presented to the High Court. . . .'
Commencement of trial.		Commencement of trial (s 331A(4)): '. . . a trial shall be taken to commence when the first witness is sworn.'
Statutory offences **Six-month** rule. In the case of statutory contraventions, unless the statute otherwise provides, proceedings must be commenced within six months of the contravention. If there is continuous contravention the last contravening point shall be taken for the application of the six-month rule, and the whole continuous contravention shall be chargeable.	*Tudhope v Lawson* 1983 SCCR 435 (Sh Ct) Offence against Trade Descriptions Act 1968. Summary proceedings 'may be commenced at any time within twelve months from the time when the offence was committed' (s 19(3) Trade Descriptions Act 1968). Date of offence was 28.6.82, proceedings commenced on 28.6.83. L pleaded proceedings incompetent as not having been commenced within prescriptive period. *Held*, that in computing period, date of offence not to be taken into account, and complaint competent.	Statutory offences regulated by the 1975 Act, s 331 Section 331(1). 'Proceedings . . . in respect of the contravention of any statute or order shall, unless the statute or order . . . fixes any other period, be commenced within six months after the contravention occurred and, in the case of a continuous contravention, within six months after the last date of such contravention, and it shall be competent . . . to include the entire period during which the contravention has occurred.'
Certain additional evidence may be considered.		Section 331(2). 'A person shall not be summarily convicted of an offence . . . unless the offence was wholly or partly committed within six months before the proceedings against him in respect of the offence where commenced; but, subject as aforesaid, evidence may be taken of acts constituting. or contributing to the offence and committed at any previous time.'
Commencement of proceedings—requirement that there be no undue delay in execution of warrant.	*Young v Smith* 1981 SCCR 85; 1981 SLT (Notes) 101 Offences against Road Traffic Act 1972. Y appeared voluntarily at court and complaint was served on him there. Convicted. Appeal on ground that proceedings time-barred because warrant not executed, dismissed. *Held*, that warrant had not been executed, but requirement for warrant to be executed without undue delay applies only where warrant requires to be and is enforced, and does not apply where, in absence of undue delay on prosecutor's part, the need for execution is elided by the voluntary act of the accused which achieves the entire objective of the warrant. *Harvey v Lockhart* 1991 SCCR 83 *Held* on appeal that when considering the question of undue delay, a sheriff should hear evidence from the Crown on its justification for delay.	Section 331(3). '. . . proceedings shall be deemed to be commenced on the date on which a warrant to apprehend or to cite the accused is granted, if such warrant is executed without undue delay.'

McGlennan v Singh 1993 SCCR 341
Undue delay. Fourteen days delay, some of which was due to the sheriff clerk's office. Sheriff said occasionally extraordinary measures were required to commence prosecutions.
Held on appeal that no special or unusual measures require to be taken, nothing to show that delay the fault of the prosecutor.

Tudhope v Mathieson 1981 SCCR 231
Contravention of Road Traffic Act 1972 on 11.1.81. Warrant for arrest granted on 19.3.81. Prosecutor did not enforce warrant during period of strike (23.3–10.8.81) by court clerks and other civil servants on court staff. M arrested on 24.8.81. Took plea to competency of complaint on ground that it was time-barred.
Held, that latitude given to prosecutors by s 331(3) did not extend to situation where prosecutor could have executed warrant timeously, but made conscious decision not to do so in order to encumber limited court facilities with cases of type in question. Complaint dismissed as incompetent.

Tudhope v Brown 1984 SCCR 163 (Sh Ct)
Statutory contraventions up to 24.9.83. On 19.3.84 sheriff assigned 30.3.84 as diet. Complaint served on *first* accused by police on 26.3.84. Accused pleaded proceedings were time-barred.
Held, that there had been undue delay. It was irrelevant that citation executed more than forty-eight hours before assigned diet; complaint dismissed as incompetent.
Statutory contraventions up to 24.9.83. On 19.3.84 sheriff assigned 30.3.84 as diet. Complaint served on *second* accused on 21.3.84. Delay was explained by reference to normal police procedure for serving citations.
Held, no undue delay. Plea to competency repelled.

Beattie v Tudhope 1984 SCCR 198; 1984 SLT 423
Contravention of Trade Descriptions Act 1968, s 1(1)(*b*). Offence allegedly committed on 18.2.82. Prosecutor obtained warrant to cite on 17.2.83 (prescriptive period is twelve months for this offence). Citation served personally, but due to intervention of weekend, this took six days. Sheriff held no undue delay. B's appeal dismissed.
Held, that question was one of fact, circumstances and degree for sheriff, 'that being so, we are unable to say that in arriving at his decision, he exercised his discretion in any manner which would justify us in disturbing his conclusion.'

McCartney v Tudhope 1985 SCCR 373
Road traffic offences allegedly committed 13.12.1984. Prescriptive period ended 13.6.1985. Warrant to cite obtained by prosecutor on 11.6 and handed to police on 13.6, but not executed until 25.6. Magistrate decided no undue delay in execution. On appeal, however, delay held unreasonable. Excessive workload of policeman responsible for serving warrant not in itself sufficient to justify delay in absence of any details as to his work priorities.
Per LJ-C Ross: '. . . I am of opinion that the stipendiary magistrate did not have material before him to justify his concluding that the delay was not undue.'

Concepts

Buchan v McNaughtan 1990 SCCR 688
Undue delay. B at sea, police not leaving citation with wife so as to cite personally.
Held on appeal that as it would not have been quicker to leave citation with wife then there was no undue delay.

Anderson v Lowe 1991 SCCR 712
Undue delay. Delay in sheriff clerk's office getting a warrant to the prosecutor.
Held not to be the fault of the prosecutor. No decision on what would have happened had the prosecutor been aware of the warrant.

References: Hume II, 136; Alison II, 96; Macdonald, 211; Renton & Brown, 7–36 and 14–10.

SPECIAL DEFENCES

The special defences of alibi, impeachment or incrimination, insanity and self-defence are those which, if established in relation to a relevant charge, are a complete answer to that charge.

Criminal Procedure (Scotland) Act 1975, s 82(1), as substituted by Criminal Justice (Scotland) Act 1980, s 13: in **solemn procedure**, for all special defences notice must be lodged ten clear days before trial, or where there is good reason, before the oath is administered to the jury.

GENERAL

COMMENTARY	CASE LAW	STATUTE LAW
Proof of special defences generally.	*Lambie v HMA* 1973 JC 53 Per LJ-G Emslie: 'The only purpose of the special defence is to give fair notice to the Crown . . . When a special defence is pleaded . . . the jury should be charged in the appropriate language and all that requires to be said of the special defence . . . is that if the evidence is believed or creates in the minds of the jury reasonable doubt as to the guilt of, the accused . . . they must acquit'. *McDonald v HMA; Valentine v McDonald* 1989 SCCR 165 McD indicted for trial in sheriff court. Purported to lodge a notice under s 82(1) of the 1975 Act of defence to the effect that the indictment was a vindictive and vexatious prosecution brought because of the knowledge of the procurator fiscal and police officers of his wrongful conviction in 1986, and was an attempt to prevent or delay him in exposing their criminal conspiracy. *Held* inter alia that as what was contained in the purported s 82(1) notice would not necessarily result in acquittal of accused even if established, it did not constitute a special defence in terms of that subsection, and proposed defence was irrelevant.	

ALIBI

This **special defence** is that at the time of the alleged offence the accused was **not at the locus libelled but at some other specified place**.

COMMENTARY	CASE LAW	STATUTE LAW
A **special defence** intimates that the defence evidence will be of a certain specific nature: the burden of proof is unaltered.	*HMA v Hayes* 1973 SLT 202 Posting packet containing explosives. Special defences of alibi and incrimination. Per Lord Cameron: 'The purpose of a special defence in Scots law is to give to the prosecution proper notice of a particular line which the defence of an accused person may take ... there is no obligation on an accused person to establish that special defence under a penalty that if he fails to do so then conviction would follow.'	Criminal Procedure (Scotland) Act 1975

Fraser v HMA 1982 SCCR 458
Assault and robbery. Special defence that F was in public house at time of crimes. Convicted. On appeal conviction sustained.
Opinion of the court: '. . . we disagree with the inherent proposition that a judge is bound to give proper and clear direction with regard to the nature, purport and effect of the special defence of alibi. The simple reason is that the special defence has played all the part it has to play in the trial when it has given notice to the Crown of a possible line of evidence which will or may be held on behalf of an accused person.'

Gilmour v HMA 1982 SCCR 590
Murder and rape. Special defence that accused was at home alone. Convicted.
Per trial judge, Lord Dunpark: 'Now, before I turn to the charge in this case let me just dismiss this so-called special defence of alibi which was read to you at the outset. It is miscalled a special defence because there is no onus on the accused, and I think you should ignore the alibi so-called special defence in this case, because if you believe the evidence of the accused that he was alone in his house between two and four o'clock on 4th November 1981, you would acquit him; and if you were left with a reasonable doubt about that you would also acquit him.'
Appeal against conviction dismissed.
Per LJ-C Wheatley: 'That direction was in line with current practice, and, rather than constituting prejudice to the appellant, it was to his advantage. We need say no more on that, and in the result we reject both branches of this ground of appeal.'

Balsillie v HMA 1993 SCCR 760
Theft by housebreaking. Sheriff not allowing B's explanation as to his whereabouts at the relevant time because no notice of special defence lodged. *Held* on appeal that notice not required where B was saying he was at the locus but did not go into the house. Only where accused saying he was at a specified other place was notice required.

At the time of the alleged offence the accused was **not at the locus libelled but at some other specified place**.
'The plea is not conclusive unless the alibi . . . makes it not only unlikely but impossible that the [accused] could have done the deed at the time and place libelled' (Alison II, 624).

William & Alex Fraser 1720 Hume II, 411
Fire raising. Alibi evidence that accused were in bed at 11 pm on night libelled, and on morning following, disregarded.

References: Hume II, 410; Alison II, 624; Macdonald, 265; Renton & Brown, 7–20 and 7–21.

IMPEACHMENT OR INCRIMINATION

This is a **special defence** that the offence was committed not by the accused but by another person, named if known. It is **competent** to call a **co-accused** as a witness.

COMMENTARY	CASE LAW	STATUTE LAW
A **special defence** intimates that the defence evidence will be of a certain, specific nature; the burden of proof is unaltered.	*Lambie v HMA* 1973 JC 53; 1973 SLT 219 Theft. Others named as responsible for crime. Per LJ-G Emslie: 'The only purpose of the special defence is to give fair notice to the Crown. . . . When a special defence is pleaded . . . the jury should be charged in the appropriate language, and all that requires to be said of the special defence, where . . . evidence in support of it has been given is that if that evidence . . . is believed, or creates in the minds of the jury reasonable doubt as to the guilt of the accused . . . they must acquit.'	
Specific reference to the special defence by the judge is unnecessary if the significance of all the evidence, including the special defence, is brought to the jury's attention.	*Mullen v HMA* 1978 SLT (Notes) 33 Rape. Defence claim that crime committed by principal Crown witness. Convicted. Appeal on misdirection refused. Per LJ-C Wheatley: 'It does not follow that failure by the trial judge to make specific reference in terms to such a special defence necessarily amounts to a misdirection such as to vitiate a conviction.' But contrast: *Donnelly v HMA* 1977 SLT 147 Assault and robbery. Special defence of incrimination. See also: *Mackie v HMA* 1990 SCCR 716 *Collins v HMA* 1991 SCCR 898	
Co-accused's evidence is **competent.**	*HMA v Ferrie* 1983 SCCR 1 Murder and serious assaults. One of the accused, Y, pled guilty to one of the assault charges. Subsequently the prosecution called Y as a witness against his co-accused. Per trial judge, Lord Stewart: '. . . the advocate-depute may call the witness subject only to any representations about delay in such call to enable the taking of defence precognitions . . . the conclusion reached [is] the witness may be called.'	Criminal Procedure (Scotland) Act 1975, ss 141 and 346, as amended by Criminal Justice (Scotland) Act 1980, s 28 **Solemn procedure:** Section 141 **Summary procedure:** Section 346 Accused on trial with others may *either* call a co-accused as a witness (only with co-accused's consent) *or* cross-examine him if he gives evidence. **Solemn and summary procedure:** 1980 Act, s 28 Prosecution or defence may call a co-accused who has pled guilty (sentenced or not) as a compellable witness without notice, but court has discretion to grant an adjournment.

There is no onus to prove a special defence of impeachment.

Lambie v HMA, supra
Per LJ-G Emslie: '. . . we have come to be of opinion that the references in [earlier cases] of *Lennie* and *Owens* to there being an onus upon the defence were unsound. It follows that [this] can now be regarded as an accurate statement of the law only in the case of the plea of insanity at the time.'

Criminal Procedure (Scotland) Act 1975.

Solemn procedure:
Section 82(1), as substituted by 1980 Act, s 13. Notice of intention to incriminate a co-accused to be given not less than ten clear days before trial, unless good reason can be shown, in which case notice to be given before jury sworn.

References: Macdonald, 265, 317; Renton & Brown, 7–21 and 18–92.

INSANITY

Insanity at the time of commission of offence

At the time of commission of offence. Where accused is found to have committed the actus reus of the offence but to have been insane at the time he may not be convicted of the offence.

COMMENTARY	CASE LAW	STATUTE LAW
'. . . an absolute alienation of reason . . . such a disease as deprives the patient of the knowledge of the true aspect and position of things . . . hinders him from distinguishing friend or foe,—and gives him up to the impulse of his own distempered fancy' (Hume I, 37).	*HMA v Kidd* 1960 JC 61 K murdered wife and child and pled special defence of insanity at time of offence. *Held* to be insane at time of offence. Per Lord Strachan: 'Must have been some mental defect . . . by which his reason was overpowered and he was thereby rendered incapable of exerting his reason to control his conduct and reactions.'	Criminal Procedure (Scotland) Act 1975, s 82, as amended by Criminal Justice (Scotland) Act 1980, s 13. In solemn procedure notice by written intimation of a special defence must be given not less than ten clear days before the trial, unless the accused can establish that there was good reason for his failure to comply.
At the time of commission of offence Accused may be insane with regard to one area of his life while appearing lucid in all others.	*HMA v Sharp* 1927 JC 66 *HMA v Kidd*, supra Per Lord Strachan: 'If his reason was alienated in relation to the act committed he was not responsible for that act, even although otherwise he may have been apparently quite rational.'	
Self-induced intoxication is not a foundation for a special defence of insanity.	*Brennan v HMA* 1977 SLT 151 B convicted of murdering his father. Defence of insanity on ground of acute intoxication rejected. Opinion of the court: 'There is nothing unethical or unfair or contrary to the general principle of our law that self-induced intoxication is not by itself defence to a criminal charge.' See also:	
	Smith v M 1983 SCCR 67 (Sh Ct) Accused was charged in the sheriff court with assault and breach of the peace. Facts of the case not disputed. Defence was that he was insane at the time. He was not suffering from mental disorder at the time of the trial. Sheriff accepted the defence and acquitted the accused. *Held* that s 376(3) had no application to a person acquitted on grounds of insanity and no hospital order could be made. Only disposal was a simple acquittal. See also: *Ebsworth v HMA* 1992 SCCR 671	Criminal Procedure (Scotland) Act 1975, s 174(3) (solemn) and s 376(3) (summary)

Note: Automatism

Ross v HMA 1991 SCCR 823
Assault. Non-insane automatism, spiked drink—involuntary intoxication.
Held (Five judge bench), automatism due to an external factor (not disease of the mind), which is not self-induced and which leads to total alienation of reason amounting to a complete absence of self control, is something which the accused is not bound to foresee and is a defence. Crown must always establish mens rea. *HMA v Cunningham* 1963 JC 80; *Clark v HMA* 1968 JC 53 and *Carmichael v Boyle* 1985 SCCR 58 overruled as far as they hold that any mental condition short of insanity relevant only to mitigation.

See also:
Cardle v Mulrainey 1992 SCCR 658

Sorley v HMA 1992 SCCR 396
Automatism, spiked drink. Held that the evidence fell far short of what will be sufficient for this defence. Need expert evidence on state of the accused, total loss of control backed up by eye witnesses.

See also:
MacLeod v Napier 1993 SCCR 303

References: Hume I, 37; Alison I, 664; Macdonald, 265; Gordon, 347; Gane and Stoddart, 291.

Insanity in bar of trial

Insanity in bar of trial. If a person is **insane** at the time of his trial he cannot be tried, whether or not he was insane at the time of the alleged crime. Insanity in this instance is based on accused's **unfitness to plead**. However, a successful plea **cannot be treated as an acquittal.**

COMMENTARY	CASE LAW	STATUTE LAW
Insane Criteria for insanity are based on accused's 'unfitness to plead' and not on those elements regarded in insanity as a special defence.		Criminal Procedure (Scotland) Act 1975 Section 375 (summary) and s 174 (indictment) Section 375(3) (summary). Notice of plea and of witnesses to maintain plea prior to calling of first prosecution witness.
Unfitness to plead A person is unfit to plead if he is incapable of understanding the charge and the proceedings or of properly instructing his defence.	*HMA v Brown* (1907) 5 Adam 312 Charged with murder of woman who had eaten poisoned shortbread intended for someone else. Jury found B to be now insane. Per Lord Dunedin: Accused must be able to 'maintain in sober sanity his plea of innocence and instruct those who defend him as a truly sane man would do'. *HMA v Wilson* 1942 JC 75 Per Lord Wark: A man is not fit to be tried if he cannot from mental or physical defect tell his counsel what his defence is and cannot instruct his counsel to defend him, or if he does not understand the proceedings and cannot intelligibly follow what it is all about.	Sections 376 and 175. Power of court to order hospital admission or guardianship.
An accused may be perfectly lucid in relation to all other matters but insane with regard to the subject-matter of the charge against him.	*HMA v Sharp* 1927 JC 66 S, otherwise intelligent and lucid, had an obsessional disorder in relation to conditions and matters regarding his family. Charged with murder of his two children. Found unfit to plead.	
Exceptionally the judge may call upon the accused to plead, leaving it to the jury to say that he is capable of pleading.	*HMA v Wilson*, supra Lord Wark's direction to the jury: 'No plea has been taken on behalf of the accused that he is unfit to plead; indeed, . . . it is to be maintained on his behalf that he is fit to do so, but the evidence which you will hear . . . will show that his mental and physical condition is such as to raise a question as to whether any plea can be accepted from him. . . .'	
Mere loss of memory by an otherwise sane person is not, however, sufficient for a plea in bar.	*Russell v HMA* 1946 JC 37 R was charged with a series of frauds. Pleaded in bar of trial that she had suffered from hysterical amnesia covering the period of four years in which the offences took place. *Held* that this amnesia was no ground for plea in bar of trial. Per Lord Sorn: 'It is enough if the accused is sane and normal now, and can rationally tell her advisers all that she knows about her defence and follow the proceedings.'	

Mental deficiency alone does not constitute a bar to trial, although the question will depend on the degree of the deficiency and its effect on the accused's ability to understand.	*HMA v Breen* 1921 JC 30 *HMA v Wilson*, supra W almost completely deaf and dumb and feeble-minded, making it difficult for him to communicate. High Court accepted that a deaf-mute could be regarded as unfit to plead although in this case accused was allowed to plead. *Barr v Herron* 1968 JC 20 Finding of unfitness to plead by reason of mental deficiency accepted by appeal court.	
Cannot be treated as an acquittal Accused cannot be treated as having tholed his assize.	*HMA v Bickerstaff* 1926 JC 65 B insane and unfit to plead. Regained sanity, whereupon he was tried.	
Where a case is remitted from a lower court because there are doubts about fitness to plead by accused.	*Herron v McCrimmon* 1969 SLT (Sh Ct) 37 Accused pled guilty in the police court to breach of the peace and was remanded in custody for probation and psychiatric reports. Case was deserted pro loco and remitted to the sheriff court. *Held*, that a plea of res judicata could not succeed since no sentence had been pronounced.	
Prosecutor may raise unfitness If the accused has not stated a plea in bar of trial the prosecutor may bring forward evidence of accused's mental condition.	*Jessop v Robertson* 1989 SCCR 600 (Sh Ct) R charged with fraud. Prosecutor submitted report from psychiatrist to effect that she was mentally disordered. *Held*, inter alia, that there was an onus on any person alleging unfitness by reason of insanity to satisfy the court by corroborated evidence on the balance of probabilities.	Sections 175(2) and 376(5)

References: Hume I, 37; Alison I, 644; Macdonald, 271; Gordon, 376; Gane and Stoddart, 301.

SENTENCING POLICY

Duff v HMA 1983 SCCR 461. Murder charge. D pled guilty to culpable homicide. Suffering from diminished responsibility. Life imprisonment. Sentence appealed.
Held that sentence in the best interests of appellant—as under life sentence, position reviewed from time to time—and in best interest of public. Appeal failed.

SELF-DEFENCE

The use of **reasonable force** against a person is **not criminal** if done in **self-defence** or **defence of others. Provocation** is not such a defence.

COMMENTARY	CASE LAW	STATUTE LAW
Reasonable force Retaliation must not exceed what is necessary in the circumstances although the matter will not be weighed too finely by the law.	*Fraser v Skinner* 1975 SLT (Notes) 84 F, a police officer, 'handed off' an aggressive motorist stopped for speeding believing himself to be under attack. Opinion of the court: 'It is only *cruel excess* which will defeat a plea of self-defence.' *HMA v Doherty* 1954 JC 1 Culpable homicide. C attacked D with a hammer and D responded by striking C in the face with a bayonet supplied to him during the affray by another. Defence of self-defence fell and D convicted of culpable homicide and sentenced to twelve months' imprisonment. Per Lord Keith's charge to the jury: 'Let me remind you ... of the limits of self-defence ... two fundamental things you will keep in mind, that there is imminent danger to life and limb and that the retaliation used is necessary for the safety of the man threatened.' *Hillan v HMA* 1937 JC 53 Assault. H accused of a minor assault. However, he claimed he was merely acting in self-defence, the case having a sexual connotation. *Held*, on appeal, that H had been acting in self-defence and acquitted. Per Lord Wark, quoting Hume: 'In deciding on pleas of this sort the judge will not insist on an exact proportion of injury and retaliation, but rather be disposed to sustain the defence unless the panel has been transported to acts of cruelty or great excess.' But see: *Crawford* 1950 JC 67	
Cruel excess of violence used.	*Fenning v HMA* 1985 SCCR 219 F killed P on a fishing trip. Alleged that P had become suspicious that there was a relationship between F and deceased's wife. P had thus threatened F with knife and in response F smashed P's head several times with rock. On appeal conviction for murder upheld as there was cruel excess of violence used. Per trial judge Lord Mayfield: '. . . there must be no cruel excess of violence on the accused's part.'	
Where there is a mistaken apprehension of danger, a plea of self-defence is not defeated if there are reasonable grounds for the belief.	*Owens v HMA* 1946 JC 119 Murder. O killed a man whom he maintained he believed to have had a dangerous object in his hand when he sprang at O. On appeal, conviction quashed. Per LJ-C Normand: 'Self-defence is made out when it is established . . . that the panel believed he was in imminent danger and that he held that belief on reasonable grounds. Grounds for such a belief may exist though they are founded on a genuine mistake of fact.'	

HMA v Kay 1970 SLT (Notes) 66
Murder. K killed her husband with a knife alleging self-defence. Notable in that Lord Wheatley allowed evidence of previous assaults by deceased on K.
Per Lord Wheatley: 'The defence . . . is to the effect that the accused was acting in self-defence, she reasonably believing that there was imminent danger to her life due to an assault intended by the deceased.'

Not criminal
If act is done in **self-defence** it is not of criminal quality.

HMA v Brogan 1964 SLT 204
Assault. B accused of assaulting W by striking him on the head with a chair. B claimed in self-defence that he was first assaulted by W.
Per Lord Cameron's charge to the jury: 'Although a plea of self-defence may be put forward . . . the burden of proof remains with the Crown throughout to prove beyond reasonable doubt . . . the charge.'

M'Cluskey v HMA 1959 JC 39
Culpable homicide. M'C claimed he had killed O when acting in self-defence in that O was forcibly attempting to effect sodomy on him. Convicted of culpable homicide on basis of provocation, self-defence being rejected. Decision upheld on appeal.
Per LJ-G Clyde: 'I can see no justification at all for extending this defence to a case where there is no apprehension of danger to the accused's life . . . but merely a threat . . . of an attack on the appellant's virtue.'

Derrett v Lockhart 1991 SCCR 109
Self-defence open in an assault-type breach of the peace but not where the accused has not looked for an opportunity to retreat before taking pre-emptive strike.

Defence of others
The special defence extends to the use of reasonable force to protect another party from unjustified attack.

HMA v Carson & Anr 1964 SLT 21
M, C's co-accused, alleged that he had struck D with a bottle, only to protect C from a homicidal knife attack by D. M alleged that he was thus acting in self-defence of C.
Per Lord Wheatley: 'If a man sees another man being unlawfully attacked, he is entitled to stop that unlawful attack.'

Provocation
Where the accused has acted in unjustifiable self-defence, he may be entitled to plead provocation, but it is not a justification of an attack that there has been provocation.

Crawford v HMA 1950 JC 67
C killed his father, stabbing him as he was preparing to shave. There had been a family quarrel the previous night and immediately before the stabbing C had been shouted at by his father. Plea of self-defence failed although plea of provocation accepted in mitigation of sentence.
Per LJ-G Cooper: 'Provocation and self-defence are . . . often I fear confused . . . but provocation *is not* a special defence.'

HMA v Hill 1941 JC 59
H shot his wife and her lover immediately after they had confessed they had committed adultery.
Per Lord Patrick: 'If a man catches his wife and her paramour in the act of adultery and, in the heat of passionate indignation, then and there kills them, his crime is a very serious one, but it is not murder, it is culpable homicide.'

See also:
McKay v HMA 1991 SCCR 364

Graham v HMA 1987 SCCR 20
G charged with murder. She had quarrel with victim who had knife and threatened to kill her. She successfully disarmed him and killed him. Convicted of murder.
Per LJ-C Ross 'What is noteworthy is that by the time the killing took place, the appellant had disarmed the victim.'

See also:
M'Cluskey v HMA, supra

Test is subjective.

Jones v HMA 1989 SCCR 726
J charged with murder. Victim had threatened J with knife previously and when J later met him in the street, he believed he had knife and stabbed him. Trial judge directed jury that test for self defence and provocation was objective. On appeal *held* to be misdirection. Test to apply is the subjective one, whether accused believed on reasonable grounds that deceased had a knife. Conviction of culpable homicide substituted.

Low v HMA 1993 SCCR 493
Provocation. Deceased inviting L to have sex with him, in following struggle the deceased cut L on the hand, L stabbed deceased fifty times. Provocation withdrawn at trial, upheld on appeal. Gross disproportion between the provocation and the retaliation.
'Gross disproportion' preferred to 'cruel excess' as in *Lennon v HMA*.

See also:
Lennon v HMA 1991 SCCR 611
Robertson v HMA 1994 SCCR 589
Murder, provocation. R had stabbed the deceased 99 times after the deceased had made a homosexual advance to him and had presented a knife at him. *Held* on appeal that the trial judge's direction that there must be a reasonable proportionate relationship between the deceased's actions and R's response was the same in effect as saying the retaliation must not be grossly disproportionate.

Withdrawal of special defence.

Williamson v HMA 1980 JC 22
Special defence of self-defence was lodged but later withdrawn prior to empanelling of jury. *Held* that Crown entitled to examine the circumstances of the withdrawal of the special defence.

References: Hume I, 217 and 333; Alison I, 132 and 176; Macdonald, 106, 116 and 265; Gordon, 750, Gane and Stoddart, 422, 505.

EVIDENCE

ADMISSIBILITY

Best evidence

The best evidence rule requires that primary evidence be given but **secondary evidence is admissible,** *quoad* **credibility in** *de recenti* **statements: of taped interview by police**; of statements by an **accused at judicial examination**; of **witness's statements different from those at trial**; but not **statements in precognition**; or if it is **impossible**, or **not reasonably practicable to produce primary evidence.**

COMMENTARY	CASE LAW	STATUTE LAW
Secondary evidence is admissible *quoad* **credibility in** *de recenti* **statements** A *de recenti* statement is of no corroborative value,	*Harrison v Mackenzie* 1923 JC 61 Illegal trawling. Only evidence of identification that of fisherman who read boat mark through telescope and reported to father immediately. *Held* evidence admissible *quoad* credibility. Appeal sustained *quoad* absence of corroboration.	
it bears only on credibility.	*Morton v HMA* 1938 JC 50 Indecent assault. Only identification that of complainer. *De recenti* statement to brother led in evidence. Objection repelled. *Held* that evidence admissible *quoad* credibility. Per LJ-C Aitchison: 'A statement made by an injured party *de recenti* . . . is admissible as bearing upon credibility only, [it is] not evidence of the fact complained of.' (Re: Evidence of distress *de recenti* and corroboration see also p 152.)	
Taped interview by police Better evidence than recollection.	*HMA v McFadden* 1981 *Scolag* 260 Murder. Police interview taped and tape produced as evidence to which defence objected and queried admissibility as to: (1) unfairness, ie, accused cross-examined by police; (2) tape contained hearsay statements and matters irrelevant to the indictment. Per Lord Jauncey: 'There is a good deal to be said for the view that where you have a tape recording, that must be the better evidence . . . than a recollection of events some months ago.'	
Conversation taped without the accused's knowledge.	*HMA v Graham* 1990 SCCR 56 Police secretly taped a meeting between G and a civilian witness with the help of the civilian; flagrant transgression of the rules of fairness. G had previously been interviewed by the police, should have had the right not to self-incriminate. Situation distinguished from that where police eavesdropping on the commission of a crime.	

Evidence

Witness's statements prior to trial.	*Morrison v HMA* 1990 SCCR 235 Where a 'mixed' statement is led in evidence, containing elements of admission as well as exonerating elements, the jury must be allowed to consider the whole statement made by the accused and not just the part on which the Crown relies as constituting an admission. *Jones v HMA* 1991 SCCR 290 Two accused admitted to police involvement in a robbery but denied being party to murder in the course of the robbery, incriminated another man. *Held* on appeal that such a 'mixed' statement could be evidence. *Morrison*, supra, followed. *Scaife v HMA* 1992 SCCR 845 'Mixed' statement. S admitted theft but denied violence. On appeal (following *Morrison*), *held* the jury should have been specifically directed to determine whether they accepted the whole, or part of it, and whether it caused reasonable doubt. See also: *Smith v HMA* 1994 SCCR 72 *Higgins v HMA* 1993 SCCR 542 H said he had stabbed the deceased but only in self-defence. *Held* that the judge was entitled to tell the jury that they could isolate parts of the statement that they wished to accept.	
Accused at judicial examination	*Howarth v HMA* 1992 SCCR 364 Judge entitled to refer to a statement made by the accused to police even though he denied making the statement at judicial examination. *Sutherland v HMA* 1994 SCCR 80 *Held* on appeal that judge correct to give a direction that jury could not draw an inference from S's failure to give evidence but could draw an inference where the facts were crying out for an explanation and none was given. Sufficiently special circumstances.	Criminal Procedure (Scotland) Act 1975, s 20, as amended by Criminal Justice (Scotland) Act 1980, s 6
Record evidence without witnesses.		**Solemn procedure:** Section 151. Record is evidence without witness. Either party can object to record or part of it being read: witnesses to it can be called. 'Record', each record, in list of productions. **Summary procedure:** Section 352. Record is evidence without witness. Either party can object to record or part of it being admitted; witnesses to it can be called. 'Record', each record, sought to be adduced. Ten days' notice to be given of application requesting court to refuse admission.

Witness's statements different from those at trial

Dunsmore v HMA 1991 SCCR 849
D giving evidence that at an earlier trial a witness had identified his co-accused not D. On appeal *held* that the jury entitled to have regard to the evidence as a direction otherwise would have meant them ignoring part of D's evidence.

Greenhalghse v HMA 1992 SCCR 311
Crown putting to witness evidence of a statement made to the police which differed from the evidence she was giving at trial. Judge making no comment about the statement in his charge.
Held on appeal that the judge should have dealt with the statement because some of it was hearsay.

See also:
McGhee v HMA 1992 SCCR 324

1975 Act, as amended by 1980 Act, s 30

Solemn procedure:
Section 147
Summary procedure:
Section 349
Witness may be examined as to whether on specified occasion he has made different statement; evidence may be led of it.

Statements in precognition

By their nature interviews of defence witnesses are precognitions.

McNeilie v HMA 1929 JC 50; 1929 SLT 145
Attempted theft. Special defence of alibi. Objection to evidence of statements made to police when they interviewed defence witnesses repelled. McN convicted. Conviction quashed on appeal.
Object had been to discover what the witness's evidence was to be, was a precognition, and therefore inadmissible.

Statements taken when a case is at the stage of active construction are precognitions,.

Kerr v HMA 1958 JC 14; 1958 SLT 82
Theft of goods. Employer gave statement to police in interview which was read as evidence in court. K convicted. Conviction quashed on appeal.
Per LJ-C Thomson: 'There is no dispute that on authority, if this statement was a precognition, it was inadmissible [a precognition] is filtered through the mind of another . . . once the police have begun to build up a case against certain people . . . we have passed beyond the stage of preliminary investigations and have got into the stage of preparation for the leading of evidence.'

Impossible to produce primary evidence

To test whether primary evidence is requisite, the questions to be asked are whether the evidence is necessary and available.

Clements v Macaulay (1866) 4 M 543
Pursuer wanted to produce copy of letter. Pursuer unable to produce original after due diligence.
Held that copy admissible.
Per Lord Cowan: 'Secondary evidence is admissible only after due exertion is proved to have been made for recovery of the principal document.'

Real evidence not essential.

Maciver v Mackenzie 1942 JC 51; 1942 SLT 144
Accused took possession of wreck without reporting it to receiver. Wreck not produced. Secondary evidence of condition admissible *quoad* marks on timber.
Per LJ-C Normand: 'The question in each case is whether the real evidence is essential for proving the case against the accused.'

Is it reasonably practicable to retain evidence?

Anderson v Laverock 1976 JC 9; 1976 SLT 62
Statutory prosecution for unlawful possession of salmon. Fish destroyed by police before defence allowed to examine them. Condition of fish material. Convicted. Conviction quashed.
Opinion of the court: 'Whether goods are perishable or whether it is reasonably practicable and convenient to retain them as primary evidence . . . will depend on the circumstances and evidence in each particular case.'

Not reasonably practicable to produce primary evidence	
Newspapers sold for trading purposes.	*Hughes v Skeen* 1980 SLT (Notes) 13 Stolen newspapers recovered and returned for distribution, but not produced at trial. Per Lord Cameron: 'Production of these newspapers . . . neither necessary nor . . . practicable in this particular case.'
No authority to impound whisky bottle and label.	*McLeod v Woodmuir Miners' Welfare Society Social Club* 1961 JC 5; (1960 SLT 349) Statutory prosecution for sale of understrength whisky. Objections to oral evidence of details on label on bottle not produced at trial sustained. Crown appeal successful. No authority to impound the bottle, not reasonably practical to produce it.
Photographs of fingerprint 'lifts'.	*Hamilton v Grant* 1984 SCCR 263 Objection taken to evidence consisting of photographs of fingerprint 'lifts'. Sheriff held photographs inadmissible and said actual 'lifts' required and best evidence rule contravened. Reversed on appeal. No opinion delivered.
Blood samples not produced.	*Williamson v Aitchison* 1982 SCCR 102; 1982 SLT 399 Drunken driving. Certification lodged re blood samples' results. Objection by defence that blood samples should have been prodced repelled. Appeal rejected. Shown that the blood analysed had been taken from the accused.
Print-out from breath testing device not available.	*McLeod v Fraser* 1986 SCCR 271 *Held* that best evidence of result of analysis of blood was that of the analyst and it was permissible for him to refer to the register of blood analyses, or the certificate, as an aide-memoire.

Competent Evidence

To be admissible, evidence must be competent; **non-compliance with statutory requirements** will make it incompetent. Competent evidence may be **compellable or non-compellable**. In the case of a **witness present during earlier evidence** it is subject to special considerations. By statutory provision evidence in **replication**, and **additional** evidence is competent.

COMMENTARY	CASE LAW	STATUTE LAW
Non-compliance with statutory requirements		Criminal Procedure (Scotland) Act 1975, as amended by Criminal Justice (Scotland) Act 1980
Service of (*a*) copy indictment, (*b*) list of prosecution witnesses.		**Solemn procedure:** Section 70 (prosecution). Accused to be served full copy of indictment and list of prosecution witnesses.
Declaration or extract conviction.		Section 79(2) (prosecution). Not necessary to list witnesses to declaration of accused or extract conviction.
Witnesses, productions, not in list—notice.		Section 81 (prosecution). Competent, with leave, to examine witnesses or put in evidence production not included in list, if written notice given not less than two clear days before jury sworn.
Special defence—ten days' notice normally required.		Section 82(1), 1980 Act, s 13 (accused). Not competent for accused to state special defence or lead evidence of it unless notice lodged ten clear days before trial diet, or on cause shown, before jury sworn.
Notice by accused if witness or production not in prosecutor's list.		Section 82(2) (accused). Not competent to examine witnesses or put in evidence productions not included in prosecutor's list unless three clear days' notice given before jury sworn (unless on cause shown).
Witness or production in other party's list competent.		Section 82A, 1980 Act, s 27 (both parties). Competent for prosecutor or accused to examine witness or put in evidence production in other party's list.
Spouse to be called—accused—notice.		Section 144 (accused). Where list of witnesses required spouse of accused not to be called for defence unless notice given in terms of s 82.
Alibi—notice in summary cases.		**Summary procedure:** Section 339 (accused). Not competent for accused to found on alibi unless notice of this plea and of witnesses proposed to prove it given to prosecutor prior to examination of first prosecution witness. Prosecutor, on notice, is entitled to adjournment.

Compellable or non-compellable Accused non-compellable either in his own, or a co-accused's defence although he may elect to give evidence.		1975 Act as amended by 1980 Act, s 28 **Solemn procedure:** Section 141(1) **Summary procedure:** Section 346(1) Accused a competent defence witness whether on trial alone or with co-accused but only upon own application.
Co-accused compellable only when giving evidence or pleading guilty.	(For evidence given by a co-accused see also p 120)	**Solemn procedure:** Section 141(2)(*b*) and (3) **Summary procedure:** Section 346(2)(*b*) and (3) If co-accused gives evidence an accused may cross-examine and if co-accused pleads guilty (sentenced or not) prosecutor or accused may call him as witness without notice.
Relatives of accused compellable.		**Solemn procedure:** Section 139 **Summary procedure:** Section 342 No objection to admissibility or compellability that witness is father, mother, son, daughter, brother, sister, by consanguinity or affinity, or uncle, aunt, nephew, niece by consanguinity of party adducing witness.
Spouse may be called by accused.	*Hunter v HMA* 1984 SCCR 306 Murder and assault. H father of deceased child. Special defence of incrimination lodged naming wife *quoad* assault. Wife warned that she need not answer any questions. Intimated that she did not wish to do so. H convicted of culpable homicide. Appeal refused. Opinion of the court that one spouse is a compellable witness in the other spouse's defence. *Bates v HMA* 1989 SCCR 338 B and C charged with drugs offences in relation to which spouse is not a compellable witness. B intended to lead evidence incriminating C. Crown called C's wife as witness and she was told by trial judge that she was not obliged to answer questions which might incriminate C. She gave evidence against B but refused to answer any questions put to her in cross-examination. On appeal, *held* that judge's direction was wrong. Ought to have instructed spouse that she could not be compelled to give evidence but that if she did she would have to answer all the questions put to her.	1975 Act as amended by 1980 Act, s 29 **Solemn procedure:** Section 143(1)(*a*) **Summary procedure:** Section 348(1)(*a*) Spouse of an accused may be called as a witness by accused.
Matrimonial communications—'special category'.	*Harper v Adair* 1945 JC 21; 1945 SLT 133 H charged with stealing property of her husband. Husband competent and compellable witness. Per LJ-G Normand: 'It is admitted that, standing the decision in *Foster* [supra] the admission of the husband's evidence cannot be impugned.'	**Solemn procedure:** Section 143(2)(*b*). Spouses non-compellable *quoad* matrimonial communications. **Summary procedure:** Section 348(2)(*b*). Spouse not compellable witness with regard to disclosure of matrimonial communications.

Spouse compellable in personal injury offences and offences against his or her property	*Foster v HMA* 1932 JC 75; 1932 SLT 482 Forgery and uttering cheques. Alleged that F forged signature of husband. Husband competent and compellable witness. Per Lord Anderson: 'If the fundamental consideration . . . is necessity—the the need for the evidence of the injured spouse to secure conviction, this would seem to operate as strongly in the case of offences against property as in the case of bodily injury.' *Hay v McClory* 1993 SCCR 1040 Section 348. Spouse compellable where she would have been at common law. Offence by accused against the house of the spouse did not make her compellable because the offence was not against her, council paid for repairs to the house. Spouse should have been warned that she need not give evidence.	**Solemn procedure:** Section 143(1)(*b*) and (2)(*a*). As complainers. **Summary procedure:** Section 348(1)(*b*) and (2)(*a*) Spouse of an accused may be called as a witness by co-accused or prosecutor without consent of accused, if compellable at common law.
Wife's evidence at previous trial may be admissible even where she is not compellable in present trial.	*Lockhart v Massie* 1989 SCCR 421.	
Socius criminis No warning need now be given to treat the evidence of a *socius criminis* with special care.	*Docherty v HMA* 1987 CO Circular A19 Appellant convicted, by majority, of assault and robbery while acting with three others who had earlier pled guilty on separate indictments, and were called as witnesses for the Crown, giving evidence that the appellant had been recruited as driver for a different criminal enterprise (an assault upon a man against whom one of the three sought retaliation for the alleged rape of his step daughter). Appeal that conviction should be quashed because no 'cum nota' warning given. A bench of nine judges was convened to reconsider the soundness of the rule referred to in *Wallace v HMA* 1952 JC 78 in these terms '(the) evidence [of a *socius criminus*] ought always to be made the subject of a specific and particular warning that . . . it is suspect evidence deserving the close scrutiny'. *Held* 'Trial judges need only give to juries in all cases, whether or not any *socius criminis* has been adduced as a witness for the Crown the familiar directions designed to assist them in dealing with the credibility of witnesses and any additional assistance which the circumstances of any particular case may require.'	
Witness present during earlier evidence Reasons to hear evidence required.	*Macdonald (Angus) v Mackenzie* 1947 JC 169; 1948 SLT 27 Reckless or careless driving. Witness for defence in court during earlier evidence. No objection by procurator fiscal. Evidence disallowed by sheriff. Per Lord Jamieson: 'It is for the party tendering the witness to satisfy the court that his presence was not due to negligence or, . . . that he had not been or was not likely to have been influenced by what he had already heard.'	1975 Act **Solemn procedure:** Section 140 **Summary procedure:** Section 343 Witness need not be rejected because of presence during earlier evidence without permission or consent if presence was not through dulpable negligence or criminal intent, if witness not unduly instructed or influenced and injustice will not follow. 1975 Act, as amended by 1987 Act **Solemn procedure:** Section 139A **Summary procedure:** Section 342A Court may permit witness to be in court prior to giving evidence if it appears to the court not to be contrary to the interests of justice.

Note: The statutory requirements do not apply to a defence solicitor as witness.

Campbell v Cochrane 1928 JC 25; 1928 SLT 394
Licensing Act prosecution. Solicitor conducting defence adduced as defence witness. Ruled inadmissible. Appealed.
Held that solicitor competent witness.

Witness not present but informed of earlier evidence.

Keenan v Scott 1990 SCCR 470
Person in court hearing evidence and then going to witness room to tell the witnesses what had been said. Trial proceeding, appeal.
Held that the sheriff was correct to allow the trial to proceed as he had repelled the submission of no case to answer holding that evidence was sufficient without the 'suspect' evidence.

Replication evidence
To contradict defence evidence where it could not have been reasonably anticipated.

Sandlan v HMA 1983 SCCR 71
Theft. S and K charged. K lodged special defence incriminating S. S lodged special defence incriminating K. In course of cross-examination by Crown, S gave evidence of shopping visit. Crown allowed evidence in replication to show trip took place two days earlier. S gave further evidence and called solicitor as witness. Argued evidence in replication incompetent on grounds that s 149A only applied to evidence led to contradict evidence of defence witness in examination in chief. Argument rejected by Lord Stewart: evidence in replication competent. On appeal conviction quashed on other matter.
Per Lord Hunter: 'I doubt whether the interpretation contended for on behalf of the appellant is well-founded.'

1975 Act, as amended by 1980 Act, s 30

Solemn procedure:
Section 149A. Judge may, after defence case closed and before speeches, permit prosecutor to lead evidence to contradict evidence prosecution could not have reasonably anticipated; or to prove witness made different statement to that at trial although witness or production not listed and witness must be recalled.

Summary procedure:
Section 350A. Judge may, before prosecutor's address on evidence, allow him to lead additional evidence to contradict evidence he could not have reasonably anticipated or to prove witness made different statement to that at trial, although witness must be recalled.

Additional evidence

1975 Act, as amended by 1980 Act, s 30
Solemn procedure:
Section 149. Judge may, before speeches, permit either party to lead additional evidence if he considers that it is *prima facie* material; was not earlier available or its materiality could not reasonably have been foreseen, although witness must be recalled.

If material, and not earlier available.

Summary procedure:
Section 350. Judge may, before prosecutor's address on evidence, permit either party to lead additional evidence if he considers it *prima facie* material; was not earlier available or its materiality could not reasonably have been foreseen, although witness must be recalled.

Fairly obtained evidence

To be admissible, evidence must have been fairly obtained. In the case of the **accused**, in determining fairness, it will be considered whether the evidence has been obtained **before suspicion: after suspicion but before charge**; or **after charge**. If **statements to persons other than the police** are made, the particular circumstances will be considered, as will **evidence disclosing previous convictions,** or **evidence of bad character**; and **illegally obtained evidence** can be admissible.

COMMENTARY	CASE LAW	STATUTE LAW
Accused, before suspicion Admissibility will be assessed on fairness and whether evidence was volunteered or elicited. Search uncovering evidence of different crime	*HMA v Hepper* 1958 JC 39; 1958 SLT 160. Theft. H gave police consent to search property in connection with a crime. While searching they found attaché case unconnected with matter under investigation. They took this suspicious article away and it founded charges re the case reported here. Evidence held to be admissible as the police had a duty to inquire further in the circumstances. See also: *HMA v Turnbull*, infra.	
Confession blurted out at early stage of investigation.	*Bell v HMA* 1945 JC 61; 1946 SLT 204 Rape. B, interviewed during enquiry, blurted out confession. *Held* admissible evidence. Until confession police had no reason to caution or charge B.	
Admission by family member at start of investigation.	*Thompson v HMA* 1968 JC 61; 1968 SLT 339 Murder. Members of victim's family were interviewed, including T who remained at police station while accommodation was being found for him. T blurted out, 'It was either her or me.' *Held* admissible evidence. Per LJ-G Clyde: '[T] had not been cautioned or charged, nor was he being asked questions by the police at the time. Nothing in the nature of bullying or cross-examining had occurred.'	
Accused, after suspicion but before charge Where there is urgency, search without a warrant may be justified.	*HMA v McGuigan* 1936 JC 16; 1936 SLT 161 Murder, rape. Evidence obtained during search without warrant led to charges of murder, rape and theft being brought. Evidence held admissible on ground of urgency.	
Search without consent or warrant justified if evidence could have been lost.	*Walsh v MacPhail* 1978 SLT (Notes) 29 Possession of drugs. Servicemen on an air base were suspected of possessing drugs. Search made without consent and on an invalid warrant. Evidence held admissible on ground that drugs could have been disposed of or lost.	
Evidence obtained improperly but in good faith admitted.	*Fairley v Fishmongers of London* 1951 JC 14; 1951 SLT 54 Salmon poaching. Evidence against F was discovered by a private inspector and a government official. *Held* that although the evidence was improperly obtained it was admissible, as they had acted in good faith.	
Genuine but mistaken belief that search authorised.	*Lawrie v Muir* 1950 JC 19; 1950 SLT 37 Illegal use of milk bottles. Two inspectors of the Scottish Milk Bottle Exchange searched L's premises believing mistakenly although in good faith that they had authority to do so; incriminating evidence found held inadmissible. Opinion of the court: 'Persons in the special position of these inspectors ought to know the precise limits of their authority and should be held to exceed these limits at their peril.'	

Reasonable belief that obtaining of warrant is necessary.	*HMA v Rae* 1992 SCCR 1 *Held* that a police officer swearing that he has reasonable grounds is sufficient to allow a justice to grant a warrant under s 23(3) of the Misuse of Drugs Act 1971.
Scope of warrant exceeded.	*Leckie v Miln* 1981 SCCR 261; 1982 SLT 177 Theft. Police told householder of L's arrest on warrant and said they wished to search house. She consented. Incriminating evidence found. *Held* inadmissible. Officers unaware of scope of warrant, consent not given for active unlimited search.
	Innes v Jessop 1989 SCCR 441 I charged with reset of driving licence and tax exemption certificate found by police while searching for firearms and ammunition. Justice repelled objection to evidence having been irregularly obtained and convicted. On appeal *held* that removal of other articles carried implication that search was random one and it would be unsafe to sustain conviction.
	Tierney v Allan 1989 SCCR 334 T charged with reset of gas cylinders and a typewriter. Police officers had searched T's house on a warrant referring only to gas cylinders. In course of search typewriter found under cot, similar to some typewriters known to have been stolen. *Held* that the evidence was admissible. Per LJ-G Emslie: 'This was not a case of random search as in *Leckie v Miln*. It was the unexpected discovery of an article which aroused suspicion during the course of a lawful search for material listed in warrant.'
	HMA v Turnbull 1951 JC 96 Fraud. Police obtained warrant and searched T. Removed property in relation to another alleged crime and kept it for six months. Inadmissible because police had acted outwith the scope of warrant.
	Davidson v Brown 1990 SCCR 304 Illegal search. Police stopping car of known shoplifters asking to see contents of a bin. *Held*, not an illegal search as the request had been voluntarily complied with.
	See also: *HMA v Hepper*, supra
	Burke v Wilson 1988 SCCR 361 Police obtained warrant for search of premises for video recordings for which no classification certificate had been obtained. In course of search they removed unlabelled videos which they subsequently found to be obscene. B charged, objected that evidence irregularly obtained. *Held* that the police had come upon videos by accident in course of authorised search and had not acted improperly.
Dental impressions taken under warrant.	*Hay v HMA* 1968 JC 40 Murder. H inmate of List D school suspected. Police took dental impressions for comparison with bite marks on body. Applied for warrant to take further impressions, granted. Upheld by High Court. '. . . obtaining of the warrant prior to the examination in question rendered the examination quite legal . . . evidence which resulted from it was therefore competent.'

Note: Police powers with regard to persons in detention under the Criminal Justice (Scotland) Act 1980.

Grant v HMA 1989 SCCR 618
G questioned by police during six-hour period, but detention not terminated until arrest after the expiry of six hours.
Held that fact that detention exceeded six hours did not invalidate things done lawfully within period.

Police may question suspect detained under s 2. Detention must not exceed six hours.

Criminal Justice (Scotland) Act 1980
Section 2: Same powers of search as available after arrest: power to take palmprints, fingerprints, or all reasonably appropriate prints. Does not include power to take samples of blood, hair or saliva. May possibly cover dental impressions.

Prisoners and Criminal Proceedings (Scotland) Act 1993 Section 28: Constable may take fingerprints, palmprints or other external prints. With the authority of an officer not below the rank of inspector, may take sample of hair, nail cuttings or blood, body fluid, tissue or other material by means of swabbing or rubbing.

The juncture at which questioning should be discontinued unless a caution is given is determined by the extent to which suspicion has been focused and having regard to fairness.

Manuel v HMA 1958 JC 41
Murder. M confessed. Gave location of corpse and commented on its condition. Convicted. Appealed. Alleged his condition motivated by inducements. Appeal rejected, no evidence of inducement.

Statement containing discrepancies, further questioning allowed.

HMA v McPhee 1966 SLT (Notes) 83
Assault and culpable homicide. McP gave statement containing discrepancies. Came under suspicion of having committed offence. No caution given. McP blurted out admissions when questioning was resumed. Evidence held admissible, mere suspicion does not mean that caution is required.

When does a person become 'a suspect'?

Miln v Cullen 1967 JC 21; 1967 SLT 35
Drunken driving. C pointed out as one of the drivers involved in a collision. Police officer asked C whether he had been the driver. Response held admissible.
Per Lord Wheatley: 'The point at which a person becomes a "suspect" in the eyes of a police officer may be difficult to define with exactitude. The test is basically a subjective one, but the police officer may have to justify his attitude by reference to the facts in his possession or the knowledge which he had at the given point of time. . . . In each case the issue is—was the question in the circumstances a fair one? . . . The question asked . . . was merely to discover whether the respondent was the driver of the car, not whether he had caused the accident or was drunk. If a question had been asked without a caution being administered, and the question had been directed to elicit an admission of culpability for the accident or an admission that he was drunk in charge of his car, then the question might have been properly objected to.'

Tonge v HMA 1982 SCCR 313
Held (1) that it is a requirement of law that a charge must be preceded by a full common law caution; (2) that where a statement is made in reply to an accusation, whether or not in the words of a formal charge, any reply induced by that accusation will be inadmissible unless preceded by a common law caution, or at least that such a caution was given as soon as it became clear that accused might be about to incriminate himself.

Questioning of a suspect.	*Chalmers v HMA* 1954 JC 66; 1954 SLT 177 Murder. C brought under suspicion to police, cautioned, then interrogated. Replied to caution and charge: 'I did it. He struck me.' Evidence held inadmissible. Conviction quashed. *Held*, that if suspicion is such that the person is viewed as the likely perpetrator of the crime then any further interrogation amounting to cross-examination may render any confession extracted inadmissible. *McClory v MacInnes* 1992 SCCR 319 MacI found asleep in vehicle at side of road, woken up by police, no caution given and asked what had happened. MacI said that he had crashed. *Held*, statement unfairly obtained, police were obviously suspicious but gave no caution. *Young v Friel* 1992 SCCR 567 F interviewed by police. F seeking incentive from police to give a statement. *Held* that sheriff correct to allow interview where the police officer had said that he was not sure whether any such offer could be made. One caution sufficient to cover statements made in relation to two different offences.
Requirement for caution depends on nature of police questioning.	*Custerson v Westwater* 1987 SCCR 389 C accused with having offensive weapon. Evidence consisted of evidence by complainer that C waved knife at him, and statement by C that he had knife with him for protection. C made statement voluntarily in response to question. C appealed on ground that he had not been cautioned (see *Tonge*). *Held* that this case distinguishable from *Tonge* in that statement made in response to unobjectionable question rather than an allegation.
Youthful suspect—is the evidence spontaneous and voluntary?	*HMA v Rigg* 1946 JC 1; 1946 SLT 49 Murder. R reported discovery of body to police and gave a statement. Later his condition being described as excited. R collapsed trembling and shuddering and gave another statement, which was held inadmissible. Statement was not spontaneous and voluntary, more like a detailed precognition. Ultimate test is fairness to the accused.
Statement by person not only possible suspect.	*Brown v HMA* 1966 SLT 105 Murder. B cautioned. Statement contained discrepancies. B warned of these and cautioned further at which he broke down saying 'I killed her.' B cautioned again and charged. Subsequently, items were recovered from where B had indicated. Evidence held admissible. Police were not cross-examining the accused or treating him as the only possible suspect.
Admission volunteered.	*Costello v Macpherson* 1922 JC 9; 1922 SLT 35 Theft. C asked by railway police to open parcel he was carrying, which contained coal. C said he obtained it from a bunker. Regular police became involved and C volunteered that he had stolen the coal. Evidence held admissible, not improper to lead evidence of a statement made voluntarily without questioning being required.

Search without warrant where crime seen to have been committed.	*Jackson v Stevenson* (1897) 2 Adam 255; 24 R(J) 38; 4 SLT 277 Assault. Water bailiffs stopped and searched J, who resisted arrest and was charged with assault. Conviction quashed. Per LJ-G Robertson: 'The right of the bailiffs is to exercise the powers . . . of constables. . . . A constable is entitled to arrest, without a warrant, any person seen by him committing a breach of the peace and [having done so] . . . search him. But it is a totally different matter to search a man in order to find evidence to determine whether you will apprehend him or not.'
Unless there is urgency, physical evidence from the person of an accused should be obtained under warrant or after charge.	*McGovern v HMA* 1950 JC 33; 1950 SLT 133 Safe blowing. McG suspected of safe blowing. Nail scrapings taken. McG subsequently charged. Evidence held inadmissible as the charge should have come before the scrapings. *Bell v Hogg* 1967 JC 49; 1967 SLT 290 Theft of telephone wires. Verdigris on B's hands. Before any charge had been preferred, police took palm rubbings without warrant but with consent. Evidence held admissible on basis of urgency.
There is no defence of entrapment in Scots law.	*HMA v Harper* 1989 SCCR 472 Police officer who suspected drugs being sold approached van, asked for and was sold drugs. Objection taken to evidence as unfairly obtained through entrapment. *Held* no defence of entrapment, and in the absence of any evidence of deception, pressure or encouragement to commit crime, evidence admissible.
Evidence from accused after charge Questioning at trial re change of plea.	*Williamson v HMA* 1980 JC 22 Assault. W pled self-defence initially but later withdrew that plea. Change of plea questioned by Crown in cross-examination. W convicted. Appeal refused. Per LJ-C Wheatley: 'This question was a legitimate and competent one. . . . The objection taken by the appellant's counsel was in anticipation of what the answer might be, and not the question itself.'
Comment by the judge on accused's failure to give evidence.	*Brown v Macpherson* 1918 JC 3 Reset. Evidence led that B had identified one of the thieves. Judge took into account fact that B did not give evidence on his own behalf. B convicted. Appeal refused. Per LJ-G Strathclyde: 'The judge may, and in my opinion ought to . . . comment on the fact [that] the only man in full possession of the facts refrains from going into the witness box for the purpose of establishing his own innocence.'
Subject to the test of fairness, evidence of the accused's actings or statements after charge is admissible.	*Forrester v HMA* 1952 JC 28 Safeblowing. F arrested, cautioned and charged. Thereafter his hand was examined for cut. Search made without F's consent. F convicted. Appeal refused.
Grant of warrants depending on the circumstances, including public interest.	*HMA v Milford* 1973 SLT 12 Rape. M charged with rape, refused to give blood sample voluntarily. Prosecutor petitioned for warrant to take sample. Granted as reasonable in these exceptionally grave circumstances. *Morris v MacNeill* 1991 SCCR 722 Sheriff granting warrant to take blood sample from accused, balancing public interest and the minimal invasion involved. Upheld on appeal.

G v Lees 1992 SCCR 252
Warrant granted to take blood sample but limited to finger pricks as the accused had a phobia of needles.

Smith v Cardle 1993 SCCR 609
Murder investigation, one of a set of twins suspected. Warrant sought and obtained to measure S and compare this with evidence from a video to eliminate twin brother. Warrant granted, non-invasive procedure, reasonable in the public interest.

Accused's answer to question not directed to him inadmissible.

HMA v Leiser 1926 JC 88
Murder. After being charged, L answered a question which was not addressed to him. Reply held inadmissible. Judge not satisfied accused had not made a mistake.

Reply to caution and charge re lesser offence.

McAdam v HMA 1960 JC 1
McA charged with assault to severe injury and subsequently attempted murder. Objection taken at trial to admissibility of reply to McA to caution and charge quoad lesser crime. Reply admitted. Admissibility confirmed on appeal. As both charges contained the element of assault they could be seen as within the same category.

Carmichael v Kinnie 1993 SCCR 751
Objection to statements made to police about the offence charged and a number of similar offences. *Held* that the police could not ask about the offence already charged but could ask about unrelated matters. Interview only inadmissible as far as matters not already charged.

Entitlement to communicate with solicitor.

HMA v Cunningham 1939 JC 61; 1939 SLT 401
Murder. C cautioned and charged. En route to the cells his attention was drawn by police officer to a notice stating that a prisoner was entitled to communicate with a law agent. Made statement after being reminded of earlier caution. Statement held admissible, police observed every requirement of fairness.

Admission by one accused put to co-accused in presence of first accused.

Stark and Smith v HMA 1938 JC 170; 1938 SLT 516
Theft. Two co-accused. Admission by one accused in reply to police interrogation repeated to other accused in presence of first. Both convicted. On appeal, statement held inadmissible against either accused.

Presence of accused when co-accused cautioned and charged.

HMA v Davidson 1968 SLT 17
Attempted murder. D cautioned and charged, brought to bar of police station where co-accused was about to be cautioned and charged. D not advised that his presence would make any incriminating reply by co-accused admissible in evidence against him.
Held that in effect the accused was providing evidence against himself contrary to the fundamental rule that he need not do so once charged, reply inadmissible.

See also:

McNicol v HMA 1993 SCCR 242
Buchan v HMA 1993 SCCR 1076

Fingerprint taken after arrest.	*Adair v McGarry* 1933 JC 72; 1933 SLT 482 Theft. McG arrested. Fingerprints taken from him hold admissible. Per LJ-G Clyde: '. . . provided a person has been legally arrested by the police, they may search him for stolen goods, or weapons, or other real evidence connecting him with the crime, and . . . neither his consent nor a magistrate's warrant is required for that purpose.' *Begley v Normand* 1992 SCCR 230 Warrant granted to take palmprints after B fully committed as the original prints taken turned out to be defective.
No further questioning after arrest.	*Wade v Robertson* 1948 JC 117; 1948 SLT 491 Theft. W arrested for theft of whisky. Police showed him bottle recovered from his lodgings and told him he would be questioned about the offence charged. Without any questions W made a self-incriminating statement. *Held*, statement inadmissible. Police not entitled to question further with regard to that particular charge. *Fraser v HMA* 1989 SCCR 82 Appellants charged with assault. In separate cells in police station. Visited by police officer, W, with whom they were friendly and made statements to him. At trial evidence of these statements left to the jury by the sheriff. Appellants appealed on ground that statements induced by W and unfairly obtained. It was conceded in the appeal that issue properly left to jury under proper directions. *Held* that in view of the concession it was not possible to say that the jury were not entitled to have regard to the statements, and that they were entitled to hold that they were not procured by inducement. Appeal refused.
Statements to persons other than the police Questioning by employer.	*Waddell v Kinnaird* 1922 JC 40; 1922 SLT 344 Theft. Quantity of oil in possession of W, a railwayman. Arrested by railway police and cautioned. Later questioned by stationmaster in presence of civilian police. W convicted. Appeal rejected, allowed to seek an explanation so long as there is nothing to suggest improper motive.
Interview by employers' investigators.	*Morrison v Burrell* 1947 JC 43; 1947 SLT 190 Fraud, attempted fraud. Horseracing bets placed by M, a sub-postmaster, who falsified date-stamping of envelopes. M interviewed under caution as suspect by Post Office investigators. Statement admitted and M convicted. Appeal rejected. *Held*, domestic investigation into public service department. Can be no objection to replies voluntarily given.
Confidentiality restricted to spouse and solicitor.	*HMA v Parker* 1944 JC 49; 1944 SLT 195 Murder. P, Canadian serviceman, visited in prison by brother to whom he made statement about how death occurred. Objection to admissibility repelled at trial. *Held*, only spouses and solicitors protected by the doctine of confidentiality.

Evidence

Incriminating remark accidentally overheard.

HMA v O'Donnell 1975 SLT (Sh Ct) 22
Assault. O'D in custody shouted incriminating remark to a co-accused which was overheard by police officers. Objection to admissibility repelled. Per Sheriff Macphail: 'It is clear that the incriminating statement was voluntarily emitted by the fourth accused, that no inducement was offered to him, that the witness who overheard the statement had not been ordered to do so but spontaneously stopped and listened when the accused shouted, and that the witness neither knew that the fourth accused was in custody, nor had any reason to suspect him of having been implicated in the assault.'

Prolonged questioning by Customs investigators.

HMA v Friel 1978 SLT (Notes) 21
Tax frauds. F, with others, interviewed by Customs and Excise investigators, first for three and a half hours, then, after caution, for another twelve and a half hours. At trial, objection to admissibility of answers in second interview sustained.
Held that questioning unfair, in the nature of cross-examination and pressure placed on the accused.

Statement made by suspected shoplifter to shop manager.

McCuaig v Annan 1986 SCCR 535
Manager saw McC put articles in pocket and leave without paying. Followed her and removed articles. She agreed to return to the office and made statements without having been cautioned.
Held that evidence admissible as the test was whether what had happened was fair to the appellant.

Evidence disclosing previous convictions

Unless evidence of previous conviction(s) is necessary to prove the offence(s) charged, it is inadmissible to elicit it.

Murphy v HMA 1978 JC 1
M pled guilty to charges of theft, assault and breach of the peace and admitted previous convictions. M induced his solicitor to make false representations which mitigated the penalty and was subsequently charged with perverting the course of justice.
Held relevant to incorporate reference to admission of previous convictions as evidence in causa of substantive charge and to show the mitigating effect of the false information.

Nelson v HMA 1994 SCCR 192
Crown leading evidence of N swallowing a substance on being approached by the police, an offence in itself, to prove a charge of supplying drugs. Allowed on appeal.
Per LJ-G Hope: 'The Crown can lead any evidence relevant to the proof of a crime charged, even though it may show or tend to show the commission of another crime not charged, unless fair notice requires that that other crime should be charged or otherwise expressly referred to in the complaint or indictment.'

Criminal Procedure (Scotland) Act 1975

Solemn procedure:
Section 141(1)(*f*)
Summary procedure:
Section 346(1)(*f*)

Accused not to be asked any questions tending to show commission of offence other than those charged, or bad character unless:
(i) proof of other offence admissible *quoad* offence charged, or
(ii) evidence of accused's good character led or character of prosecution or prosecution witness impugned, or
(iii) accused has given evidence against any co-accused.

In case of prison breaking disclosure of previous convictions is inevitable.

Varey v HMA 1985 SCCR 425
V and others charged with prison breaking. Indictment specified length of sentences and crimes for which imposed.
Held that to prove appellants were lawfully confined at date of charge, Crown required to prove date and length of sentences, and appeals dismissed.

Solemn procedure:
Section 160(1), (2). Previous convictions not to be laid before jury or reference made to them before verdict unless as evidence in causa in support of substantive charge or accused leads evidence of previous good character. See also s 161.

Admissibility

Road traffic disqualification listing of previous convictions where not competently supporting substantive charge not allowed.

Mitchell v Dean 1979 JC 62; 1979 SLT (Notes) 12
Driving while disqualified and without insurance. Trial evidence included extract conviction *quoad* disqualification which referred to admission of six previous convictions. M convicted.
Held, on appeal, that evidence in relation to six previous convictions not competent to support substantive charge and conviction quashed.

Boustead v M'Leod 1979 JC 70; 1979 SLT (Notes) 48
Driving while disqualified and without insurance. Trial evidence included extract conviction referring to public mischief offence. B convicted.
Held, on appeal, evidence inadmissible and conviction quashed. Prejudice to be confined within the narrowest limits.

Summary procedure:
Section 357(1)(*b*). Previous convictions not to be laid before judge until charge proved.
Section 357(5). 'Nothing in this section shall prevent evidence of previous convictions being led in causa where such evidence is competent in support of a substantive charge.'

But see:
Sexual Offences (Scotland) Act 1976, s 4(2)(*b*): defence that there was reasonable cause to believe girl sixteen or over if accused not previously charged with like offence. (An equiparation with the provisions of ss 141 and 346(1)(*f*)(ii), supra.)

Strictly construed.

Robertson and Anr v Aitchison 1981 SCCR 149; 1981 SLT (Notes) 127
Driving while disqualified. At trial evidence incorporated extract conviction which referred to an offence additional to that which had led to R's disqualification. R convicted.
Held, on appeal, that reference to previous conviction was a fatal flaw and conviction quashed.
Opinion of the court: 'The words of the statute are clear, the risk of prejudice is guarded against by the strictness of its prohibition which operates "in any proceedings".'

Criminal Procedure (Scotland) Act 1975
Section 357(1)(*b*), supra

Breach of statutory prohibition not necessarily sufficient to constitute miscarriage of justice.

McAvoy and Jackson v HMA 1982 SCCR 263; 1983 SLT 16
Theft by housebreaking. J, in a voluntary statement to police, made reference to 'two guys who I know from the jail'. Statement given in evidence. No direction in charge to jury to disregard implied reference to previous convictions. Jury, on sheriff's suggestion, took voluntary statement to jury room while deliberating. J convicted.
Held, on appeal, that the reference to previous conviction had been a breach of a s 160(1), but no miscarriage of justice and appeal refused. No objection raised by the defence at the time.

Section 160(1), supra

Disclosure of previous convictions creating no risk of prejudice.

Moffat v Smith 1983 SCCR 392
Driving while disqualified. M convicted. Trial evidence incorporated extract conviction referring to two offences (for driving without licence and without insurance) in respect of which M disqualifed. Submission, that reference to one would have been sufficient, repelled and appeal dismissed. No risk of prejudice.

Section 357(5), supra

Where credibility in issue.

Graham v HMA 1983 SCCR 315; 1984 SLT 67
G tried on four charges. Offer of plea of guilty to charges 2, 3 and 4 rejected. On first charge, wife assault, credibility at issue. Evidence elicited of reply to caution and charge *quoad* charge 2 (breach of the peace) which was :'That cow's got me the jail again.' Jury directed to disregard reply.
Held deliberate eliciting of evidence irredeemably prejudicial, and conviction on charge 1 quashed.
Per LJ-G Emslie: 'So grave was the breach, and so important was the issue of credibility, that we are satisfied that the effect of the breach of the peremptory direction in section 160(1) upon the minds of the jurors could not reasonably be expected to have been obliterated by anything the sheriff tried to do. . . .'

Previous convictions elicited by questioning.	*Slane v HMA* 1984 SCCR 77 S tried for conspiracy to rob with two others. During Crown evidence, counsel for one of the co-accused elicited in cross-examination of a Crown witness that S had previous convictions. 'Ample evidence' of S's guilt. Judge gave direction to jury to disregard evidence of previous convictions. *Held* that questions should not have been asked, action of counsel inexcusable, but no miscarriage of justice.

McLean v Tudhope 1982 SCCR 555
McL charged with breach of the peace. On cross-examination by prosecutor, McL was asked whether he regarded himself as honest with a previous conviction. No reply. On re-examination by defence solicitor McL stated one previous conviction. Because of revelation of earlier conviction, McL liberated on appeal. Violation of section 346(1)(*f*).

Section 346(1)(*f*)

Kepple v HMA 1936 JC 76
Assault on wife. Libel evincing previous violence and malice. At trial wife made reference to 'previous convictions'. K convicted. Appeal refused, it being *held* that the information had been volunteered not elicited.

Haslam v HMA 1936 JC 82
Fraud. H charged with fraud offences had at police station at first given false name. At trial evidence by police witness that H had been asked if name was Haslam and that witness, for identification purposes, had then examined hand wound. H convicted. Appeal refused but in the course of his judgment LJ-C Aitchison observed obiter. 'When a reference is made to a previous conviction by an officer of the police, who ought to know better, it is obviously prejudicial to a fair trial . . . an accused is not fairly tried if an inspector of police, when he gets an opening in a question inadvertently addressed to him, makes a reference, direct or indirect, to the record of the man who is standing his trial.'

See also:

Armstrong v HMA 1993 SCCR 311

Special rules re reset.	*Deighan v Macleod* 1959 JC 25 Theft. Two accused. Police witness speaking of accused being 'known thieves'. Conviction upheld, not act of prosecutor.

Watson v HMA (1894) Adam 355
Reset. W charged with reset. During trial evidence of previous conviction for reset tendered. W convicted. Appeal dismissed.
Per Lord Rutherford Clark: 'Under the statute the previous conviction may be given in evidence in order to prove guilty knowledge . . . at any stage in the proceedings provided only that evidence has been given that the stolen property has been found in the possession of the accused. . . .'

Prevention of Crimes Act 1871, s 19. In prosecution for reset competent to lead evidence that accused in possession of other stolen property within previous twelve months. Previous offence of fraud or dishonesty within the preceding five years may be taken into consideration.

Disclosure of manner of accused's identification no reference to previous conviction.	*Corcoran v HMA* 1932 JC 40 Housebreaking. C convicted. Fact that C's arrest based upon identification from a police photograph album disclosed in court. *Held*, on appeal, that disclosure fell short of reference to previous conviction.

HMA v McIlwain 1965 JC 40
Assault and robbery. Special defence of alibi. Objection to leading of evidence *quoad* identification by police officers repelled. Not always incompetent to lead evidence just because it may incidentally reveal previous convictions.

Exception to general prohibition: reference rebutting defence of innocence.	*Carberry v HMA* 1975 JC 40; 1976 SLT 38 C and two others charged with conspiracy to rob. Evidence led at trial that co-accused of C had made voluntary statement, before arrest, that he had obtained car, allegedly used in furtherance of conspiracy, from man 'met in Barlinnie'. C convicted. Appeal refused. Opinion of the court: 'The jurisdiction is a delicate one and in its exercise it is necessary to keep firmly in view that the statutory prohibition is designed in the interests and for the protection of accused persons and, therefore, that there is a heavy onus on a prosecutor who seeks to support the competence of evidence which directly or indirectly brings to the knowledge of judge or jury or leads to the drawing of the inference, that the accused has been previously convicted. One of the categories of possible exception from the consequences of breach of the statutory prohibition is where the reference tends to rebut a defence of innocence which might otherwise be open to the accused . . . each case must depend on its own facts and circumstances. . .'
Police referring to accused as a housebreaker.	*Smith v HMA* 1975 SLT (Notes) 89 S, charged with theft, identified by police witness who referred to him twice as, 'known to me as Smith, a housebreaker'. No warning to jury to disregard evidence. S convicted, quashed on appeal. *Held* that the trial judge should have directed the jury to ignore such evidence.
Relevant evidence of collateral matters will be admitted if fairness requires it.	*HMA v Kay* 1970 JC 68; 1970 SLT (Notes) 66 Murder of K's husband. Indictment libelled previous evincing of malice and ill-will. At trial K's counsel allowed to lodge hospital records relating to treatment after alleged assaults by deceased. *Held* admissible to lead evidence of these to show the accused had reason to apprehend danger. Departure from general rule justified.
Accused forced to admit he was in prison at specified time.	*Cordiner v HMA* 1978 JC 64; 1978 SLT 118 Extortion. C, with another, indicted *inter alia* on a charge of extortion. Special defence of alibi that he was in prison at the time. At trial, evidence of date of conversations grounding charge imprecise and charge withdrawn. C convicted on other charges. *Held*, on appeal, that C had been compelled to disclose record, and conviction quashed. Opinion of the court: 'We cannot say that the jury would have convicted if the Crown had not erred at the outset in forcing the appellant to admit that he was in prison in June 1976.'
Evidence revealing previous assaults bearing on conclusions in medical reports.	*Gemmill v HMA* 1980 JC 16; 1979 SLT 217 Murder. G's mental condition at issue *quoad* diminished responsibility. Medical evidence disclosed previous assaults on females. G convicted by jury. *Held*, on appeal, that evidence introduced for purposes connected with G's medical history not admissible *quoad* guilt and that the judge should thus have directed the jury to disregard this evidence. However, not misdirection sufficient to require quashing of conviction. *Note:* G was convicted of culpable homicide, not murder.
Caution and charge referring to previous convictions—insufficient miscarriage of justice.	*McCuaig v HMA* 1982 SCCR 125; 1982 SLT 383 McC convicted on a number of charges. Police witness speaking to caution and charge disclosed to jury that charge referred to previous convictions. *Held*, on appeal, that there had been a breach of the statutory provisions, but miscarriage of justice not sufficient to set aside conviction.

Disclosure accidental.

Johnston v Allan 1983 SCCR 500
Driving without licence. J tried on a number of road traffic contraventions including driving without a licence.
During trial a computer printout was production to
establish J did not hold a licence. Sheriff asked for and
was handed printout he saw on 'production table',
which was, however, a different printout disclosing previous convictions. J convicted. Appeal refused, previous convictions not 'laid before the court' by the
prosecutor, just an unfortunate accident.

Grugen v HMA 1991 SCCR 526
Witness spontaneously implicating G in a crime with
which he was not charged. Prosecutor commenting
on this matter in his charge to the jury. Conviction
upheld on appeal. Prosecutor entitled to make such
comment as evidence spontaneous.

Cross-examination on character.

Leggate v HMA 1988 SCCR 391
L charged with assault and robbery. Evidence came
from two police officers who spoke to an admission
by L and two other officers who said that L took them
to where weapon hidden. L alleged that police had
'fitted him up' and were lying. Trial judge, relying on
Templeton v HMA 1985 SCCR 357, allowed Crown
to cross-examine L as to character, and he admitted
various analogous convictions.
Held by bench of seven judges
(1) where nature or conduct of defence is such as to
involve imputations on the character of Crown
witnesses, accused is liable to cross-examination
on his character in terms of s 141(1)(*f*)(ii), and
whether or not it was necessary for an accused to
conduct his defence in this way in order to establish
his defence fairly is irrelevant, but that s 141(1)(*f*)(ii)
does not apply where the accused merely asserts
that a Crown witness is lying;
(2) that a trial judge has a wide discretion to refuse to
allow an accused to be cross-examined on his character, that the fundamental test is one of fairness,
having regard both to the position of the accused
and the public interest in bringing wrongdoers to
justice, and that a significant factor in the exercise of
the discretion is whether the questions asked of the
Crown witnesses were integral and necessary to
the defence or were a deliberate attack on the character of the witness;
(3) that while s 161(1) of Crimninal Procedure
(Scotland) Act 1975 prohibits the prosecutor from
laying a list of the accused's previous convictions
before a judge, it does not prevent him making
reference to them by giving judge relevant information; and
(4) trial judge had erred in not exercising his
discretion and there had been miscarriage of
justice. Appeal allowed and conviction quashed.

Penalty notice applicable to second offence.

Bryce v Gardiner 1951 JC 134; 1952 SLT 90
Licensing Act offences. B, a licence holder, charged
with breach of conditions of certificate and contravention of statute. Penalty liability referred to in
complaint disclosed implicitly that it was a second
offence which was alleged. Conviction quashed on
appeal.
Held that an alert judge would have seen the penalty
and known there was a previous conviction.

Separate libelling of charges.

McGregor v Macdonald 1952 JC 4; 1952 SLT 94
Theft. McG and others charged with theft and, being
'known thieves' loitering with intent to steal. List of
previous convictions annexed to indictment. Conviction on theft charge quashed.
Held that charges should have been separately
libelled. Statutory provision designed to exclude
prejudice but effect here was to nullify that purpose
since one charge within general rule and other not.

Inadvertent disclosure of endorsement on licence.	*Clark v Connell* 1952 JC 119; 1952 SLT 421 Comparison drawn between Connell's handwriting and signature on licence. Examination of licence by sheriff inadvertently disclosed endorsement, although not offence for which imposed. Connell's objection to evidence upheld by sheriff and Connell acquitted. On appeal by Crown court held sheriff to have been mistaken in sustaining objection to competency as information not 'laid before' the sheriff, but appeal dismissed on other grounds.
Evidence of bad character (i) of the accused Cross-examination of wife—who was accused—on fidelity.	*HMA v Grudins* 1976 SLT (Notes) 10 Murder of husband. G asked by Crown whether she had remained faithful to husband during separation. Defence objection on basis that question attempted to impugn G's character sustained. Per Lord Stewart (quoting LJ-C Thomson in *O'Hara v HMA* 1948 JC 90; 1948 SLT 372): '"The fundamental consideration is a fair trial and there may be cases where the price which the accused may be called upon to pay if cross-examined will be out of all proportion to the extent and nature of the imputations cast on the witnesses who testify against him." I would have no hesitation here in using my discretion in favour of disallowing the line of cross-examination. . . . There must be a limit to what can be explored.'
Accused giving evidence against co-accused is open to question on record.	*McCourtney v HMA* 1977 JC 68; 1978 SLT 10 Manufacture of controlled drug. McC convicted along with four co-accused. Appealed on basis that judge had allowed a co-accused's counsel to ask questions of McC which elicited his previous convictions, McC having given evidence already against co-accused. Conviction upheld. Opinion of the court: 'Once an accused has given evidence against a co-accused there is no discretion in the trial judge to refuse to the co-accused the right to cross-examine him as to his criminal record.' *Burton v HMA* 1979 SLT (Notes) 59 B and co-accused J tried on charge of attempted extortion. J acquitted, B convicted. B appealed on basis that J's counsel had been allowed to cross-examine B on issue of character, B having given evidence already against J. Appeal dismissed. *Held*, B's evidence against J was damaging, J entitled to cross-examine.
Reluctant witness—evidence relevant to explain reluctance.	*Manson v HMA* 1951 JC 49; 1951 SLT 181 Assault. M charged with assault (razor slashing). At trial hesitant witness claimed she had been threatened by, allegedly, M's wife about giving evidence. M convicted. On appeal submitted that jury should have been directed to disregard evidence of intimidation, presumably as suggesting bad character of M. Appeal refused. *Held*, not evidence against M but evidence to explain the reluctance of the witness.
(ii) of the witness Witness's conversation with complainer relevant *quoad* credibility.	*Donald McFarlane* (1834) 6 SJ 321 Assault with intent to ravish. *Held* competent to ask witness about his conversation with victim with a view to testing her credibility, but not competent to ask another witness what first witness had repeated to him in an attempt to prove 'latent acts of individual unchastity'. Per Lord Neaves: 'Such a course would be contrary to the principles of justice, and of judicial inquiry.'

One witness not to be asked about character of another.	*Thomas Wight* (1836) 1 Swin 47 Theft and horsestealing. *Held* incompetent for prosecutor to ask prosecution witness about general character of one of defence witnesses. Per Lord Meadowbank: 'Even in cases of rape, where the character of the woman is so material a point, such questions are not allowed, unless a special defence impugning her character has been given in.'
Evidence of general disposition but not specific acts of violence.	*James Irving* (1838) 2 Swin 109 Cutting and stabbing. I attempted to prove that his alleged victim had perpetrated specific acts of violence on other occasions, and led evidence to show 'passionate disposition' of victim in support of claim that offence committed in self-defence. *Held* competent to lead evidence of victim's 'passionate disposition' having given notice in his defences of intention to do so, but not to prove specific acts of violence committed by victim. *Brady v HMA* 1986 SCCR 191 B convicted of attempted murder and pleaded self-defence. Sought to lead evidence of assaults by complainer on third parties. Appealed on ground that trial judge was wrong to reject this evidence. *Held*, following *Irving* (supra) that evidence of specific acts of violence by complainer against third parties was inadmissible except in exceptional circumstances, as in *HMA v Kay* supra at p 141. *Robert Porteous* (1841) Bell's Notes 293 Murder. *Held* competent for Crown to ask whether deceased was quarrelsome or inoffensive, although his character had not been impugned by P, but incompetent to ask whether another individual involved, who was not an injured party, was quarrelsome or inoffensive.
General character, but not specific acts of unchastity.	*David Allan* (1842) 1 Broun 500 Rape or assault with intent to ravish. A pled not guilty. Gave in special defences that alleged victim was of unchaste character and had previously had sexual intercourse with other men. *Held* (1) principal witness in such a charge not bound to answer questions whether on particular previous occasions she had intercourse with other men; (2) incompetent for panel to prove this by evidence of witnesses although notice had been given in special defences that the proof was proposed; (3) proof of general reputation of witness in respect of chastity allowed. *Walter Blair* (1844) 2 Broun 167 Rape, murder, assault with intent to ravish. B submitted special defences setting forth that attack on character of victim would be made. *Held* (1) incompetent to prove by examination of mother of injured party in rape charge that her daughter, since deceased, and from whom a dying declaration had been taken, had been convicted of theft; (2) proof tending to show in terms of special defences lodged that victim had shortly before had voluntary intercourse with B admissible. Opinion of the court: On special notice being given, competent for party accused of rape to prove that alleged victim had previously had criminal intercourse with other men.

John McMillan (1846) Ark 209
Rape.
Held competent for prosecutor to lead evidence of alleged victim's good character, even although McM had not lodged special defences impugning her character, but this evidence should not be brought forward at commencement of trial.
Held, character relevant as making it likely the woman did or did not consent.

James Reid and Others (1861) 4 Irv 124
Rape or assault with intent to ravish. Special defence of alibi, and statement that victim of unchaste character and unfaithful to her husband with other men.
Held (1) in a charge of rape, although the unchaste character of the woman said to have been ravished is not matter of defence, due notice must be given to prosecutor if panel intends to lead evidence of a woman's unchastity; (2) incompetent to lead evidence in respect of character other than that at or about time of alleged offence; (3) incompetent to lead evidence of character on points collateral to the issue, not forming part of *res gestae*.
Per Lord Ardmillan: 'It would be most unfair to the woman to admit evidence of what is said to have taken place, it may be 12, 15, or 18 years ago. . . . The rule [as applicable to charges of rape] applies to proof of unchastity at, and immediately before, the time when the rape is said to have been committed.'

See aso 1985 Act which specifies restrictions on questioning victims of alleged sex attacks.

Bremner v HMA 1992 SCCR 476
Rape. Character of the complainer, s 141B. B wished to lead evidence of a previous sexual relationship with the complainer. Leave refused, appeal.
Held that it was a matter for the trial judge to decide in the interests of justice. No interference here. Time gap of eight months between the relationship ending and the alleged offence.

Law Reform (Miscellaneous Provisions) (Scotland) Act 1985, s 36

Illegally obtained evidence may be admissible
Urgency

Bell v Hogg 1967 JC 49; 1967 SLT 290
Theft of copper wire. Police intercepted van carrying B and others and cautioned but did not charge them. Palm rubbings taken but B not told expressly that he was entitled to refuse. B convicted. Appeal refused.
Per LJ-G Clyde: 'The urgency of the matter is its justification.'

HMA v McGuigan, supra, p 131

Walsh v MacPhail, supra, p 131

Fairley v Fishmongers of London, supra, p 131

Lawrie v Muir, supra, p 131

Leckie v Miln, supra, p 132

Hay v HMA, supra, p 132

Non-urgency

McGovern v HMA 1950 JC 33; 1950 SLT 133
Theft by opening lockfast place. McG not charged or apprehended in connection with safe blowing, but kept in police station for six hours during which police obtained scrapings from fingernails of McG for chemical analysis. McG later charged.
Held evidence inadmissible, as no question of urgency, and no knowledge by police as to whether scrapings would yield any evidence of McG's connection with offence.

Forrester v HMA, supra, p 135.

SUFFICIENCY

As evidence requires to be sufficient, there must be corroboration of the essential facts of **the identification of the accused** and **the commission of the crime**, except when there is a **statutory non-requirement for corroboration**. There need not be corroboration of **procedural matters** or **incidental matters**. Special considerations apply in the case of **the *Moorov* doctrine** and **the circumstantial confession**. There may be **inferential corroboration from *de recenti* possession**.

COMMENTARY	CASE LAW	STATUTE LAW
The identification of the accused It is essential that identification of the accused be explicit.	*Bruce v HMA* 1936 JC 39 Wilful fire raising. B convicted on evidence of witnesses not asked expressly to identify B, but certain of whom referred 'to the accused James Bruce'. On appeal conviction quashed because B not directly identified in court. *Wilson v Brown* 1947 JC 81 Sale of adulterated whisky. W convicted on evidence of witnesses not asked expressly to identify her. One witness said he knew the owner of the hotel to be Mrs Wilson, another that he knew licence holder to be Mrs J W S Wilson. On appeal conviction quashed because no express identification of accused by witnesses.	
During trial, accused under no duty to facilitate ID.	*Beattie v Scott* 1990 SCCR 296 *Held* on appeal that the sheriff erred in requiring the accused to stand up to assist the Crown with the ID. Accused had no duty to do so, so long as not taking positive steps to conceal his identity.	
Evidence of earlier identification is admissible.	*Muldoon v Herron* 1970 JC 30; 1970 SLT 228 Breach of the peace. Witnesses could not identify M in court and one denied having identified M to police previously. Police evidence of previous identification by witnesses held to corroborate evidence by witnesses that identification made to police at the time of the offence. Per LJ-C Grant: 'The evidence of the police as to who was identified is primary and direct evidence of that matter and no question arises of hearsay evidence in the sense of evidence designed to establish the truth of a statement by proving that the statement was made.' *Bennett v HMA* 1976 JC 1; 1976 SLT (Notes) 90 Assault to severe injury. D identified on day of assault by victim and two other witnesses none of whom able to identify him at the trial. Police officer gave evidence of previous identification of B by witnesses and victim. B convicted. Appeal refused. *Held*, identification need not be visual. Concurrences of independent fact even if each spoken to by only one witness may be enough when taken together. *McGaharon v HMA* 1968 SLT (Notes) 99 Breach of the peace and assault. Two witnesses unable to identify McG at trial. Police evidence of identification by these witnesses to police at time of the incident held to be sufficient identification. McG convicted. Per Sheriff Middleton: '. . . evidence by policeman that a particular witness identified a particular person at the time may be very much better than identification by a witness himself six months later in the witness box.'	

Neeson v HMA 1984 SCCR 72
Murder. Two police witnesses gave evidence that N identified at identification parade by witness. This witness unable to identify N in court. N convicted and appeal dismissed.
Held, corroborative material from what happened at the identification parade.

See also:

Maxwell v HMA 1990 SCCR 363
Hawkins v Carmichael 1992 SCCR 348
McEwan v HMA 1990 SCCR 409

Corroboration of identification normally required unless there is statutory provision to the contrary.

Morton v HMA 1938 JC 50; 1938 SLT 27
Indecent assault. M identified by complainer at identification parade and at trial. The only other witness failed to identify M. M convicted. On appeal conviction quashed.
Held, insufficient evidence.
Opinion of the court: '. . . by the law of Scotland no person can be convicted of a crime or a statutory offence except where the legislature otherwise directs unless there is evidence of at least two witnesses implicating the person accused with the commission of the crime or offence with which he is charged.'

Harrison v Mackenzie 1923 JC 61; 1923 SLT 565
Illegal trawling. Name of vessel read through telescope by only one witness. H convicted. Quashed on appeal.
Per Lord Hunter: '. . . it is always essential that vital testimony given by a single witness against the person accused should be corroborated, either by the testimony of other witnesses, or by facts and circumstances.'

Bainbridge v Scott 1968 SLT 871
Criminal damage. B admitted to police that he had damaged car and van with paint stripper. B had also freely admitted to owners of two vehicles that he was responsible for the damage.
Held that the accused's special knowledge sufficient to corroborate admission to the police but observed that evidence of confession to the owners did not corroborate evidence of confession made to the police.

Sinclair v MacLeod 1962 JC 19
Careless driving. Driver of the car owned by S not identified at locus. Later, police arrived at S's house to find wife locking the car door. S in bed admitted to police he was the driver. S convicted. Quashed on appeal, insufficient corroboration.

Reilly and Ors v HMA 1981 SCCR 201
Assault and robbery. Corroboration relied on by Crown consisted of weak sometimes contradictory pieces of circumstantial evidence. Conviction quashed on appeal.
Opinion of the court: 'The question . . . is whether that evidence, in character, quality and strength, is apt to entitle the jury to treat it as corroborative of the evidence of [the witness]. We have come to be of the opinion that it was not.'

Ralston v HMA 1987 SCCR 467
R convicted of assaulting a security guard and attempting to rob him. Evidence consisted of positive identification at identification parade and in court by victim and weak evidence from two other guards that R's face resembled that of the assailant.

Held that where one starts with a positive emphatic identification by one witness, very little else is required provided that it is consistent with the positive evidence. Appeal refused.

Nelson v HMA 1988 SCCR 536
One positive identification sufficiently corroborated by identification by build.

Fisher v Guild 1991 SCCR 308
Road traffic. Passenger identifying accused as the driver. Only two in the car and as passenger held to be credible there was sufficient identification.

See also:

Cuthbert v Hingston 1993 SCCR 87

Contradictory evidence of identifying witnesses.

Robertson v HMA 1990 SCCR 142
R identified by two witnesses who differed as to his clothing. Convicted.
Held on appeal, up to jury to assess reliability, one reliable witness alone would have been sufficient to corroborate the special knowledge admission R had made.

See also:

McDonald v Scott 1993 SCCR 78
Gilmour v HMA 1994 SCCR 133
McGeoch v HMA 1991 SCCR 487

Evidence of identification can be corroborated by the accused's actings at the time of the offence.

O'Donnell v HMA 1979 SLT (Notes) 64
Assault. Evidence of principal eyewitness held by sheriff as corroborated only by circumstantial evidence of O'D being seen at the locus at least ten minutes after crime. O'D convicted. Conviction quashed on appeal.
Per LJ-C Wheatley: 'No reasonable jury could have accepted that evidence as corroboration. . . .'

Gracie v Allan 1987 SCCR 364
G convicted of theft by housebreaking. Principal evidence that of Mrs F who identified him as being in the back garden of the house in question. Mrs F said accused very like the person she saw. For corroboration Crown relied on evidence that G found acting suspiciously a quarter of a mile away twenty minutes after the housebreaking.
Held that it was not necessary that identification witness be 100 per cent certain and there was sufficient other evidence to corroborate that identification.

MacNeill v Wilson 1981 SCCR 80
Use of lorry carrying insecure load. W identified by one of his passengers as driver of the lorry, also seen by another witness examining the lorry after accident. W made no admissions to the police but produced damaged strop and said this was being used at the time the load fell from the lorry. W acquitted. On Crown's appeal conviction ordered, evidence that the respondent was the driver.

Maclennan v Macdonald 1988 SCCR 133
Road traffic offences. Question of whether M had been driving his car when it collided with parked car. Witness gave evidence of seeing M walking from his car to the parked car. No other traffic present. Damage to parked car consistent with M's car having reversed into it. M's explanation that someone else had been driving his car was not believed by sheriff and witnesses had not heard anyone running off.

Held that the evidence showed that car involved in collision was the appellant's, seen walking towards the car and no-one else present.

Proctor v Tudhope 1985 SCCR 403
P convicted of housebreaking with intent to steal. Clear identification by householder some hours after offence. In addition to this R ran off when pointed out while walking along the street by householder to policeman.
Held, witness credible and P's reaction sufficiently eloquent of guilt to be corroboration.

Stillie v HMA 1990 SCCR 719
Robbery. Complainer identified S. Corroboration in that police officers identified two persons running as or similar to the two accused. Conviction upheld on appeal. Complainer was a debt collector on his rounds, reasonable inference that the purpose of the attack was robbery.

Henderson v HMA 1993 SCCR 1005
Mobbing and rioting. Complainer identified H as did a witness who spoke to H telling him of the proposed riot and inviting him to join in.
Held, sufficient corroboration of H's identification.

Identification by voice.

McGiveran v Auld (1894) 1 Adam 448; 21 R (J) 69
Causing street obstruction. McG alleged to have made statements earlier to witnesses through telephone. Only means of identification of speaker was similarity of voice. McG convicted. Upheld on appeal.
Per LJ-C Macdonald: 'The evidence is practically the same as that given by a person outside a house who identifies his voice, and such evidence has never been held incompetent.'

See also:

Lees v Roy 1990 SCCR 310

Identification by video recording.

Bowie v Tudhope 1986 SCCR 205
Assault and robbery incident recorded on video tape. Video viewed by two police officers who identified B as one of the men seen committing the offence on film.
Held that evidence of constables sufficient to identify appellant.

Fingerprint identification.

HMA v Hamilton 1934 JC 1
Opening lockfast place, theft. H convicted on evidence of two fingerprint identification experts who found prints on bottle in shop. No other evidence. Appeal dismissed.
Per LJ-G Clyde: '. . . no chain is stronger than its weakest link. . . . Accordingly the strength of the link provided by the finger-mark depends on the degree of reliability which—on the evidence presented to them—the jury thought should be attributed to the finger-mark method as applied by the police and the experts in the present case.'

Langan v HMA 1989 SCCR 379
L charged with murder. Only evidence consisted of bloodstained fingerprint on tap in sink of house where crime committed. Fingerprint identified as L's. L claimed to have never been in the house but offered no explanation for presence of the print.
Held that in the absence of any explanation the jury were entitled to hold that it was made by the murderer.

Handwriting identification.

Richardson v Clark 1957 JC 7
Forgery and uttering. R and his wife convicted on the evidence of handwriting analysis experts in relation to wife's handwriting. Appeal refused.
Per LJ-C Thomson: '. . . it was for the sheriff, as a jury question, to decide whether and to what extent, the handwriting evidence led before him was careful, reliable and scientific, having in view . . . the skill and experience of the investigators and the amount and nature of the materials available to them for comparison.'

Campbell v Mackenzie 1974 SLT (Notes) 46
Fraud. C convicted of writing letters to chief constable making unfounded allegations about other persons and subscribed by false signature. Appeal rejected, competent and sufficient expert evidence not contradicted.

Palm print identification.

HMA v Rolley 1945 JC 155
Theft by housebreaking. Palm print found in house identified with palm print of R. Police evidence that no case of identity between prints of two different person's palms had ever been found. R convicted.
Per LJ-C Cooper: ' . . the evidence in its quality and substance [must be] of a character to carry conviction to the jury, whose duty it is to determine upon its value.'

DNA identification.

Welsh v HMA 1992 SCCR 108
Murder. Blood found at the scene matched to that of W by use of DNA profiling.
Held on appeal that DNA could be used. While DNA is not unique as with fingerprinting there was only a chance of 1 and between 88 and 99 million that the blood not that of W. No set statistical mark must be reached, up to jury whether to accept an identification using this process.

Identification by blind person.

Hill v Copeland (1976) SCCR Supp 103
H convicted of assaulting a blind person. Complainer said he had been assaulted by person who had brought him home. Threads found in complainer's house similar to those used to repair H's jacket. H had admitted taking complainer home but stated that he had left him in the close and not entered the house. Sheriff believed the complainer and determined that the threads constituted sufficient corroboration.

Identification by admissions of guilt—unequivocal

Keane v Horne (1978) SCCR Supp 225
Theft by opening lockfast car. Accused seen near locus but ran off. Described by owner of car. Two sets of car keys found on the accused's person, who said on apprehension, 'Honest we didn't take anything', and replied to caution and charge, 'I'm sorry, I didn't mean to take anything'.
Held, sufficient corroboration.
Opinion of the court: 'It has been said time and time again that when you are dealing with an unequivocal and clear admission of responsibility, only a very little evidence in corroboration of such an admission is required in law.'

McNab v Culligan (1978) SCCR Supp 222
Careless driving. Collision. Two occupants of car ran off. Later, respondent seen with facial injuries. Car belonged to respondent's father. Registered driver not driving, had handed car over to respondent who said, 'I might as well tell you the truth, it was me', to the police.
Held sufficient corroboration, even a clear admission requires some element of independent evidence.

	Meredith v Lees 1992 SCCR 459 Lewd practices. Sheriff holding that the evidence of the four-year-old complainer provided the 'very little' required to corroborate the confession of M. *Held*, appeal sustained, even a clear and unequivocal confession required corroboration.	
—equivocal.	*Sinclair v Clark* 1962 JC 57 Careless driving. S admitted to two witnesses that he was the driver. Other evidence showed S one of those in car and that he reported to the police station. S convicted. On appeal *held* sufficient corroboration. Per LJ-C Thomson: '. . . short of a solemn plea of guilt, an admission of guilt by an accused is not conclusive against him unless it is corroborated by something beyond the actual admission.'	
	Greenshields v HMA 1989 SCCR 637 G charged with murder and attempting to pervert the course of justice. Replied 'You don't think I did it myself do you; but I'm telling you nothing about it until I see my lawyer.' Appealed on the ground of insufficiency of evidence. *Held*, even when confession is not clear and unequivocal it is of evidential value and in present case constituted critical ingredient of case based on circumstantial evidence. Appeal refused.	
	See also:	
	King v Normand 1993 SCCR 896 *McDonald v Normand* 1994 SCCR 121	
Inconsistent account by the accused.	*Wright v Tudhope* 1983 SCCR 403 Careless driving. Collision with parked car. W identified by driver of parked car did not deny then that he was driver. Later W said that he was passenger and actual driver could not be traced. W convicted. Appeal dismissed.	
Identification established by answering summary complaint.	*Smith v Paterson* 1982 SCCR 295 Breach of the peace. Witnessed by two policemen who arrested P but were not asked to identify him in court. Defence submitted 'No case to answer'. Fiscal founded on statutory presumption that person who answers summary complaint is person charged by police unless the contrary is alleged and argued that there was sufficient evidence to convict. P acquitted. Crown appeal by stated case allowed. Per LJ-G Emslie: 'In most cases the presumption of limited scope provided by [the statute] will have no part to play at all in proof of the essential facts in a prosecution, viz (i) that the offence libelled was committed and, (ii) that the person who committed it was the accused.'	Criminal Justice (Scotland) Act 1980, s 26(5)
	See also:	
	Hamilton v Ross 1991 SCCR 409	
Extract conviction and police evidence as proof of disqualification.	*Andrews v McLeod* 1982 SCCR 254 Driving while disqualified. Extract conviction showed disqualification, police evidence identified A as driver. *Held*, sufficient evidence.	
The commission of the crime	*Hay v HMA* 1968 JC 40 Murder. Suspicion fell on H because impression of bite marks on deceased's body corresponded with impression of H's teeth. H convicted.	

Cause of death—postmortem evidence desirable.

Brown v HMA 1964 JC 10
Causing death by dangerous driving. Evidence of only one doctor that death caused by multiple injuries and shock. Evidence from other witnesses of prior good health provided corroboration of this.
Per LJ-C Grant: 'It is unfortunate that the Crown did not follow the normal and proper practice of proving the cause of . . . death by medical evidence based on a postmortem dissection. Such evidence, where the cause of death is in issue, is not a sine qua non, but it is highly desirable that it should be led, and grave difficulties may arise if it is not.'

Police evidence may corroborate evidence of *socius criminis*.

O'Hara v Tudhope 1986 SCCR 283
Car theft. O convicted on evidence of I who pled guilty but incriminated O. Car was stopped after a chase and O was sitting in the back seat.
Held that I's evidence was sufficiently corroborated by police evidence that O was a passenger in the car.

It is necessary that there be evidence that the crime was carried out in the manner described.

McDonald v Herron 1986 SLT 61
Theft. Witness said McD had been on premises acting suspiciously. No evidence that stolen property found in McD's possession. McD convicted.
Held on appeal, not enough corroboration to establish that the theft took place and conviction quashed.

McLeod v Mason & Ors 1981 SCCR 75
Forcing open lockfast cars with intent to steal and attempting to steal. Sheriff acquitted, holding complaint should have indicated intent to steal either the contents of the car or the car itself and insufficient evidence to show attempt to steal the car not just drive it away unlawfully. Crown appealed successfully.
Opinion of the court: 'There was no need for the Crown in order to establish the commission of a completed crime to show that it was the intention of the respondents to steal the car or its contents or both. It is quite sufficient to libel the opening of a lockfast motor car with the criminal intent of theft and in many cases it will be impossible to prove more.'

Distress of the complainer may corroborate complaint.

Gracey v HMA 1987 SCCR 260
Rape. G charged with rape and his defence was that the complainer had consented to intercourse.
Held that where evidence is led of the distressed state of the complainer it is for the jury to assess that evidence, and if accepted as genuine, it is capable of corroborating the complainer.

Moore v HMA 1990 SCCR 586
Rape. Distress of the complainer witnessed twelve hours after the alleged incident. No distress witnessed in the time gap. Conviction quashed on appeal.
Per LJ-G Hope: 'What matters is not the time interval as such but whether the shocked condition or the distress of the complainer was caused by the rape. Only then can it be said that it provides separate and independent testimony to corroborate what she herself has said in her evidence. The shorter the interval, the more likely it is that the condition is spontaneous and independent, and thus evidence in itself of what had occurred. The longer the interval, the more important it becomes to examine what happened during that period.'

Sufficiency

See also:

Cannon v HMA 1992 SCCR 505
Martin v HMA 1993 SCCR 803

McLellan v HMA 1992 SCCR 171
Lewd practices. Crown leading evidence of child complainer's distress. Judge not directing the jury on a possible alternative source of distress that the complainer was not supposed to be visiting M's house. Conviction quashed on appeal. Direction in terms of *Moore v HMA* required.

Stobo v HMA 1993 SCCR 1105
Indecent assault. Distress evidence. Argued that distress evidence could only corroborate actings proved by other evidence.
Held on appeal that distress evidence is circumstantial, provides support for the complainer's account of events. Up to jury to assess its weight and quality. Distress cannot corroborate evidence of the identity of the accused or penetration because the acts surrounding an attempt to rape are enough to explain the distress.

Vetters v HMA 1994 SCCR 305
Indecent assault. Crown alleged distress as corroboration. Sheriff did not specifically direct the jury on the distress evidence. Conviction quashed on appeal.
Held that judges must give the jury directions where there is distress evidence.

Distress in non-rape cases.

Horne v HMA 1991 SCCR 174
Abduction.
Held that distress evidence also relevant in cases other than rape. (Following *Mongan v HMA* 1989 SCCR 25 and *Bennett v HMA* 1989 SCCR 608.)

Insufficient evidence that an individual committed a specific crime.

Shannon v HMA 1985 SCCR 14
Reset. S's conviction of possessing illegal sawn-off shotgun upheld on appeal.
Held, however, that although S's actings inferred knowledge of possessing the shotgun there was insufficient evidence to infer that he knew gun had been stolen.

See also:
West v HMA 1985 SCCR 248 (Conspiracy, p 93)

Statutory non-requirement for corroboration

Criminal Justice (Scotland) Act 1980

Solemn and summary procedure:

Autopsy report.

Section 26(6). Autopsy report presumed to relate to deceased identified therein unless contrary is alleged by defence by notice not less than six days before trial or later in special circumstances.

Signatories to autopsy or forensic science report.

Section 26(7). Evidence of one of two signatories to autopsy or forensic science report sufficient on contents and signatories' qualifications if intimation to accused of intention to call only one specified signatory given when report lodged as production unless notice given by accused requiring other signatory, not less than six days before trial, or later in special circumstances.

Forensic science report need not be spoken to in certain circumstances.	**Summary procedure:** Section 26(2). Forensic science report need not be spoken to if (*a*) a copy served on accused not less than fourteen days before trial, and (*b*) no notice given by defence of challenge thereto not less than six days before trial, or later in special circumstances.
	Solemn and summary procedure: Section 26(1) and Sched 1. Speedometer, odometer, radar meter, measuring apparatus—signatories: two police testers. Substance allegedly controlled drug—signatories: two qualified/authorised analysts. Benefits payments, eg, social security, child and supplementary benefits—signatory: authorised officer.
	Forgery and Counterfeiting Act 1981 Section 26. Arrival, entry particulars—signatory: authorised officer.
	Criminal Justice (Scotland) Act 1980
Conviction or extract sufficient to show disqualification.	**Solemn and summary procedure:** Section 26(8). Conviction or extract of disqualification is sufficient evidence if copy served on accused not later than fourteen days before trial, purportedly signed by clerk of court, and showing named person disqualified, unless notice denying application of conviction given by accused not less than six days before trial.
Bail—extract of minutes.	Bail etc (Scotland) Act 1980 Section 3(11). Extract of minutes bearing to be signed by clerk of court sufficient evidence; section 7(5) undertaking sufficient evidence.
Road traffic—blood specimen; analyst's report.	Road Traffic Offenders Act 1988 Section 16(3) and (4). Certificate of medical practitioner taking blood specimen and analyst's report thereon sufficient evidence only if copy served on accused not less than seven days before trial, and accused does not serve notice that certificate's signatory required to attend trial. This notice to be served not less than three days before trial, or later in special circumstances.

There is provision by statute that one witness is sufficient to prove certain offences.

Poaching

Game offences.

Lees v Macdonald (1893) 20 R(J) 55
Trespass in pursuit of game. Appeal by prosecutor from decision of sheriff that title to shooting rights required corroboration sustained.
Held, day poaching, one credible witness sufficient.

Game (Scotland) Act 1832
Sections 1, 2 and 6. Contraventions may be proved by the evidence of one credible witness.

Anderson v Macdonald 1910 SC(J) 65
Unlawful pursuit of game. Sheriff dismissed complaint against M found in possession of rabbits on grounds that evidence of only one witness was led. Crown appeal sustained.
Per Lord Ardwall: 'Section 3 of the Act of 1862 imports into that Act the whole provisions regarding procedure in the Act of 1832.'

Poaching Prevention Act 1862
Section 3. Conviction of offences on evidence of single credible witness, by way of adopting the terms of the Game (Scotland) Act 1832.

Salmon poaching.

Jopp v Pirie (1869) 7 M 755
Taking salmon during closed time. Appeal from decision of sheriff that proof by one witness only applied where there was a 'paucity of evidence' sustained.
Per Lord Neaves: 'By the common law of Scotland, the evidence of one witness, however credible, is not sufficient for a conviction, but this Act has said it shall be sufficient. The sheriff seems to have thought this was only where there was a *penuria testium*; but there is nothing to that effect in the Act.'

Salmon Fisheries (Scotland) Act 1868
Section 30. 'All offences' under the Act (found in ss 15, 17 to 24) can be proved by one credible witness.

Salmon and Freshwater Fisheries (Protection) (Scotland) Act 1951
Section 7(3). Conviction is lawful on evidence of one witness (for illegal possession of salmon or trout or means for taking them).

Road traffic.

Road Traffic Regulation Act 1984
Section 120(1). In respect of any of the offences described in s 120(2) conviction is lawful on the evidence of one witness.

Road Traffic Offenders Act 1988
Section 21(3). Conviction is lawful on the evidence of one witness for contravention of the Road Traffic Act 1988, s 35(1) (failure to obey traffic direction by police constable or traffic sign).

Procedural matters
Rights re medical examination

Farrell v Concannon 1957 JC 12; 1957 SLT 60
Drunken driving. Sheriff returned 'not proven' verdict. Appeal by Crown allowed.
Held, on appeal, that the fact that an accused was told he need not consent to medical examination should be proven, but could be done by only one witness.

Breath test procedure.

MacLeod v Nicol; *Torrance v Thaw* 1970 JC 58; 1970 SLT 304
Drunken driving. At trial of N one police witness spoke to circumstances of breath test. At trial of To one policeman spoke to fact he was in uniform and device used was of approved style. Sheriff found charge against N not proven. To convicted. In N's case, Crown appealed and in To's case accused appealed.
Held, that procedural steps in issue could be spoken to by one credible witness.
Per LJ-C Grant: '. . . in any case any fact can be proved by one witness although the whole case cannot be so proved. . . . All that the law demands is that there should be two witnesses to prove a case; and provided that is so, any fact in the case may be provided by the testimony of one credible witness.'

Incidental matters
Security of premises.

Cameron (1839) 2 Swin 447
Theft by housebreaking. Only one witness to wash-house being locked up before offence took place. Aggravation proved. Conviction upheld on appeal.

Davidson (1841) 2 Swin 630
Theft by opening lockfast place. Locking spoken to by only one witness.
Held only one witness necessary, now fixed law.

Evidence of real facts.

Ryrie v Campbell 1964 JC 33
Driving without due care and attention. No eye witness but tyre marks on the wrong side of the road observed by the police. Paint marks on lamp standard matched car. Appeal refused.
Held evidence of eyewitness not essential, real facts eloquent of what happened.

The *Moorov* doctrine
The interlinking of evidence on separate charges, if sufficiently idiosyncratic, will furnish corroboration even if there is only one witness speaking to matters.

HMA v Moorov 1930 JC 68
Indecent assault. M convicted of series of indecent assault over a period of years. On appeal, *held* evidence in support of any one charge was competent corroboration of evidence in support of other charges.
Per LJ-G Clyde: 'Before the evidence of a single credible witness to separate acts can be used as providing material for mutual corroboration, the connection between the separate acts indicated by the external relation in time, character or circumstance must be such as to exhibit them as subordinates in some particular and ascertained unity of project, campaign, or adventure, which lies beyond or behind, but is related to, the separate acts.'

Pettigrew v Lees 1991 SCCR 304
Two charges of indecent exposure. In both incidents only one witness could identify the accused. The presence of others at one incident did not make the doctrine inapplicable as there was only one identification on each occasion.

Quinn v Lowe 1991 SCCR 881
Held on appeal that *Moorov* could apply to two incidents arising out of the same matter in each of which the same complainer was the only witness.

See also:

Lindsay v HMA 1993 SCCR 868
Carpenter v Hamilton 1994 SCCR 10

Offences connected in time.

Ogg v HMA 1938 JC 152
Sexual offences. Ten charges over seven years. In first three, complainer the only witness.
Held that *Moorov* not applicable in view of the time between offences and lack of corroboration.
Per LJ-C Aitchison: '*Moorov* . . .—laid down the general proposition in relation to sexual crimes, although not entirely limited to such crimes, that similar sexual crimes each deponed to by a single credible witness may afford mutual corroboration, provided always that they are so inter-related by character, circumstances and time—the presence of all these features is not essential—as to justify an inference that they are instances of a course of criminal conduct systematically pursued by the accused person.'

Russell v HMA 1990 SCCR 18
Interval of two years between two incidents held to be fatal to the application of the doctrine.

See also:

Coffey v Houston 1992 SCCR 265

Offences must be of the same *genus*

HMA v WB 1969 JC 72
Incest and lewd, indecent and libidinous practices. Five offences over some years. Two incidents separated by interval of fifteen months. *Moorov* applied despite time interval.
Held, evidence of incest included indecency and could corroborate evidence of lewd practices but not vice versa as incest much more serious than lewd practices.

Mackintosh v HMA 1991 SCCR 776
Held on appeal that *Moorov* could not apply to a charge of theft by housebreaking and assault with intent to rob because one incident involved violence and the other did not.

P v HMA 1991 SCCR 993
Trial judge holding that *Moorov* could be applied to two charges of sexual offences against a young boy and girl. Course of criminal penetrative abuse.

See also:

Russell v HMA 1992 SCCR 257
Farrell v Normand 1992 SCCR 859

An attempted crime may corroborate a completed one

PM v Jessop 1989 SCCR 324
PM charged with sodomy and attempted sodomy in relation to two boys. Convicted using *Moorov*.
Held that the sodomy and attempted sodomy so closely related that evidence of attempted act may corroborate evidence of completed act.

Moorov also applied to non-sexual crimes

McDudden v HMA 1952 JC 86—bribery
HMA v McQuade 1951 JC 143—razor attacks
Harris v Clark 1958 JC 3—reset
McIntosh v HMA 1986 SCCR 496—supply of drugs

The circumstantial confession
Where a confession by an accused or a suspect details information which would have been in the possession of the perpetrator of the crime, the terms of the confession supply corroboration of it.

Manuel v HMA 1958 JC 41
Murder. Statement by M as to whereabouts of victim's body which was subsequently discovered by police held sufficient corroboration and conviction upheld on appeal.

Connolly v HMA 1958 SLT 79
Theft. Particularised and detailed confession with extraneous evidence of its accuracy. Independent evidence of the accused acting suspiciously in car near locus held sufficient corroboration.
Held, confession shows crime committed and accused must have been the perpetator or privy to its perpetration.

Woodland v Hamilton 1990 SCCR 166
Held not to be special knowledge admission where the alleged special knowledge could have been given to W by his co-accused.

Robertson v HMA 1990 SCCR 345
Art and part assault. Statement by R to police, 'You've got this wrong, I've never stabbed anyone' consistent with R knowing of the incident in question but not sufficient to infer she knew or ought to have known that a knife was to be used.

Smith v HMA (1978) SCCR Supp 203
Theft by housebreaking. Confession amounting to account of offence and some of the items stolen held sufficient corroboration.
Per LJ-G Emslie: 'A confession can receive corroboration if there is not only proof of the commission of the crime to which it related but proof *aliunde* of the truth of the confession.'

Wilson v McAughey 1982 SCCR 398
Vandalism. Details in confession as to how mechanical digger had been started and what thereafter occurred held sufficient corroboration.
Per LJ-C Wheatley: 'The law in the situation here could be summarised in the phrase that the respondent could not have been able to make the statement which he did if he had not been present at the time when the offence libelled had been committed.'

Admissions partly consistent with facts.

Gilmour v HMA 1982 SCCR 590
Rape and murder. Two admissions of guilt by G incorporating information, some consistent, some inconsistent with the proved facts. On appeal held sufficient corroboration of investigating officers' existing information.
Held on appeal, corroboration found in that the statement contained material facts, established independently, which accused could have known if he had been present when the offence occured.

See also:

Hutchison v Valentine 1990 SCCR 569

Confession must be corroborated by findings in fact.

Allan v Hamilton 1972 SLT (Notes) 2
Theft. A told police where stolen savings stamps were cashed and admitted theft. A convicted. Appeal dismissed.
LJ-C Wheatley observed that there had been a very full confession by the accused admitting the theft, and that was corroborated by findings in fact.

Admission by one accused may be corroborated by another accused.

Annan v Bain 1986 SCCR 60
Theft. B and H charged with theft of car. Respondents seen in car and subsequently chased by police. B admitted that he 'stole white car' before police had indicated that this was the reason for apprehension. H also admitted 'We stole it'.
Held that confessions contained special knowledge and were sufficiently corroborated by presence in car; and that statement of each respondent corroborated that of the other.

See also:

Low v HMA 1993 SCCR 493

Inferential corroboration from *de recenti* possession
In the absence of an explanation, an inference of guilt can be drawn from the possession in criminative circumstances of recently stolen property.

Christie v HMA 1939 JC 72; 1939 SLT 558
Theft by housebreaking. C found in possession of part of stolen property and evidence of *de recenti* pawning of stolen article. On arrest C gave detailed statement that goods were obtained from named person, who denied it. No evidence given by C at trial. Appeal against conviction refused.
Per Lord Fleming: 'According to the authorities, which extend over a long period of time, it has in practice been recognised that where there is no reasonable explanation of such possession, the jury are entitled not merely to infer that the accused is guilty of reset, but to go further and hold that he was actor or art and part in the actual theft charged.'

Corroboration not necessary to establish that items stolen (Alison p 324).

Findlay v HMA (1953) SCCR Supp 1
Theft by housebreaking. Crown relied on evidence of recent possession of stolen articles, the only evidence that the articles were stolen being that of the householder
Held that the finding of articles in accused's possession in suspicious circumstances sufficient to corroborate evidence of owner as to their having been stolen.

but compare:
Bennet v HMA 1989 SCCR 608
Appellants charged inter alia with robbing taxi driver of a watch and £35. No corroboration of complainer's evidence that he had a watch. There was evidence that complainer had money at outset of journey but no evidence that he had no money when he reported the incident.
Held to be no corroboration of robbery.

Other criminative circumstances in addition to possession necessary.

Fox v Patterson 1948 JC 104; 1948 SLT 547
Reset. P, scrap merchant, sold stolen metal. P had receipt for his purchase of the metal.
Held that there was no presumption of guilt to be rebutted. Eventual conviction for reset quashed on appeal.
Per LJ-C Cooper: '[For the doctrine of recent possession to apply] three conditions must concur: (*a*) that the stolen goods should be found in the possession of the accused; (*b*) that the interval between the theft of the goods and their discovery in the accused's possession should be short . . .; and (*c*) that there should be "other criminative circumstances" over and above the bare fact of possession.'

Watt v Annan 1990 SCCR 55
Six months is too great an interval for application of doctrine of recent possession, but may be sufficient to convict of reset.

De recenti possession must not merely be transporting of items on another's behalf.

HMA v Simpson 1952 JC 1; 1952 SLT 85
Theft by opening lockfast place. Stolen goods found in possession of dealer to whom S had taken them as another's servant. Conviction quashed on appeal because no presumption of guilt to be rebutted as S not in 'possession' of the goods.

Gilchrist v HMA 1992 SCCR 98
Theft. G spotted by police driving car similar to one seen at the scene of a crime, pursued by police. Car slowed to allow a person to jump from the car. G stopped and jewellery found in the back seat.
Held on appeal that given the discovery of the jewellery and the manner in which G drove the car there was sufficient evidence to infer that G was aware of the stolen goods.

Present possession not required—past possession sufficient.

Brannan v HMA 1954 JC 87; 1954 SLT 255
Theft by housebreaking and opening lockfast place. Evidence that B had possession of stolen goods initially although recovered elsewhere. B convicted. Appeal refused because held that presumption of guilt arising from recent possession had not in this case been rebutted.
Per LJ-G Cooper: 'Possession may be constructive, and it does not necessarily follow that possession which has been parted with need not be explained.'

Stolen goods not 'in person's possession' as premises open to other people.

Cryans v Nixon 1955 JC 1; 1954 SLT 311
Theft. C occupier of two sheds kept unlocked, with customers having access. Part of stolen property found concealed in C's premises. C denied all knowledge. C convicted. Conviction quashed on appeal. *Held* no presumption of guilt to be rebutted, other people had access to premises, goods not in accused's possession.

Silence, when charged, not a criminative circumstance.	*Wightman and Anr v HMA* 1959 JC 44; 1959 SLT (Notes) 27 (*sub nom* Collins) Theft. Scrap metal found in W's possession. When cautioned and charged W replied: 'I am saying nothing, not one iota.' Other appellant did not reply, neither did he give evidence. Both convicted. On appeal, held that neither the failure to reply nor the failure to give evidence could constitute a criminative circumstance and no presumption of guilt to be rebutted. Per LJ-G Clyde: (quoting LJ-G Cooper in *Robertson v Maxwell* 1951 JC 11): '. . . no legitimate inference in favour of a prosecutor can be drawn from the fact that a person, when charged with crime, either says nothing or says that he has nothing to say. He is entitled to reserve his defence, and is usually wise if he does so.'
Fingerprints and attempt to dispose of items—*de recenti* possession.	*Cameron v HMA* 1959 JC 59 Theft by opening lockfast place. Box of stolen goods thrown out of window when police arrived at C's house. C's fingerprints found on stolen articles in box. C convicted. Appeal refused. *Held*, evidence of the box confirming evidence as regards possession.
Fingerprint evidence alone—not *de recenti* possession.	*Reilly v HMA* 1959 JC 59 Theft. R co-appellant with Cameron (supra). Only evidence of possession fingerprints on sheets of stamps. Conviction quashed on appeal beause no presumption of guilt to be rebutted. Per LJ-G Clyde: '. . . the presence of fingerprints alone is not sufficient to establish possession . . . of the articles alleged to have been stolen . . . one of the three necessary conditions for applying the doctrine of recent possession has not been satisfied.'

SENTENCING

ABSOLUTE DISCHARGE

Criminal Procedure (Scotland) Act 1975 (fractionally amended by Criminal Justice (Scotland) Act 1980, ss 55, 58)

FLOW CHART	COMMENTARY	STATUTE LAW	
		Solemn	**Summary**
Solemn—Conviction for offence in question. **Summary**—Court satisfied that offender committed offence in question.	Offence other than one for which sentence is fixed by law.	Section 182	Section 383
	Nature of offence to be considered.		
	Character of offender to be considered.		
	Probation order not appropriate.		
Absolute discharge.	Inexpedient to inflict punishment.		
Other sentence.	Sentence for offence may be one fixed by law.		
Not a conviction.	But can be laid before court as previous conviction in subsequent proceedings.	Section 191(1) and (4)	Section 392(1) and (5)
Appeal.	Right of appeal not affected.	Section 191(3)(a)	Section 392(3)(a) and (4)

Flow chart: From "Solemn—Conviction for offence in question." / "Summary—Court satisfied that offender committed offence in question." to "Absolute discharge." — NO → Other sentence. YES → Not a conviction. Both lead to Appeal.

ADMONITION

Criminal Procedure (Scotland) Act 1975

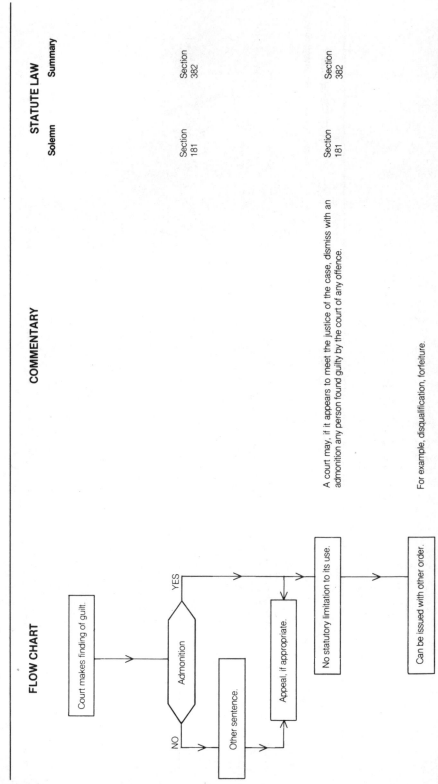

| | STATUTE LAW | |
| FLOW CHART | COMMENTARY | Solemn | Summary |

FLOW CHART

Court makes finding of guilt.

Admonition — YES / NO

Other sentence.

Appeal, if appropriate.

No statutory limitation to its use.

Can be issued with other order.

COMMENTARY

A court may, if it appears to meet the justice of the case, dismiss with an admonition any person found guilty by the court of any offence.

For example, disqualification, forfeiture.

STATUTE LAW

Solemn
Section 181

Summary
Section 382

Solemn
Section 181

Summary
Section 382

CAUTION

Criminal Procedure (Scotland) Act 1975; Criminal Justice Act 1982; Criminal Justice Act 1991

FLOW CHART

Conviction

Power to require caution restricted to courts of summary jurisdiction.

Caution consists of a specified amount of money as security for good behaviour over a specified period of time.

Failure to find caution within specified period.

YES → Alternative of imprisonment may be imposed.

NO →

Caution is consigned.

Further offence.

YES → Caution forfeit.

NO →

End of period—caution refunded plus accumulated interest.

COMMENTARY

District court	Sheriff court
Period not exceeding six months.	Period not exceeding twelve months.
Maximum not exceeding level 4 on standard scale (at present £2,500).	Maximum amount £5,000.
May be ordered in lieu of, or in addition to, imprisonment or a fine.	
Must be consigned in total to sheriff clerk or district court clerk.	
Specified period of time usually allowed by court to enable offender to lodge the amount.	
Earns interest for offender during period of caution.	

STATUTE LAW

District court	Sheriff court
1975 Act, s 284	1975 Act, s 289
1991 Act, s 17(1)	1991 Act, s 17(2)
1975 Act, s 303	1975 Act, s 303
1975 Act, s 284	1975 Act, s 289

Notes: (1) Instead of consignation of the amount there can be a bond of caution.

(2) Caution can be recovered by civil diligence and imprisonment is still competent, see Criminal Justice (Scotland) Act 1980, s 52.

COMMUNITY SERVICE ORDER

Community Service by Offenders (Scotland) Act 1978

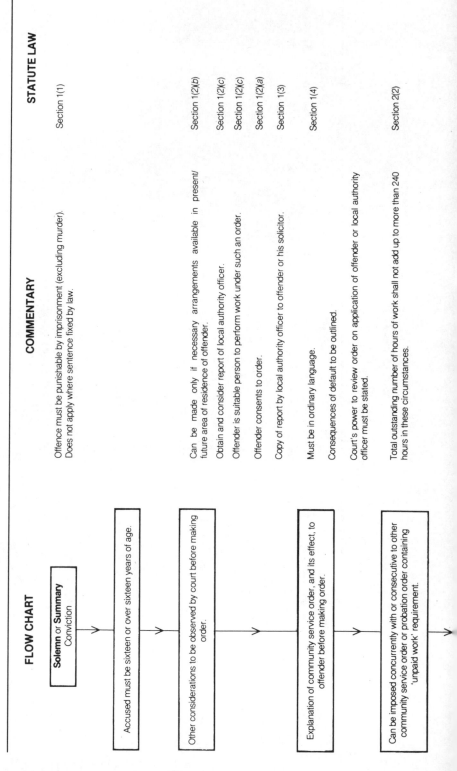

FLOW CHART	COMMENTARY	STATUTE LAW
Solemn or **Summary** Conviction	Offence must be punishable by imprisonment (excluding murder). Does not apply where sentence fixed by law.	Section 1(1)
Accused must be sixteen or over sixteen years of age.		
Other considerations to be observed by court before making order.	Can be made only if necessary arrangements available in present/future area of residence of offender.	Section 1(2)(b)
	Obtain and consider report of local authority officer.	Section 1(2)(c)
	Offender is suitable person to perform work under such an order.	Section 1(2)(c)
	Offender consents to order.	Section 1(2)(a)
	Copy of report by local authority officer to offender or his solicitor.	Section 1(3)
Explanation of community service order, and its effect, to offender before making order.	Must be in ordinary language.	Section 1(4)
	Consequences of default to be outlined.	
	Court's power to review order on application of offender or local authority officer must be stated.	
Can be imposed concurrently with or consecutive to other community service order or probation order containing 'unpaid work' requirement.	Total outstanding number of hours of work shall not add up to more than 240 hours in these circumstances.	Section 2(2)

Flowchart	Description	Section
Requires unpaid work for certain number of hours.	Not less than forty hours.	Section 1(1)
	Not more than 240 hours (includes consecutive sentences).	Sections 1(1) and 2(2)
	Disqualification may be imposed in addition to community service order.	Section 1(7)(a)
Court makes order. (YES / NO)	Must specify locality of residence.	Section 2(1)(a)
	Must require local authority to appoint a supervising officer.	Section 2(1)(b)
	Must state the number of hours of work.	Section 2(1)(c)
	Copy order must go to offender, local authority and 'appropriate court'.	Section 2(3) (and s 12(1))
Other disposal. / Appeal	Right of appeal is not affected by making of order.	
Obligations on person subject to order.	Must advise supervising local authority officer of any change of address or of any change in times of work.	Section 3(1)(a)
	Must perform specified hours on such work and at such times as instructed by local authority officer.	Section 3(1)(b)
	Work to be completed within twelve months but if not, order will stand until revoked or full number of hours worked.	Section 3(2)
	Instructions must avoid conflict with offender's religious beliefs.	Section 3(3)
Obligations on local authority supervising officer.	Must not interfere with normal working hours or attendance at educational establishments.	Section 3(3)

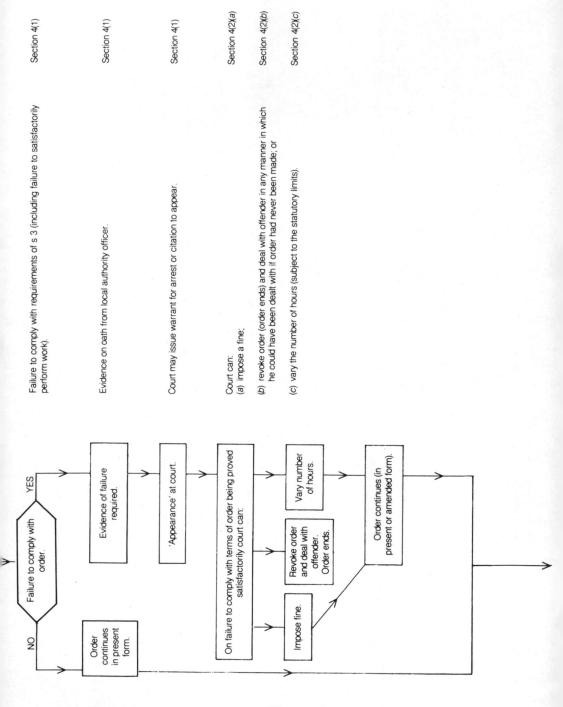

Failure to comply with requirements of s 3 (including failure to satisfactorily perform work).

Section 4(1)

Evidence on oath from local authority officer.

Section 4(1)

Court may issue warrant for arrest or citation to appear.

Section 4(1)

Court can:
(a) impose a fine;

Section 4(2)(a)

(b) revoke order (order ends) and deal with offender in any manner in which he could have been dealt with if order had never been made; or

Section 4(2)(b)

(c) vary the number of hours (subject to the statutory limits).

Section 4(2)(c)

Community Service Order

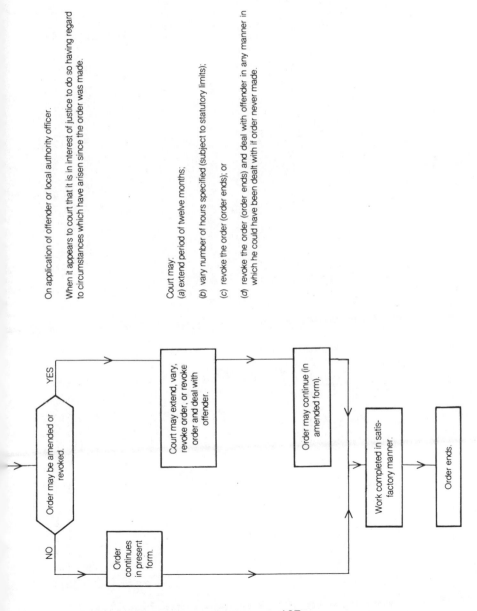

On application of offender or local authority officer. — Section 5(1)

When it appears to court that it is in interest of justice to do so having regard to circumstances which have arisen since the order was made. — Section 5(1)

Court may:
(a) extend period of twelve months; — Section 5(1)(a)

(b) vary number of hours specified (subject to statutory limits); — Section 5(1)(b)

(c) revoke the order (order ends); or — Section 5(1)(c)

(d) revoke the order (order ends) and deal with offender in any manner in which he could have been dealt with if order never made. — Section 5(1)(d)

167

COMPENSATION ORDER

Criminal Justice (Scotland) Act 1980

FLOW CHART	COMMENTARY	STATUTE LAW
Conviction	If going to make compensation order, court to consider means of offender.	Section 59(1)
Compensation order. — YES / NO	May be made instead of, or in addition to, other disposal. Cannot be made on (a) absolute discharge, (b) probation order, or (c) deferred sentence.	Section 58(1)
Covers: personal injury, loss or damage caused by acts constituting offence.	Personal injury, loss or damage may be caused directly or indirectly.	Section 58(1)
	(a) Solemn proceedings: no limit to amount.	Section 59(2) of the 1980 Act
	(b) Summary proceedings before sheriff or stipendiary magistrate: amount not exceeding prescribed sum within meaning of s 289B of Criminal Procedure (Scotland) Act 1975, (ie, presently £5,000).	Section 59(3)(a) of the 1980 Act, s 289B of the 1975 Act as amended by the Criminal Justice Act 1991, s 17(2)
As per s 58(3)—Does not cover loss because of death of person; or arising due to motor vehicle accident (except under s 58(2)).	(c) District court before lay magistrate: amount not exceeding level 4 on standard scale (presently £2,500).	Section 59(3)(b) of the 1980 Act, s 289G of the 1975 Act as amended by the Criminal Justice Act 1991, s 17(1)
	Damage caused in case of offence under Road Traffic Act 1988, s 178(1), is included.	Section 58(2)
Appeal	Order is a sentence for purposes of appeal or review.	Section 63(1)
	Payments to court retained until determination of appeal.	Section 63(2)
Where order and fine are concurrent, order takes precedence over fine.	Where there is both a fine and a compensation order, payment by convicted person shall first be applied in satisfaction of the compensation order.	Section 62

Review of order on application of person against whom order made.

If it appears to the court either that the injury, loss or damage has been held in civil proceedings to be less than it was taken to be for the purposes of the compensation order, or that property lost has been recovered, then order can be reduced or discharged.

Court has power to enforce order generally as if it were a fine.

A court may impose imprisonment in respect of a fine and decline to impose imprisonment in respect of a compensation order, but not vice versa.

Where a court imposes imprisonment both in respect of a fine and a compensation order, the amounts are to be aggregated for the purpose of calculating the maximum period imposed.

All the provisions of the 1975 Act relative to the payment, remission, transfer and enforcement of fines apply to compensation orders, as appropriate.

Section 64
Section 64

Section 66
Section 66(2)

Section 66(2)(a)

Section 66(1) and (2)

See list in s 66(2)

Review of compensation order. → Reduction of amount possible. → Discharge of order.
- YES → Order ends.
- NO → Order continues. → Failure to comply.
  - YES → Alternative disposal. → Order ends.
  - NO → Order continues. → Payment in full. → Order ends.

DEFERRED SENTENCE

Criminal Procedure (Scotland) Act 1975, as amended by Criminal Justice (Scotland) Act 1980, ss 53, 54

FLOW CHART

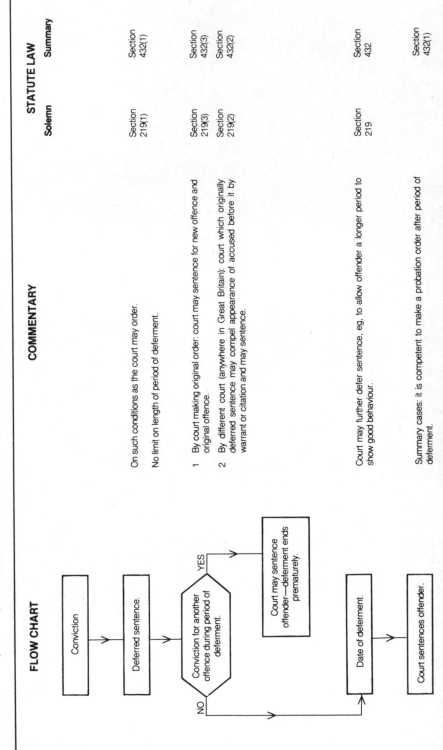

Conviction

↓

Deferred sentence.

↓

Conviction for another offence during period of deferment.

— YES → Court may sentence offender—deferment ends prematurely.

— NO → Date of deferment.

↓

Court sentences offender.

COMMENTARY

On such conditions as the court may order.

No limit on length of period of deferment.

1 By court making original order: court may sentence for new offence and original offence.

2 By different court (anywhere in Great Britain): court which originally deferred sentence may compel appearance of accused before it by warrant or citation and may sentence.

Court may further defer sentence, eg, to allow offender a longer period to show good behaviour.

Summary cases: it is competent to make a probation order after period of deferment.

COMMENTARY	STATUTE LAW	
	Solemn	Summary
On such conditions as the court may order.	Section 219(1)	Section 432(1)
1 By court making original order	Section 219(3)	Section 432(3)
2 By different court	Section 219(2)	Section 432(2)
Court may further defer sentence	Section 219	Section 432
Summary cases: probation order		Section 432(1)

FINES

Criminal Procedure (Scotland) Act 1975 ('1975 Act'), as amended by Criminal Justice (Scotland) Act 1980, ss 47-52. Criminal Law Act 1977; Criminal Justice Act 1982; Criminal Justice (Scotland) Act 1987; Criminal Justice Act 1991

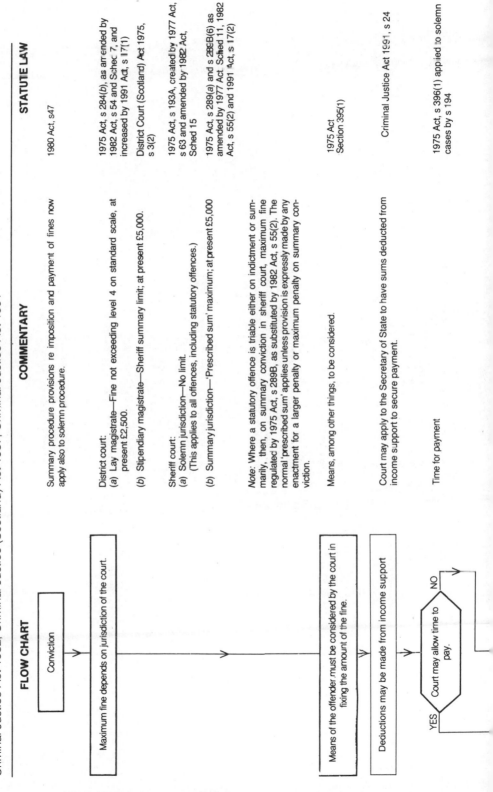

FLOW CHART	COMMENTARY	STATUTE LAW
Conviction	Summary procedure provisions re imposition and payment of fines now apply also to solemn procedure.	1980 Act, s47
Maximum fine depends on jurisdiction of the court.	District court: (a) Lay magistrate—Fine not exceeding level 4 on standard scale, at present £2,500.	1975 Act, s 284(b), as amended by 1982 Act, s 54 and Sched 7, and increased by 1991 Act, s 17(1)
	(b) Stipendiary magistrate—Sheriff summary limit; at present £5,000.	District Court (Scotland) Act 1975, s 3(2)
	Sheriff court: (a) Solemn jurisdiction—No limit. (This applies to all offences, including statutory offences.)	1975 Act, s 193A, created by 1977 Act, s 63 and amended by 1982 Act, Sched 15
	(b) Summary jurisdiction—Prescribed sum' maximum; at present £5,000.	1975 Act, s 289(a) and s 289B(6) as amended by 1977 Act, Sched 11, 1982 Act, s 55(2) and 1991 Act, s 17(2)
	Note: Where a statutory offence is triable either on indictment or summarily, then, on summary conviction in sheriff court, maximum fine regulated by 1975 Act, s 289B, as substituted by 1982 Act, s 55(2). The normal 'prescribed sum' applies unless provision is expressly made by any enactment for a larger penalty or maximum penalty on summary conviction.	
Means of the offender must be considered by the court in fixing the amount of the fine.	Means, among other things, to be considered.	1975 Act Section 395(1)
Deductions may be made from income support	Court may apply to the Secretary of State to have sums deducted from income support to secure payment.	Criminal Justice Act 1991, s 24
Court may allow time to pay. YES / NO	Time for payment	1975 Act, s 396(1) applied to solemn cases by s 194

171

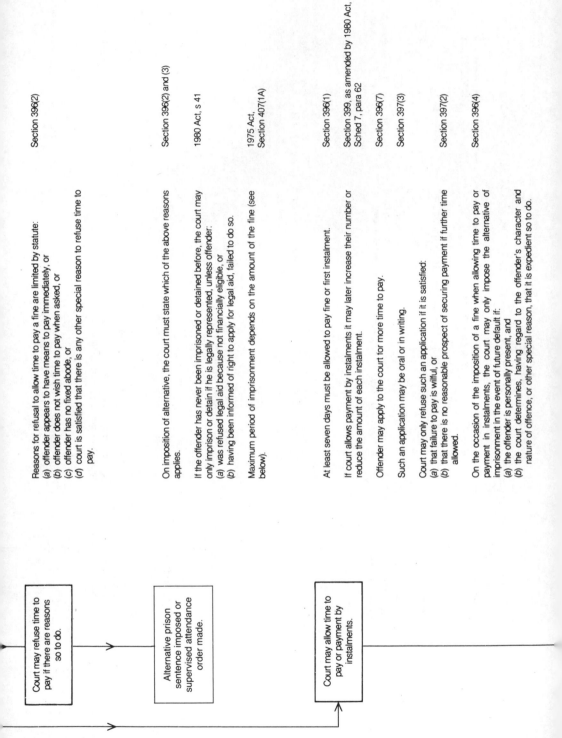

Court may refuse time to pay if there are reasons so to do.

Reasons for refusal to allow time to pay a fine are limited by statute:
(a) offender appears to have means to pay immediately, or
(b) offender does not wish time to pay when asked, or
(c) offender has no fixed abode, or
(d) court is satisfied that there is any other special reason to refuse time to pay.

Section 396(2)

Alternative prison sentence imposed or supervised attendance order made.

On imposition of alternative, the court must state which of the above reasons applies.

Section 396(2) and (3)

If the offender has never been imprisoned or detained before, the court may only imprison or detain if he is legally represented, unless offender:
(a) was refused legal aid because not financially eligible, or
(b) having been informed of right to apply for legal aid, failed to do so.

1980 Act, s 41

Maximum period of imprisonment depends on the amount of the fine (see below).

1975 Act, Section 407(1A)

Court may allow time to pay or payment by instalments.

At least seven days must be allowed to pay fine or first instalment.

Section 396(1)

If court allows payment by instalments it may later increase their number or reduce the amount of each instalment.

Section 399, as amended by 1980 Act, Sched 7, para 62

Offender may apply to the court for more time to pay.

Section 396(7)

Such an application may be oral or in writing.

Section 397(3)

Court may only refuse such an application if it is satisfied:
(a) that failure to pay is wilful, or
(b) that there is no reasonable prospect of securing payment if further time allowed.

Section 397(2)

On the occasion of the imposition of a fine when allowing time to pay or payment in instalments, the court may only impose the alternative of imprisonment in the event of future default if:
(a) the offender is personally present, and
(b) the court determines, having regard to the offender's character and nature of offence, or other special reason, that it is expedient so to do.

Section 396(4)

172

If court allows time to pay, it may impose the alternative of imprisonment in default of payment

YES / NO

or

make a fines supervision order (FSO).

Default in payment.

Imprisonment

Default in payment.

Means enquiry court.

In the event of failure to pay, the offender will only serve the period of imprisonment which relates to the unpaid portion of the fine.

Section 407, as substituted by 1980 Act, s 50

When given time to pay the offender may be under supervision of the local Social Work Department while paying.

Section 400

Normally, detention of an offender under twenty-one as an alternative disposal when a fine is unpaid is not competent unless an FSO has been made.

Section 400(4) and (5)

Where an FSO has been made, the court must obtain a report from the supervising authority before imposing the alternative.

Section 400(6)

In the event of imprisonment being imposed as an alternative the offender may secure his release or reduce the period spent in prison by making payment in whole or in part while in prison.

Section 409(1)

Most sheriff courts issue warning letters on default before issuing a citation to a means enquiry court.

Section 398(1)

Unless the alternative was imposed when the fine was originally imposed, a court may not imprison a defaulter without an enquiry in his presence into the reasons for his failure to pay.

A fine defaulter may be cited to attend a means enquiry court or a warrant may be issued for his apprehension, either initially or if he fails to appear when cited.

Section 398(2),(3)

Court may make suypervised attendance order.

Court may order imprisonment. — YES / NO

Further time to pay allowed.

Maximum period is determined by amount of fine still unpaid.

Alternative imprisonment served.

Offender aged 16 years or over convicted, fine imposed, offender has failed to pay, the court instead of ordering the alternative imprisonment may make a supervised attendance order. Offender must attend a place of supervision for 10, 20, 30, 40, 50 or 60 hours and carry out instructions of supervising officer.

Law Reform (Miscellaneous Provisions) (Scotland) Act 1990, s 62(2) and Sched 6

Offender's consent required and order must be considered more appropriate than imprisonment.

1990 Act, s 62(3)(c)

Section 396(7)

Amount of fine	Alternative
Not exceeding £200	7 days
Exceeding £200 but not £500	14 days
Exceeding £500 but not £1,000	28 days
Exceeding £1,000 but not £2,500	45 days
Exceeding £2,500 but not £5,000	3 months
Exceeding £5,000 but not £10,000	6 months
Exceeding £10,000 but not £20,000	12 months
Exceeding £20,000 but not £50,000	18 months
Exceeding £50,000 but not £100,000	2 years
Exceeding £100,000 but not £250,000	3 years
Exceeding £250,000 but not £1,000,000	5 years
Exceeding £1,000,000	10 years

Section 407(1A), as substituted by 1980 Act, s 50 and amended by Criminal Justice (Scotland) Act 1987, s 67(1) and 1991 Act, s 23(2)

If the fines were imposed by the same court on the same day, the period of imprisonment will be determined by the total of the fines imposed.

Section 407(1B), as substituted by 1980 Act, s 50

Offender may secure his release or reduce the period spent in prison by making payment in whole or in part while in prison.

Section 409(1)

Note: Other financial penalties

FORFEITURE
Property in offender's possession or under his control at the time of apprehension, used or intended for use in committing the crime, court may order forfeiture and disposal of the property.

Solemn:
1975 Act, s 223
Summary:
1975 Act, s 436

Now also applied to various road traffic offences.

Solemn:
1975 Act, s 223(1A)
Summary:
1975 Act, s 436(1A) (as inserted by Road Traffic Act 1991, s 37)

CONFISCATION
Confiscation of the proceeds of drug trafficking: see—Misuse of Drugs.

Criminal Justice (Scotland) Act 1987, ss 1–7

IMPRISONMENT AND DETENTION

Mostly regulated by Criminal Justice (Scotland) Act 1980, Part III as amended by Criminal Justice Act 1988, s 124

FLOW CHART	COMMENTARY	STATUTE LAW
Conviction	Young offender: not less than sixteen, but under twenty-one years of age. Adult offender: twenty-one years or over.	Section 45(1)
Adult offender not previously sentenced to imprisonment or detention. / Young offender not previously sentenced to imprisonment or detention.	Court must, when taking account of previous sentences, (i) Disregard suspended sentence (English/Irish) which has not been brought into effect. (ii) Interpret detention as meaning detention in a young offenders institution or detention centre, but not borstal training (except in England and Wales).	Section 41(2)(a) Section 41(2)(b)
Custodial sentence being considered. / Custodial sentence being considered.	Criminal Justice Act 1988, s 124 abolishes the sentence of detention while retaining the definition of detention for the purposes of s 41(2) where court is having regard to previous sentences. All references to detention centres are amended to young offenders' institutions.	
Alternative / Alternative		
Court must *first* consider background reports.	Report by officer of local authority or otherwise. Court must take account of any information before it relating to offender's character, and his/her physical/mental condition.	Sections 42(1), 45(1)

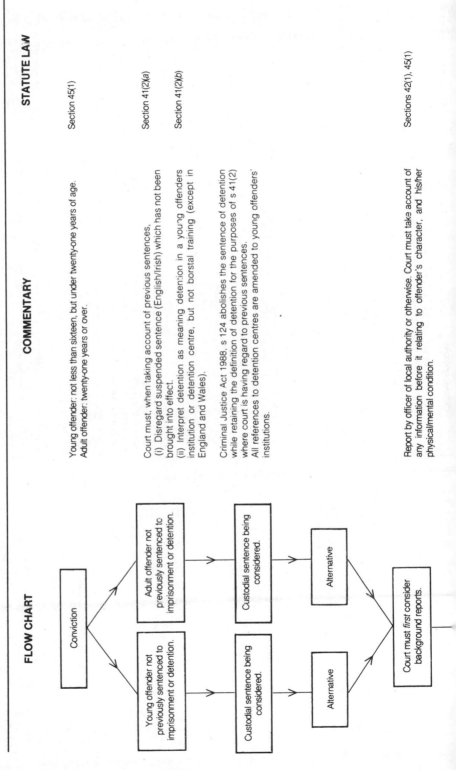

175

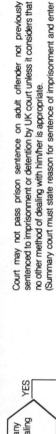

Is there available any other method of dealing with offender appropriately?

YES → Alternative imposed.

NO → First sentence of imprisonment or detention.

If first sentence, offender should be allowed legal representation irrespective of offender's age.

Place of imprisonment or detention

Young offender: young offenders institution.

Adult offender: HM Prison institution.

Court may not pass prison sentence on adult offender not previously sentenced to imprisonment or detention by UK court unless it considers that no other method of dealing with him/her is appropriate. (Summary court must state reason for sentence of imprisonment and enter reason in record of proceedings.) — **Section 42(1)**

A young offender not to be sentenced to detention unless no other way of dealing with that person is appropriate. Reason for imposing detention to be given and, except in High Court, entered in record of proceedings. — **Section 42(2)**

Deferment should be granted if necessary to allow accused to apply for legal aid and for consideration of reports. — **Section 45(1)**

No court may pass sentence of imprisonment or detention (or impose such sentence as immediate alternative to fine under s 396(2) of the 1975 Act) if the offender is not legally represented and has not previously been sentenced to imprisonment or detention by a UK court. — **Section 41 (1)**

But
Legal representation not prerequisite if offender either
(a) has been refused legal aid on financial grounds, or
(b) has failed to apply for legal aid after having been informed of his right and having had the opportunity to do so. — **Section 41 (1)(a), (b)**

And
Where imposition of alternative occurs in cases of future default where time to pay has been allowed or imposition of alternative occurs at a means enquiry whether further time to pay is allowed or not, legal representation is not necessary, nor does it matter whether or not the offender has previously suffered a custodial sentence.

Applies to all courts and all sentences of imprisonment or detention, except those fixed by law. — **Section 41(3)**

All young offenders serve sentence in young offenders institution.

Consecutive sentences imposed at same time are treated as single sentences. — **Criminal Justice Act 1988, s 124**

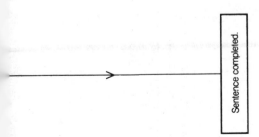

Sentence completed.

PROBATION ORDER

Criminal Procedure (Scotland) Act 1975, as variously amended

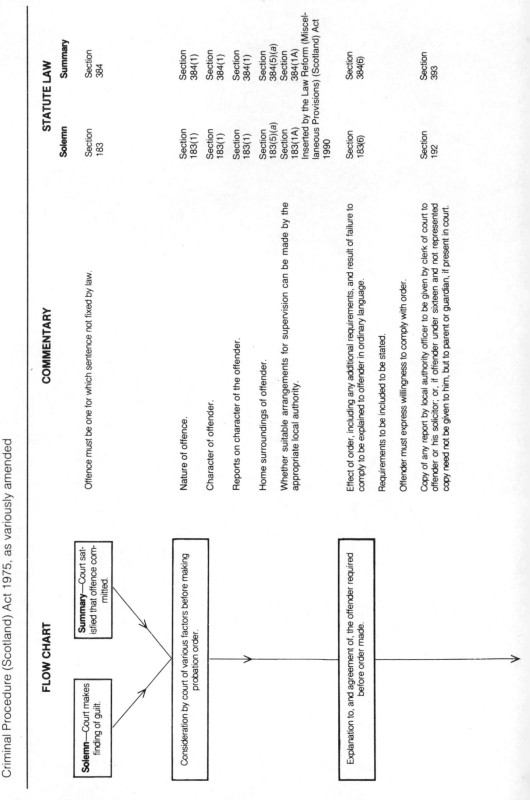

FLOW CHART	COMMENTARY	STATUTE LAW Solemn	STATUTE LAW Summary
Solemn—Court makes finding of guilt. / **Summary**—Court satisfied that offence committed.	Offence must be one for which sentence not fixed by law.	Section 183	Section 384
Consideration by court of various factors before making probation order.	Nature of offence.	Section 183(1)	Section 384(1)
	Character of offender.	Section 183(1)	Section 384(1)
	Reports on character of the offender.	Section 183(1)	Section 384(1)
	Home surroundings of offender.		
	Whether suitable arrangements for supervision can be made by the appropriate local authority.	Section 183(5)(a) Section 183(1A)	Section 384(5)(a) Section 384(1A) Inserted by the Law Reform (Miscellaneous Provisions) (Scotland) Act 1990
Explanation to, and agreement of, the offender required before order made.	Effect of order, including any additional requirements, and result of failure to comply to be explained to offender in ordinary language.	Section 183(6)	Section 384(6)
	Requirements to be included to be stated.		
	Offender must express willingness to comply with order.		
	Copy of any report by local authority officer to be given by clerk of court to offender or his solicitor; or, if offender under sixteen and not represented copy need not be given to him, but to parent or guardian, if present in court.	Section 192	Section 393

Statement	Act of Adjournal (Probation Orders) 1969 SI 1969/1597	1975 Act, Section 183(7)	1975 Act, Section 384(7)
Order to be as nearly as may be in form prescribed.	✓		
Clerk of court gives copy of order to supervising officer, probationer, person supervising place of residence (if necessary).		Section 183(7)	Section 384(7)
Right of appeal not affected.		Section 191(3)(a)	Section 392(3)(a)
Not deemed conviction unless offender subsequently sentenced for that offence.		Section 191(1)	Section 392(1)
Period not less than six months. Not more than three years.		Section 183(1)	Section 384(1)
Local authority area in which offender resides or is to reside is named.		Section 183(2)	Section 384(2)
Discretion continues during whole or part of order and such requirements as are necessary may be made to secure good conduct.		Section 183(4)	Section 384(4)
Name of residence must be specified and may involve enforced change of residence.		Section 183(5)(b)	Section 384(5)(b)
Period of residence to be for not more than twelve months from date requirement made or beyond expiry date of order.		Section 183(5)(b)	Section 384(5)(b)
Not less than forty hours. Not more than 240 hours.		Section 183(5A) inserted by Community Service by Offenders (Scotland) Act 1978, s 7	Section 384(5A)

Flowchart:

- **Probation order.** (decision: NO / YES)
  - NO → **Other disposal.**
  - YES → **Appeal against conviction.**
  - YES → **Supervision for specified period by officer of local authority.**
- **Court has discretion re additional requirements.**
- **Residential requirement may be added.**
- **Unpaid work requirement may be included.**

Section 184(1) and Mental Health (Scotland) Act 1984, s 20 or s 39	Section 385(1)
Section 184(1)	Section 385(1)
Section 184(5), (5B),(6)(a) as substituted by Mental Health (Amendment) (Scotland) Act 1983, s 36	Section 385(5), (5B), (6)(a)
Section 184(2)(a), (b) and (c)	Section 385(2)(a),(b) and (c)
Section 186(4)	Section 387(4)
Section 183(5B) inserted by Criminal Justice (Scotland) Act 1987, s 65	Section 384(5B)
Section 186(5)	Section 387(5)
Section 186(1)	Section 387(1)

Evidence *re* mental condition of offender to be given by registered medical practitioner.

Period of treatment not to extend beyond twelve months from date of requirement specified.

Treatment or place of treatment may be changed with consent of probationer and supervising officer and officer must notify the court of new arrangements.

Treatment will be one of the following:
(a) as a resident patient in hospital (not State hospital);
(b) as a non-resident patient;
(c) by or under direction of specified registered medical practitioner.

Refusal of probationer to undergo any surgical, electrical or other treatment will not be failure to comply with order if court considers refusal reasonable.

Lump sum or instalments for any personal injury, loss or damage caused. Compensation provisions of the Criminal Justice (Scotland) Act 1980 applied.

Without prejudice to s 187 and s 388 of the 1975 Act, failure to comply will not include probationer being convicted of offence committed during probation period.

Treatment for mental condition requirement may be included.

Compensation requirement may be included

Failure to comply with requirements of order.

YES

Order continues.

Warrant for arrest or citation to appear.

	Section	Section
Information on oath by supervising officer—proof to satisfaction of court.	Section 186(1), (2)	Section 387(1), (2)
Fine may be levied without prejudice to continuation of probation order (not exceeding level 3 on the standard scale).	Section 186(2)(a)	Section 387(2)(a)
Any extension of probation period must terminate not later than three years from the date of the probation order.	Section 186(2)(c)	Section 387(2)(c)
To run with probation order.	Section 186(2)(d) added by Community Service by Offenders (Scotland) Act 1978, s 8	Section 387(2)(d)
On failure to comply with terms of order: (i) where probationer has been convicted for offence in respect of which probation order was made, he can be sentenced; (ii) where probationer not convicted court may convict and sentence him.	Section 186(2)(b)(i) Section 186(2)(b)(ii)	Section 387(2)(b)(i) Section 387(2)(b)(ii)
	Section 187	Section 388
Conviction for offence by court other than that which made order (see Failure to comply with requirements, supra).	Section 187(1)	Section 388(1)

Flowchart:

NO ← Proof of failure. → YES

Court may impose fine or vary requirements or make community service order.
- YES
- NO → or impose other sentence → Order ceases.

Commission of further offence.
- YES → Warrant for arrest. Citation to appear.
- NO → Order continues.

Description	Section	Section
Conviction for offence by court which made order, (see Failure to comply with requirements, supra).	Section 187(2)	Section 388(2)
May require offender to give security for good behaviour.	Section 190(1)	Section 391(1)
Security may be forfeited and recovered in like manner as caution.	Section 190(2)	Section 391(2)
	Section 187	Section 388
At request of probationer or supervising officer.	Section 185(2)	Section 386(2)
	Sections 183, 185, Schedule 5, paras 2 and 3	Sections 384, 386
At request of probationer or supervising officer. Or Time period expires.	Schedule 5, para 1	

Flowchart:

Court may: fine or vary requirements or make community service order. — YES / NO

May impose supplementary provisions. — YES / NO

Sentence for offence for which placed on probation. — YES / NO

Probation order ceases to have effect.

Amendment of order. — YES / NO

Order continues.

Discharge of order.

END

MISCELLANEOUS

CHILDREN'S HEARINGS

I Applications to sheriff for finding under Social Work (Scotland) Act 1968, s 42

COMMENTARY	CASE LAW	STATUTE LAW
Applies only to child of eight years or over.	*Merrim v S* 1987 SLT 193 Sheriff dismissed application by reporter to sheriff on grounds that s 32(2)(*g*) of the Act had no application to persons of non-age.	
Jurisdiction—children's hearing and sheriff.	*L v McGregor* 1980 SLT 17 *Held* (2nd Div, Ct of Session) that the reporter has a discretion to make application to any sheriff, at least within the area of the reporter's jurisdiction	Social Work (Scotland) Act 1968, ss 32(2)(*g*), 42(2)(*c*), and s 42(2A), which provides that sheriff in whose area alleged offence would be prosecuted has jurisdiction.
Application to sheriff—time limit.	*H v Mearns* 1974 SC 152; 1974 SLT 184 *Held* (2nd Div, Ct of Session): a hearing is incompetent if outwith the statutory twenty-eight days allowed for the lodging of an application to the sheriff.	Section 42(4)
Second proceedings brought by reporter because of intervening strike.	*McGregor v L* 1983 SLT (Sh Ct) 7 *Held* that the reporter was not barred from bringing proceedings five months after his first instructions to apply because of intervening strike of sheriff court staff.	Act of Sederunt (Social Work) (Sheriff Court Procedure Rules) 1971 (SI No 92) Social Work (Scotland) Act 1968, s 42(4)
Continuation by sheriff.	*H v Mearns*, supra *Held* (2nd Div, Ct of Session) that provisions re continuation of hearing by sheriff applied only where initial hearing had actually begun.	Rule 9 Section 42
Dismissal of application for finding by sheriff.	*McGregor v D* 1977 SC 330; 1977 SLT 182 *Held* (1st Div, Ct of Session) that sheriff not entitled to dismiss application as irrelevant, to discharge referral before he had heard evidence which the reporter sought to lead and that sheriff further not entitled to permit amendment of grounds of referral. *Observed* that proceedings before sheriff are 'civil proceedings *sui generis*' and that 'basic rules of evidence' to be observed, but that 'ordinary codes of civil and criminal procedure do not apply'.	Rules 8 and 10 Sections 32(2)(*g*) and 42(2)(*c*) Children's Hearings (Scotland) Rules 1971 (SI No 492), Rules 14 and 15
Grounds disposed of previously (not *res judicata*).	*McGregor v D* 1981 SLT (Notes) 97 *Held* (2nd Div, Ct of Session) that sheriff was bound to hear all the evidence which reporter proposed to tender in relation to a referral, even if that evidence had been led in relation to other grounds disposed of previously. See also: *Kennedy v S* 1986 SLT 679	Sections 32(2)(*c*) and 42(7)
Grounds of referral—incorrect reference to statutory provision in statement of grounds of referral.	*McGregor v A* 1982 SLT 45 Circumstances in which held (2nd Div, Ct of Session) that technically defective statutory reference did not invalidate referral when meaning clear.	
Summary procedure—prosecution of child—consent of Lord Advocate may be given by general directions.	*M v Dean* 1974 SLT 229 *Held* (2nd Div, Ct of Session) that general directions given by Lord Advocate, which did not appear on face of complaint, sufficient to comply with s 31(1) of 1968 Act.	Section 31(1)

Proof of grounds for referral.	*McGregor v H* 1983 SLT 626 *Held* (1st Div, Ct of Session) that ground for referral established in one application may be sufficiently proved in subsequent applications on same common factual basis by production of certified copy interlocutor.	Sections 32(2)(*d*) and 42(6)
Consideration of referral on alternative 'offence' grounds.	*McGregor v A*, supra *Held* (2nd Div, Ct of Session) that Rule 10 permits—but does not require—sheriff to make an alternative finding on the facts, where offence alleged in original ground of referral was unproved, and the facts prove that another offence has been committed.	Sections 32(2)(*d*) and 42(7) Act of Sederunt (Social Work) (Sheriff Court Procedure Rules) 1971, Rule 10
Change of circumstances to be considered in application to sheriff for finding—evidential weight of unsworn statement to sheriff—duty of sheriff when new matter suddenly disclosed.	*Kennedy v B* 1973 SLT 38 *Held* (2nd Div, Ct of Session) that in reaching his decision sheriff had to take into account (1) change of circumstances of family in period of time between decision of hearing and date of proof, and (2) that sheriff was entitled to give weight to unsworn statement. *Observed* that when faced with a 'surprise disclosure' sheriff should consider adjourning to allow other side chance to reply.	Sections 32, 39(3) and 42(2)
Decision—whether founded on the established grounds of referral.	*K v Finlayson* 1974 SLT (Sh Ct) 51 *Held* that when case is remitted back to children's hearing after finding by sheriff, children's hearing should base its decision on information laid before sheriff and not on additional information not available to sheriff: observations re what constitutes adequate 'reasons' stated by hearing.	Sections 42(6), 43(1) and 49

II Appeals against decision of children's hearing

COMMENTARY	CASE LAW	STATUTE LAW
Time limit for lodging appeal.	*S, Appellants* 1979 SLT (Sh Ct) 37 *Held* that time for appeal must be computed to include date of children's hearing whose decision is being appealed against. *Kennedy v H* 1988 SLT 586 Discretion to extend time limit only available to a prospective appellant if he/she had right to appeal within time limits prescribed in s 49. But contrast: *Tudhope v Lawson* 1983 SCCR 435 (Sh Ct)	Social Work (Scotland) Act 1968, s 49(1)
Meaning of 'decision' of a children's hearing.	*H v McGregor* 1973 SLT 110 *Held*, that a 'decision' for the purposes of an appeal under s 49(1) is a decision by a children's hearing as to the final disposal of the referral to the hearing.	Section 49(1)
Change of circumstances between hearings.	*D v Sinclair* 1973 SLT (Sh Ct) 47 *Held* that two-month interval between hearings long enough to allow circumstances to change materially and this should be taken into consideration when final decision being made. *Observed* that sheriff should not allow appeal merely because he thought another disposal preferable, but only if satisfied there had been flaw in procedure or proper consideration not given to some factor.	Section 49(2)

III Evidence

COMMENTARY	CASE LAW	STATUTE LAW
Hearing before sheriff—nature of proceedings.	*McGregor v T* 1975 SC 14; 1975 SLT 70 *Held* (1st Div, Ct of Session) that proceedings before sheriff (on application by reporter under s 42) are judicial, but not criminal proceedings, and therefore normal rules of evidence, as regards competence and compellability of witnesses apply. See also: *McGregor v D* 1977 SLT 182, supra under I	Social Work (Scotland) Act 1968, ss 32(2) and 42(6)
Competency and compellability of parent.	*McGregor v T*, supra *Held* (1st Div, Ct of Session) that parents of children involved in proceedings under 1968 Act are competent and compellable witnesses. *Observed* that when objection taken sheriff should normally allow evidence subject to relevance and competency.	Evidence (Scotland) Act 1840, s 1
Unsworn statement—weight of evidence.	*Kennedy v B* 1973 SLT 38 *Held* (2nd Div, Ct of Session) that unsworn statement of child's parent entitled to have some weight given to it, if accepted. (See supra under I.)	Act of Sederunt (Social Work) (Sheriff Court Procedure Rules) 1971 (SI No 92), Rule 8(2)
Identification and corroboration.	*D v Kennedy* 1974 SLT 168 *Held* (2nd Div, Ct of Session) that evidence given about identification and corroboration had to be specific.	Social Work (Scotland) Act 1968, ss 42 and 50
Proof of previous decisions by production of certified copy documents.	*McGregor v H* 1983 SLT 626 *Held* (1st Div, Ct of Session) that in subsequent application concerning another child in same family, certified copies of the sheriff's decision in earlier case sufficiently proved existence of common ground of referral. (See also infra, and supra under I.)	Sections 32(2)(*d*) and 42(6)
Offences under Sched 1, Criminal Procedure (Scotland) Act 1975.	*McGregor v K* 1982 SLT 293 *Held* (2nd Div, Ct of Session) that when child referred under s 32(2)(*d*), it is not necessary to specify person who is alleged to have committed offence against child in terms of 1975 Act.	Criminal Procedure (Scotland) Act 1975, Sched 1 Social Work (Scotland) Act 1968, s 32(2)(*d*)
Re 'Membership of household' in terms of s 32(2)(*d*).	*McGregor v H* supra *Held* (1st Div, Ct of Session) that test to be applied is membership of household, not whether child is, at relevant time, living in same household as relevant offence. (See also supra.)	Section 32(2)(*d*)
'Likely to cause unnecessary suffering'— proper test includes whole facts.	*M v McGregor* 1982 SLT 41 *Held* (2nd Div, Ct of Session) that in reaching his decision, sheriff must consider whole facts of the case. Circumstances in which appellate court held that sheriff not entitled to hold grounds established. Observations of sheriff tending to 'pre-empt the disposal of the case by the children's hearing' *disapproved*.	Section 32(2)(*c*)
'Likely lack of parental care'— whether competent ground for referral.	*McGregor v L* 1981 SLT 194 *Held* (2nd Div, Ct of Session) that 'likely lack of parental care' was a competent ground under 1968 Act. Circumstances in which inference of likely lack of parental care entitled to be drawn from parents' previous mode of life, even although child had never been in parents' care.	Section 32(2)(*c*)

IV Assumption of parental rights—resolution by local authority under Social Work (Scotland) Act 1968, s 16

COMMENTARY	CASE LAW	STATUTE LAW
Effect of passing of a section 16 resolution by local authority.	*Strathclyde Regional Council v M* 1982 SLT (Sh Ct) 106 *Held* that child ceased to be in care of local authority under s 15 when resolution under s 16 was passed. (See also infra.)	Social Work (Scotland) Act 1968, ss 15 and 16
Section 16 resolution—three-year period—date of commencement.	*Strathclyde Regional Council v M*, supra *Held* that the period of three years in s 16 was not intended to run after a litigation had started, for to hold otherwise would result in the outcome of the case depending on the length of the litigation. (See also supra.) But contrast: *Strathclyde Regional Council v H and Anr* (Sh Prin J. A. Dick, QC) at Glasgow, 23rd December 1981, unreported.	Section 16(1)(*a*)(iv), (2)(*d*) and (2)(*e*), as substituted by Children Act 1975, s 74
Satisfaction of sheriff re need for section 16 resolution by local authority.	*Strathclyde Regional Council v T* 1984 SLT (Sh Ct) 18 *Held* (Sh Prin) that it is unnecessary for sheriff to see all material laid before local authority committee passing resolution; it is only necessary to satisfy sheriff that state of affairs at date of resolution entitled local authority to pass resolution.	Section 16(2) and (8), as substituted by Children Act 1975, s 74
Intention behind passing of section 16 resolution by local authority.	*Lothian Regional Council v H* 1982 SLT (Sh Ct) 65 *Held* (Sh Prin) that in decisions concerning resolutions under 1968 Act to assume parental rights, sheriff is entitled to give weight to purpose behind resolution (in this instance adoption). *Observed* that 'an *onus* of some weight' rests on local authority to satisfy sheriff that statutory requirements for assumption of parental rights had been met: circumstances in which court refused to sustain assumption of parental rights because not satisfied it was in child's interests even when other statutory grounds established.	Section 16(1)(*a*), (2), (5), (6), (7) and (8), as substituted by Children Act 1975, s 74
Rights and powers.	*Beagley v Beagley* 1982 SLT 331 *Held* (1st Div, Ct of Session) that all rights and powers of person on whose account a resolution under 1968 Act is passed shall vest in the local authority.	Section 16(1), as substituted by Children Act 1975, s 74
Access	*Beagley v Beagley* 1984 SLT 202 *Held* (HL) that when parental rights assumed, the divested parent not entitled to apply to Court of Session for custody or access but *observed* that right of other person (eg, grandparent) so to apply remained unaffected. *Observed* that right of parent to apply to Court of Session regarding matters other than custody and access (eg, property rights) also probably remain unaffected. *Observations* (per Lord Fraser) on extent of sheriff's powers under s 18(3) of 1968 Act.	Section 16(1), as substituted by Children Act 1975, s 74 NB: see s 17B of 1968 Act (now in force) for up-to-date statutory position re access to child in care.
Access	*MacInnes v Highland Regional Council* 1982 SLT 288 *Held* (OH) that where local authority has assumed parental rights in terms of s 16, a third party relation (in this case the grandmother) of the child may competently apply to the court for access.	Sections 16(1) and 17(2) But see s 17A-17E of 1968 Act, as inserted by Health and Social Services and Social Security Adjudications Act 1983, s 7(2).

V Supervision order made by children's hearing—condition of residence

COMMENTARY	CASE LAW	STATUTE LAW
Residential condition prevails over contrary decision by court re custody.	*Grant v Grampian Regional Council* May 1983, unreported *Held* (Sh Ct) that a residential condition of supervision order made by children's hearing in favour of one party could not be overridden by any court making custody order in favour of another party.	Social Work (Scotland) Act 1968, s 44(1)(*a*)
'Place of supervision'—precise specification required.	*R v Children's Hearing for the Borders Region* 1984 SLT 65 *Held* (2nd Div, Ct of Session) that 'place' (where child under supervision to reside) had to be narrowly construed and that therefore children's hearing acted *ultra vires* by including in supervision requirement a condition that child 'to reside in a pre-adoptive home chosen by local authority'. Hearing's action also in contravention of ss 29(1) and 57(2) of Adoption Act 1958.	Section 44(1)(*a*) Adoption Act 1958, ss 29(1) and 57(2)

VI *Nobile officium*—extension of local authority care orders

COMMENTARY	CASE LAW	STATUTE LAW
Extension of warrants.	*Humphries*, Petitioner 1982 SLT 481 *Held* (1st Div, Ct of Session) that extension of warrants (authorising two children who were in care, to be kept by foster parents) via *nobile officium* not contrary to the intention of 1968 Act; in the instant case the children's father was awaiting trial for the murder of their sibling.	Social Work (Scotland) Act 1968, ss 32(2)(*d*) and 37(2)(*b*) Criminal Procedure (Scotland) Act 1975, Sched 1

In general see Kearney *Children's Hearings and the Sheriff Court*.

BIBLIOGRAPHY

Publications referred to in the text

Alison, A.   I *Principles of the Criminal Law of Scotland* (1832).

Alison, A.   II *Practice of the Criminal Law of Scotland* (1833).

Bovey, K.   *Misuse of Drugs* (1986).

Gane, C. H. W. and Stoddart, C. N.   *A Casebook on Scottish Criminal Law* (2nd edn, 1988).

Gordon, G. H.   *The Criminal Law of Scotland* (2nd edn, 1978, with second supplement, 1992).

Hume, D.   *Commentaries on the Law of Scotland Respecting Crimes* (with supplement by B. R. Bell, in two volumes, 4th edn, 1844).

Kearney, B.   *Children's Hearings and the Sheriff Court* (1987).

McCall Smith, R. A. A. and Sheldon, D.   *Scots Criminal Law* (1992)

Macdonald, Sir J. H. A.   *A Practical Treatise on the Criminal Law of Scotland* (5th edn, 1948).

Murdoch, J. L.   'The Civic Government Act and Public Processions' (1984) *Scolag* 97, 144.

Renton and Brown   *Criminal Procedure according to the Law of Scotland* (by G. H. Gordon, Looseleaf, 1993).

Williams, G.   *Criminal Law* (2nd edn, 1961).

Wheatley, J.   *Road Traffic Law in Scotland* (2nd edn, 1993).

Books for additional reference

Archbold   *Pleadings, Evidence and Practice in Criminal Cases* (43rd edn, 1988).

Dickson, W. G.   *A Treatise on the Law of Evidence in Scotland* (two volumes, 1887).

Field, D.   *Law of Evidence in Scotland* (1988).

Gane, C. H. W. and Stoddart, C. N.   *Criminal Procedure in Scotland: Cases and Materials* (1988).

Harper, J. R.   *A Practitioner's Guide to the Criminal Courts* (1985).

Lewis, W. J.   *Manual of the Law of Evidence in Scotland* (1925).

Macphail, I. D.   *A Revised Version of a Research Paper on the Law of Evidence in Scotland* (1987).

Nicholson, C. G. B.   *Sentencing: The Law and Practice in Scotland* (2nd edn, 1992).

Walker, A. and Walker, N.   *The Law of Evidence in Scotland* (1964, reprinted 1980).

Wilkinson, A. B.   *The Scottish Law of Evidence* (1986).

Wilkinson's Road Traffic Offences   (P. Halnan and J. Spencer, eds, two volumes, 13th edn, 1987).

INDEX